AF571886

A User Guide to the VAX/VMS System

L. de Chernatony
MSc, PhD, CPhys, MinstP
Senior Lecturer
School of Computer Science
The Polytechnic of Central London

R. Pretty
PgradC
VAX/VMS Systems Manager
PCL Computer Services
The Polytechnic of Central London

M. Newens
BA(hons), PhD
Chief Applications Programmer
PCL Computer Services
The Polytechnic of Central London

McGRAW-HILL BOOK COMPANY

London · New York · St Louis · San Francisco · Auckland · Bogotá
Caracas · Hamburg · Lisbon · Madrid · Mexico · Milan · Montreal
New Delhi · Panama · Paris · San Juan · São Paulo
Singapore · Sydney · Tokyo · Toronto

Published by
McGRAW-HILL Book Company Europe
SHOPPENHANGERS ROAD · MAIDENHEAD · BERKSHIRE
ENGLAND
Telephone: 0628 23432
FAX: 0628 770224

British Library Cataloguing in Publication Data
de Chernatony, L. (Leslie)
A user guide to the VAX/VMS system – (J. Ranade DEC series).
1. Computer systems. Operating systems
I. Title II. Pretty, R. (Ray) III. Newens, M. (Mike) IV. Series
005.43

ISBN 0–07–707220–0

Library of Congress Cataloging-in-Publication Data
de Chernatony, L. (Leslie)
A user guide to the VAX/VMS system / L. de Chernatony, R. Pretty, and M. Newens.
p. cm. – (J. Ranade DEC series)
Includes bibliographical references and index.
ISBN 0–07–707220–0
1. VAX/VMS I. Pretty, R. (Ray) II. Newens, M. (Michael)
III. Title. IV. Series.
QA76.76.063D43 1991
005.4′44—dc20 90–48239
CIP

1234CUP9321

Typeset by Paston Press, Loddon, Norfolk
and printed and bound in Great Britain at the University Press, Cambridge

Contents

Preface vii

Acknowledgement xi

Chapter 1. Introduction to the VAX/VMS Operating System 1

Chapter 2. Accessing VAX/VMS 4
2.1 Introduction 4
2.2 Getting an Account 5
2.3 Logging On and Off 6
2.4 Issuing VAX/VMS Commands 8
2.5 Simple VAX/VMS Commands 8
2.6 Setting the Terminal Type 9
2.7 Using the Keyboard 11
2.8 Setting and Changing Passwords 12
2.9 Disk Quota 14
2.10 The LOGOUT Command 15

Chapter 3. Using the VAX/VMS Command Language—DCL 17
3.1 Introduction 17
3.2 DCL Commands and their Structure 18
3.3 Some Useful DCL Commands 22
3.4 The Help Library 33

Chapter 4. Obtaining Output **42**
4.1 Introduction 42
4.2 Output from VAX/VMS 43

Chapter 5. A First Visit to the Editor EVE **48**
5.1 Introduction 48
5.2 What Is an Editor? 48
5.3 Requirements of an Editor 49
5.4 Entering EVE 50
5.5 The EVE Status Line 50
5.6 EVE Keyboard Layouts and Keypad Commands 51
5.7 Entering EVE Commands 51
5.8 Getting Help 52
5.9 Insert and Overstrike Modes 53
5.10 Changing Direction 54
5.11 Moving the Cursor 55
5.12 Simple Deletion of Text 55
5.13 Leaving EVE 56

Chapter 6. A Second Visit to the Editor EVE **59**
6.1 Introduction 59
6.2 The /RECOVER Qualifier 60
6.3 The EVE Keypad 60
6.4 Entering EVE Commands 66
6.5 Accessing Buffers 81
6.6 Using Windows 87
6.7 Incorporating Text Created by DCL Commands into a File 90

Chapter 7. Files and Directories **91**
7.1 Introduction 91
7.2 File Characteristics (Classification) 93
7.3 File Specifications and Naming Conventions 94
7.4 Directories 98
7.5 Subdirectories 99
7.6 File Manipulation Commands 107
7.7 File and Directory Protection 117
7.8 Differences between Files 119
7.9 The SORT Utility 122

Chapter 8. Process Creation—the SPAWN Command **125**
8.1 Introduction 125
8.2 Creating Subprocesses 126
8.3 Useful Qualifiers 130
8.4 Attaching to Processes 131

Chapter 9. Batch and Print Queues **135**
9.1 Introduction 135
9.2 Batch Queues 136
9.3 Print Queues 146

Chapter 10. Program Development **158**
10.1 Introduction 158
10.2 Inputting the Program 159
10.3 Compiling or Assembling the Program 160
10.4 Linking the files 162
10.5 Running the Programs 163
10.6 Summary 163
10.7 Development of a Simple Program 164
10.8 The VAX/VMS Debugger 170

Chapter 11. Communicating with other Users **174**
11.1 Introduction 174
11.2 MAIL 174
11.3 The PHONE Utility 193

Chapter 12. Using VAX/VMS Libraries **201**
12.1 Introduction 201
12.2 The Help Library 201
12.3 Adding and Deleting Library Information 202
12.4 Other Libraries 207
12.5 The VMS Common Run-Time Library 208
12.6 Using the Run-Time Library 213

Chapter 13. Symbols and Logical Names **216**
13.1 Introduction 216
13.2 Symbols 217
13.3 Logical Names 233
13.4 Customizing the VAX/VMS Environment—The LOGIN.COM File 249

Chapter 14. Writing Command Procedures **253**
14.1 Introduction 253
14.2 A Simple Command Procedure 254
14.3 Executing Command Procedures 256
14.4 Command Procedure Levels 259
14.5 Default Input/Output Logical Names 259
14.6 Major Command Procedure Statements 260
14.7 Examples of Command Procedures 275

Chapter 15. An Introduction to DECwindows 280
15.1 Introduction 280
15.2 Overview of DECwindows 280
15.3 The Need for X Windows 281
15.4 Using DECwindows 283

Appendix A. Major File Types on VAX/VMS 286

Appendix B. Terminal Session 287

Appendix C. Reference Data 293
C.1 General Notes 293
C.2 Alphabetical List of Useful Commands 294
C.3 Frequently Used VAX/VMS Commands 298
C.4 Alphabetical List of Terminal Key Functions 301

Index 304

Preface

All computers run a special program called the *Operating system*. It is this program that provides the interface between the user and the rest of the programs and the peripherals (i.e. printers and so on). It is the responsibility of this program to ensure the overall integrity of the operation of the computer. This can include the organization of a multi-user system, making comparison with a set of internal rules and only executing the user's commands if they are "valid". In addition to these tasks, the operating system runs "built-in" useful (utility) programs, (i.e. programs provided by the manufacturer), which are available to all users. Furthermore, each user can write, at this level, his or her own tailor-made programs, which the system recognizes to be the property of that particular user and therefore not available to other users. It is thus recognized that the operating system is a very powerful program and a good grasp of it is a prerequisite for all users of the system. The level of comprehension, i.e. knowledge of the commands and their valid combination, determines the ease of usage and the benefit one can gain from fully exploiting the power of that particular computer system. In general, the more powerful is the computer system, the larger is the associated operating system. The DEC (Digital Equipment Corporation) VAX Computer Operating System is recognized as being very versatile—it can be used with a limited set of simple commands to carry out commonly encountered operations. However, only with proficiency of a much larger set of commands can one really appreciate its inherent facilities. The manufacturer's manuals consist of many volumes, are expensive, and are usually not directly available to individual users. Thus, information about the commands and their use is passed on within organizations by "word of mouth" and as such is of limited use.

Recognizing the need for a text that bridges the gap between the above extremes, our search for such a book for this particular computer system was of no avail. Subsequent discussions with Mr Andrew Ware of McGraw-Hill Book Company led to the writing of this volume.

The organization and the content of this text was selected with the aim of being immediately useful for both the newcomer to computing and for the experienced programmers who are not familiar with this particular system. A reader will probably familiarize him or herself with the content by browsing through it once or twice. Thereafter, with the help of the index and the contents list, the user will locate the specific topic of current interest and study in detail the description and the examples provided.

The topics selected and the depth of coverage is, of necessity, a compromise between the amount of information needed and the amount of space available. Our selection was based on the likely action encountered during a typical computer session: firstly, by a newcomer and therefore at the simplest level; and secondly, by a more advanced user who is prepared initially to devote additional time, in order to be able to use techniques that on subsequent occasions will provide simpler and time-saving operations.

The order of presentation proceeds from the simpler concepts towards the more advanced topics. Thus the topics include a description of how to enter and exit from a session, using editors to write programs and divers methods to enter data into the computer ("input and output"). Next the special VAX/VMS Command Language (DCL) is introduced. This is extended to show the techniques of retaining and organizing individual files into convenient storage systems, "the directories". Housekeeping and maintenance are important aspects, we show how to dispose of material that is no longer needed and how to reorganize the content of the directories to suit the latest requirements. Further topics include consideration of input/output techniques, more advanced use of the editor, process creation, and queue organization. This is followed by a brief demonstration of program development, communication with other users, the use of VAX/VMS libraries, and more advanced DCL techniques. Because of their importance, this is extended to include writing DCL command procedures.

The final section presents only a brief introduction to DECwindow (interface) operation, whereby a symbolic menu appears on the screen and the user makes a choice by using a special pointer to activate the symbol (e.g. wastepaper basket, to represent disposal). This interface can display and run more than one program (or even, computer) and simultaneously shows the status of each window (and each process). The description of this important technique is restricted because the necessary terminal is considerably more expensive, in line with its capabilities, and thus not widely available. Finally, in a set of appendices, data for special purposes are collected.

The topics and their coverage might be considered to be of levels 1 and 2. Further, more specialized topics are reserved for a possible second volume on "advanced techniques". The software of the operating system undergoes continuous revision and extension. Our discussion is based on the current version 5.3. It is expected that any differences in later versions can be readily assimilated by using the HELP and library facilities described here. However, it is envisaged that certain spelling and other errors have crept in and we would be pleased to be informed of their presence.

Trademarks

The following are trademarks of Digital Equipment Corporation:

DECnet
DECwriter
DIBOL
VAX
VMS
VAX/VMS
VAXcluster
VT

™

This book makes extensive use of the VMS HELP facility. The whole of this facility is copyright Digital Equipment Corporation.

Acknowledgement

This book is a condensation and selection of topics, based on many years of experience of running VAX/VMS in a teaching environment.

The experience described is, of necessity, based on the design of the VAX/VMS operating system by Digital, and we have relied on their excellent documentation and technical support.

This book is to complement and not supercede the existing VAX documentation and on line help facility.

We wish to thank the Polytechnic of Central London for making it possible for us to produce this work.

L. de Chernatony
R. Pretty
M. Newens

Chapter

1

Introduction to the VAX/VMS Operating System

VAX/VMS is an interactive, multi-user operating system. That is, users type commands to the operating system, which then responds with an action, waits for another command, and so on. Many users can type commands simultaneously to the same computer, at any instant in time—hence multi-user—without being aware of the existence of the other users. The computer achieves this by allowing each user a chance to use the CPU (central processing unit)—it is this that runs all the programs and commands in turn. Since these timeslices are very small amounts of time (of the order of microseconds) and the computer executes millions of instructions each second, the user's timeslice, known as a quantum, soon comes round again. The overall impression created to each individual user is that of a computer dedicated solely to their own use. This technique is called "timesharing", since the computer shares its processing (or CPU) time between all current users.

When a user wishes to run a command, a program, or a utility, VAX/VMS loads the appropriate program from the disk into the computer's memory. Some VAX/VMS commands are stored permanently in memory in order to make access to them faster. The computer's CPU then starts running the program, on the user's next timeslice. If the program has not finished running by the time the timeslice ends, then the program is kept in the computer's memory to wait for the next timeslice when it can continue running. Thus the memory, as well as the CPU, is shared among all the active users. In addition, the VAX/VMS operating system performs all the functions necessary to keep the system operational; it too is allocated a portion of the computer's memory.

When a program has finished running, VAX/VMS then copies it back to that program's storage area on the disk.

What would happen if a program were too big to fit into the computer's memory? Then VAX/VMS would organize the program so that the parts that did not need to be run by the CPU, on that timeslice, were stored in a special area on the disk called the "pagefile". Both, the section in the computer's memory and the section on disk are divided into "pages", which are then "paged in" or "paged out" between the memory and the pagefile, as required. *Virtual memory* is the name given to this technique of paging. The method allows even those programs that require far more memory than the computer can provide to run. It is by employing this method that VAX/VMS derived its name. VMS stands for Virtual Memory System and VAX for Virtual Address eXtended, the name of the range of computers on which the VMS operating system runs.

At this point, it is useful to view how the user–machine interface is constructed of various functional layers, consisting of the operating system, the computer hardware, and of other software as shown in Figure 1-1. Figure 1-1 shows how software on the VAX (and computers in general) is layered. Each level of software is built upon the lower level, and can interact with both the level below and the level above. At the bottom of the diagram is the VAX computer itself, containing memory, CPU, disks, etc. Also built into the VAX are computer chips which contain programs (written in machine code). They are used by VAX/VMS to perform *low-level** system functions. At the next level, VAX/VMS itself provides an interface to these lower functions. VAX/VMS also provides a platform for the running of higher-level software, sometimes referred to as "layered products". The next level, "system support software", contains the programming languages, which provide the users with a means of writing their own programs in *high-level* languages, i.e. in a format where the instructions are expressed in an English-like format. At the top level are the "applications software". These programs usually perform only a specific function and are available for all users.

VAX/VMS is capable of running on a wide range of VAX computers, from small, single-user VAX stations, to large computers capable of supporting over 1000 concurrent users. From the users' point of view, VAX/VMS is exactly the same to use on any VAX computer. Any program developed and run on one VAX computer works without any modification on any other VAX computer. A constant user interface across such a wide range of computers, which are capable of running the same packages, commands, and utilities, is considered an essential feature of VMS. Each VAX computer running VAX/VMS is

* Low level: this is associated with the value of each memory location. It can have only two values: 0 or 1. Low-level programming is concerned with allocating specific values (of 0 or 1) to their locations, which in turn the computer interprets as a particular operation or value.

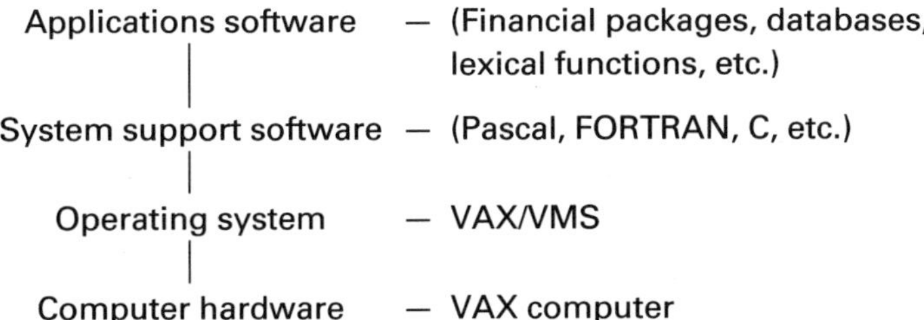

Fig. 1-1 The layered computer model.

exactly the same to use as any other VAX running VAX/VMS, although there may be some variation in the availability of programming languages and development tools.

In this book we consider and describe those aspects of VAX/VMS that form part of the basic operating system supplied by the Digital Equipment Corporation (DEC).

Chapter

2

Accessing VAX/VMS

2.1 Introduction

In this chapter we introduce the initial stages you have to go through to become a VAX/VMS system user. This chapter provides an insight to the main topics, which include obtaining a user account, how to access (log in) and leave (log out) the computer, and how to issue commands to VAX/VMS while you are connected.

Two simple, but very important commands are introduced: SHOW and SET. The SHOW command provides us with information about the system, while SET provides us with a mechanism for altering or modifying existing conditions. These two commands, and in general any command, require an "argument", i.e. an entity with which to be associated. There are some arguments known as "defaults" that the system automatically uses in commands, without the user needing to specify them. To use a value other than the default, we need to specify that new value as an argument to the command. Alternatively, some defaults can be permanently altered by use of the SET command. A command can also have associated with it a "qualifier" or "switch". An example would be the LOGOUT command, which can be used in conjunction with the /FULL qualifier (i.e. LOGOUT/FULL) to provide greater information when leaving the system.

This chapter contains examples of arguments for the SHOW command, such as to show the time and to show the current users. Arguments for the SET command are illustrated for changing the system prompt, i.e. the prompt which informs us that the system is ready to execute the next command, and for

Table 2-1 Response to Selected Control Key Commands

Key Sequence	Action
⟨Ctrl⟩Y	Causes VMS immediately to stop running the current program and return to the $ prompt.
⟨Ctrl⟩C	For compatibility with other Digital operating systems, such as the TOPS 10 and RSX, ⟨Ctrl⟩C will generally perform the same function as ⟨Ctrl⟩Y (above).
⟨Ctrl⟩S	Freezes the terminal display, so that you can inspect its current output. This key is associated with ⟨Ctrl⟩Q.
⟨Ctrl⟩Q	Resumes output to a terminal after ⟨Ctrl⟩S has been pressed.
⟨Ctrl⟩O	Pressing ⟨Ctrl⟩O once prevents the output from the current operation, appearing on the screen. Pressing ⟨Ctrl⟩O a second time, resumes the display. When the current operation has been completed, normal output is automatically resumed. While scanning lengthy terminal output for information, repeated use of ⟨Ctrl⟩O can be used to overcome the need to see all the display.
⟨Ctrl⟩R	Redisplays the current command line on the screen.
⟨Ctrl⟩U	Deletes the current command line.
⟨Ctrl⟩B	Recalls the last command line typed.
⟨Ctrl⟩T	Causes VAX/VMS to display a status message, which provides a summary of CPU and memory, as well as the amount of page faults and input/output performed so far.

setting the terminal type. The terminal type is set in one of two ways: either by using the qualifier /INQUIRE (i.e. SET TERMINAL/INQUIRE) which automatically sets the terminal type; or by the use of the /DEVICE=terminal_type qualifier, i.e. SET TERMINAL/DEVICE=VT100, where VT100 is the type of terminal you are assumed to be using, which allows us to specify the terminal type directly. The chapter then continues by discussing aspects of the keyboard and the special control sequences we can generate to get VAX/VMS to perform various actions (Table 2-1).

System security is discussed and changing the user's password is described. The disk quota system is explained and this is followed by a description of the corrective action to take if you exceed your allocated disk quota.

2.2 Getting an Account

VAX/VMS is a timesharing operating system, i.e. it is sharing the computer's resources with several users at any one time. In order to do this and ensure the computer's (and the users') integrity, each user is given their own individual account. With any multi-user computer, the activities of each individual user may have an effect on the computer's overall performance; for this reason and because of security, accounts are usually administered by the System Manager.

In order to get an account on the computer, you need to contact the person responsible for running your computer systems. You may have to offer a brief description of the activities you wish to perform on the computer so that the account can be tailored to your own requirements. Accounts consist of a username, a password, a UIC (User Identification Code), and a disk quota.

The username is generally what it implies—the name of the user—although it can be any text string. Each username has a password associated with it. In order to ensure that there is no violation of the content of the user's programs, the password must be kept secret. After you have received your password, it is a good idea to change it when you first log in. Once modified, there is no way that other users, including the System Manager, can find out what the new password is.

If your password does fall into the wrong hands, another person can log in to your account and do all sorts of damage, such as, for instance, deleting all your files and/or changing the password so even you are not able to log in to your account.

A UIC is used to tag the files and programs you create, and through this you are known as their owner. Any free storage space allocated to you is also shown as belonging to your UIC.

The amount of space your files can occupy on the computer's disk is specified by the disk quota. Since all users have to share computer resources, some devices, such as disks, are given quotas to limit the amount each individual user can use on that device. If quotas were not enforced on disks, then a single user would be able to occupy the entire disk or disks with their programs, denying other users their disk space facility.

Armed with a username and password, we are now ready to log in as described in the next section.

2.3 Logging On and Off

In order to do any work you must go through the process of logging on. This involves typing in a valid username and a password to identify yourself, to the VAX/VMS operating system, as an authorized user.

The username uniquely identifies you and distinguishes you from the many other people who are authorized to use the computer, some of whom may be working at the same time as you.

If you have not got a username you need to ask your System Manager for one. This involves the System Manager in setting up an account for you and giving you a username and password. You should change your password to your own choice, as described in Section 2.8.

2.3.1 Logging In

To start the log in process, you press the key labeled "return" or "enter". In future, we shall show such keys in angle-brackets, (⟨ ⟩), to avoid confusion with actually typing the characters "R E T U R N". So to start, we press the ⟨Return⟩ key. VAX/VMS now prompts you for your username and password, which you type in followed by pressing the ⟨Return⟩ key.

You will notice that when you type the password, it does not appear on your terminal screen. This is to ensure that people nearby cannot observe your password.

The following example shows a user with username MIKE logging in. Note that the user's commands are in **bold** type.

```
Username: MIKE ⟨Return⟩
Password:      ⟨Return⟩

       Welcome to VAX/VMS version 5.0

  Last interactive login on Wednesday, 27-APR-1988 08:32
  Last non-interactive login on Monday, 25-APR-1988 20:51

***********************************************************
* The VAX 6220 will be down tomorrow for Software Updates.*
***********************************************************

$
```

The computer then responds by displaying the date and time your account last used the computer. This is shown by "last interactive login". The "non-interactive login" message refers to your last batch job, a topic that we will discuss in Chapter 9. Following that is a message which the System Manager has set-up on the system; this will vary from time to time, usually providing news on how to use the computer, or advanced warning of computer down-time. Finally, the logging in process terminates and we are presented with the dollar ($) prompt. This prompt indicates that VAX is ready to accept a VAX/VMS command from you.

2.3.2 Logging out

An example of a VAX/VMS command is LOGOUT, which logs you off the VAX computer. On receiving this command, VAX/VMS carries out a "housekeeping" operation, closing any open files and terminating processes as required, so that the system is able to function in an orderly manner when the user next logs in.

To exit the system, we issue the command:

```
$ logout ⟨Return⟩

MIKE   logged out at 22-APR-1989 12:23:38.10
```

VAX/VMS responds with the time and date you logged out of the computer.

2.4 Issuing VAX/VMS Commands

We have so far seen two commands: LOGIN, to start your terminal session, and the command LOGOUT, to end it.

Note that having introduced the use of the ⟨Return⟩ or ⟨Enter⟩ key, it is now assumed that all command lines must terminate with the use of the ⟨Return⟩ (or ⟨Enter⟩) key in order to transmit the command to the computer. Therefore from here on, the use of ⟨Return⟩ will only be shown explicitly in cases where its use is not clear.

2.5 Simple VAX/VMS Commands

We will look in Chapter 3 at VAX/VMS commands that are necessary for you to do some of the more obviously useful things. But while we are logged in, let us take the opportunity to try out a few of the more common VAX/VMS commands.

The first command to try shows us the date and time as set by the computer's clock. Not surprisingly this command is SHOW TIME. To execute the command, we simply type after the dollar prompt as follows:

```
$ show time
```

The system responds with a message of the form shown below:

```
22-APR-1989 12:40:32
```

Another command, SHOW USERS, shows the usernames, together with some additional information, of all the users currently logged on to the system:

```
$ show users

          VAX/VMS Interactive Users
           22-MAR-1989 08:47:56.18
     Total number of interactive users = 4
Username      Process Name     PID        Terminal
OPERATORS     JACK             00001876   OPA0:
ENGINEERS     ENGINEERS        00001A7F   TXA4:
BARBARA       BLACK SHEEP      00001880   TXA5:
ROGER         Roger            00001A81   TXA7:
```

There is even a command to change the prompt if we want to. We are able to change the prompt from a $ to any character, or characters, we choose. For example, to set the prompt to Ray⟩ and then change it back to the default, we type in the following:

```
$

$

$ set prompt = "Ray⟩ "

Ray⟩
```

Here we have changed the prompt to Ray⟩; the following operation sets it back to the default value:

```
Ray⟩

Ray⟩ set prompt = "$"

$
```

This does not change the function of the prompt; VAX/VMS is still waiting for you to type commands. Throughout this book we shall use the default prompt, the dollar sign.

These commands work on any type of Digital terminal. Some commands, however, require the computer to know the terminal's exact model type. We review this aspect in the next section.

2.6 Setting the Terminal Type

In order for VAX/VMS to run certain of its utilities correctly, it needs to know the type and model of the terminal you are using. This is so that it knows which special codes to send in order to update the screen and to enable the keyboard to function correctly. When you first log in, the terminal type is unknown to VAX/VMS. If the terminal you are using is not a Digital or Digital compatible terminal, it is best to leave it set to UNKNOWN. Digital terminals are identified by a VT badge; members in this series include the types VT52, VT100, VT200, and VT300. Printer terminals are usually in the LA series.

The easiest way of setting the terminal type is by using the command:

```
$ set terminal/inquire
```

This causes a short dialog between the computer and the terminal, in which the terminal passes back to VAX/VMS a code to identify its type.

Another method is by specifying the terminal type directly. If the terminal is a VT100, then to set it correctly type in the following command:

```
$ set terminal/device=vt100
```

When using a Digital terminal, a badge located on the equipment gives its exact type; with compatible terminals manufactured by another company you may have to ask someone for this information.

In order to obtain a listing of the terminal settings from VMS, type the command:

```
$ show terminal
```

Figure 2-1 shows a typical response. We are informed that we are using terminal line RTA3 and the terminal type has been set to VT100. We can also see that the screen size—80 characters wide by 24 lines deep—has also been set. Other details about the terminal session are also displayed.

The above settings are referred to as "default" settings. They may be altered individually using the SET TERMINAL command. Let us look at a few examples:

```
$ set terminal/width=132
```

Changes the screen width of the terminal from 80 to 132 characters; it does this by making the characters smaller.

```
$ show terminal
Terminal: _RTA3:          Device_Type: VT100          Owner: Ray Pretty
                                                   Username: RAY
   Input:  9600          LFfill: 0          Width: 80          Parity: None
   Output: 9600          CRfill: 0          Page:  24
Terminal Characteristics:
 Interactive          Echo                 Type_ahead      No Escape
 No Hostsync          TTsync               Lowercase       Tab
 Wrap                 Scope                No Remote       No Eightbit
 Broadcast            No Readsync          No Form         Fulldup
 No Modem             No Local_echo        No Autobaud     Hangup
 No Brdcstnbx         No DMA               No Altypeahd    Set_speed
 No Line Editing      Overstrike editing   No Fallback     Dialup
 No Secure server     No Disconnect        No Pasthru      No Syspassword
 No SIXEL Graphics    No Soft Characters   Printer Port    Numeric Keypad
 ANSI_CRT             No Regis             Block_mode      Advanced_video
 Edit_mode            DEC_CRT              No DEC_CRT2     No DEC_CRT3
```

Fig. 2-1 Typical display of VT100 terminal characteristics.

```
$ set terminal/speed=1200
```

sets the terminal speed to 1200 baud (bits per second). This is a measure of the speed at which the characters are sent along the communication cable between the VAX and the terminal.

You may need to reset the terminal type each time you log in.

2.7 Using the Keyboard

2.7.1 Introduction to key functions

The position of some of the keys varies depending on the model of terminal you are using. Computer keyboards incorporate a basic typewriter QWERTY keyboard, together with other more specialized keys. It is the location and function of these keys that varies. The VT100 is the simplest model. The VT200 and VT300 series terminals have identical keyboards, consisting of 20 function keys located in a row along the top of the keyboard, with additional keys for cursor movement, help, previous screen, next screen, etc., and editing functions. The earlier VT100 series keyboards do not have separate function keys but have their four function keys incorporated into the top row of the keypad.

Let us now look in more detail at the purpose of some of the more specialized keys.

2.7.2 The Shift key

The characters typed in are all normally displayed in lowercase mode. Pressing the ⟨Shift⟩ key while typing causes uppercase characters to be typed. Keys that have two characters, or symbols, on them normally display the lower character on the key. However, holding down the ⟨Shift⟩ key and simultaneously pressing a dual-symbol key causes the upper character on the key to be generated.

2.7.3 The Return or Enter key

This is the key that sends, or transmits, all the messages typed at the keyboard to VAX/VMS.

This key must be pressed at the end of each command line that is typed to VAX/VMS. The operating system cannot run the command until the ⟨Return⟩ or ⟨Enter⟩ key has been pressed.

2.7.4 The Delete key

The ⟨Delete⟩ key is sometimes labeled as DEL, ←, or RUBOUT. Pressing this key deletes the character to the left of the cursor.

2.7.5 The Tab key

Pressing this key causes the cursor to move to the next tab position. Tab positions are usually at eight-character intervals across the screen. A tab can also be generated by pressing simultaneously the "control" key, shown on the keyboard as "Ctrl", and the character "I" key.

2.7.6 The Control key

The control key is used to generate control characters from the standard keyboard. These keystrokes are interpreted by VAX/VMS to have a special meaning. By holding down the control (⟨Ctrl⟩) key and pressing the specified keys, the computer, as shown in Table 2-1, can be made to carry out selected processes. Since these operations are regularly carried out, it is advisable to familiarize yourself with this table. For example pressing the ⟨Ctrl⟩ and "T" keys simultaneously causes VAX/VMS to display a status message. See Table 2-1 for a brief description of this message.

```
$ ⟨Ctrl⟩T
MOLE::RAY 17:32:02 (DCL) CPU=00:02:01.57 PF=234 IO=153 MEM=410
```

The above control codes work on all the terminals, although VT200 and VT300 series terminals have some of their function keys already preprogrammed to perform some of these functions. These functions are clearly labeled along the top of the key, e.g. the F1 key labeled "HOLD SCREEN" toggles between ⟨Ctrl⟩S and ⟨Ctrl⟩Q, to stop and to restart the screen scrolling.

2.8 Setting and Changing Passwords

It is good practice to change your password regularly. Modifying the original password, given with the computer account, means you can choose one that is easy for you to remember and one that only you know. There are a few guidelines that may be useful in choosing a good password:

1. Choose one that is difficult for other people to guess. Do not choose your name, or make your password the same as your username.

2. The longer the password, the more time it takes to guess it.
3. Mix characters, underscores, spaces and numbers in the password. Numbers are not as obvious a choice. Car license plates can sometimes be a good choice.
4. Put two usually unassociated words together, such as dog_apple for a password. Even two associated words can be a good choice, dogcollar for example.
5. Do not write your password down, but if you do, never keep your password together with your username.

Obviously you can follow all the above suggestions and take choosing a password to extremes; however, if you are sensible with your choice, there should not be any problems.

A password, once set, has a fixed life span on VAX/VMS; this time interval is preset by the System Manager. When this lifespan is coming towards its end VAX/VMS gives you warnings of the form:

```
Warning - Your password expires on 22-Apr-1990
```

If you ignore these warnings and let the password expire, when you next log in you will be greeted with the message:

```
Your password expired - update it immediately with SET PASSWORD
```

If you log out without changing the password, you will be allowed to log in again, but this time you will receive the message:

```
Your password has expired; you must set a new password to log in
```

VMS will then automatically run the SET PASSWORD command for you, and prompt you to type in your existing, expired password and then the new password of your choice.

To change the password on VAX/VMS, we use the command following:

```
$ set password

Old password:   - type existing password, press ⟨Return⟩
New password:   - type in new password, press ⟨Return⟩
Verification:   - type in new password again, press ⟨Return⟩
```

Notice that the passwords are not displayed on the screen. Furthermore, you are prompted for the new password twice, to check that it has been spelt correctly the first time. VAX/VMS can be forced to choose a password for you, although these are usually sequences of random numbers and difficult to remember. To get VMS to choose a password, type in:

```
$ set password/generate

Old password:

oayaydeu     oa-yay-deu
proscs       proscs
asseabem     as-sea-bem
anefam       a-ne-fam
okajeba      o-ka-je-ba
Choose a password from this list, or press RETURN to get a new list

New password:  <Return>

lacoca       la-co-ca
ubdeifen     ub-dei-fen
ewdonja      ewd-on-ja
engundko     en-gund-ko
blyerrir     blyer-rir
Choose a password from this list, or press RETURN to get a new list

New password:

Verification:
```

As shown above, this generates a list of five random passwords. If you do not like any of the passwords shown, you can press ⟨Return⟩ to have VAX/VMS generate five more.

Some accounts may be set up with two passwords. To alter the "secondary" password, type:

```
$ set password/secondary
```

2.9 Disk Quota

Associated with each account is an amount of storage space that the account can use, on the computer's disk, to store files. Care must be taken to ensure this quota is not exceeded, or files may be deleted by the system in order to bring the account back under this level. Storage space is measured in blocks. Each block is equivalent to half a (computer) page, or 512 characters (each character occupies one byte of storage space).

Disk quotas are based on the UIC (User Identification Code) part of the username, as it is this that identifies the owner of a file or a program. If files are copied from one account to another, then the original account still owns that file, the file being tagged with the first owner's UIC. We will explain about file ownership and protection later (see Chapter 7).

The SHOW QUOTA command displays our quota allocation and the amount already used:

```
$ show quota

User [12,5] has 18504 blocks used, 1496 available,
of 20000 authorized and permitted overdraft of 500 blocks on DUA0
```

The computer responds by showing the account's UIC, in this case 12,5. Here 12 corresponds to the number of a particular group of users, which we are a member of, and 5 is the user number within that group. The amount of quota we have already used (18 504 blocks), the amount we have still available to use (1496 blocks), and the sum of the these two—the total amount of space we have been allocated (18 504 + 1496 = 20 000 blocks). The overdraft is an extra allowance for any existing file, allowing it to increase in size up to this limit. However, once the "authorized" quota has been exceeded no new files can be created. DUA0 is the name of the disk on which the files are stored.

If we exceed our quota allocation, we receive the message:

```
SYSTEM-F-EXDISKQUOTA, disk quota exceeded
```

If this happens, we must delete some of our files. Aspects of the DELETE and PURGE commands are described in detail in Chapter 7. VAX/VMS does not allow us to log out if we are over quota. First, delete any unnecessary files, then any files with the extension.TMP. To delete all old copies of existing files in the current directory use the PURGE command (directories are discussed in Chapter 7):

```
$ purge
```

2.10 The LOGOUT Command

When you have finished your session on the terminal, you must always log out. Failure to do so may result in the loss of some of the files and programs. Another user, seeing the account logged in, could use the SET PASSWORD command to change the password and then log out, effectively locking you out of your own account.

There are two main forms of the log out command: LOGOUT/BRIEF and LOGOUT/FULL, the former being the default. So if we type LOGOUT:

```
$ logout

RAY     logged out at 22-APR-1990 12:23:38.10
```

However, if we wish to display accounting information for this session, we can use the /FULL qualifier:

```
$ logout/full

RAY     logged out at 22-APR-1990 12:32:17.42

Accounting information:
Buffered I/O count:       4234     Peak working set size:  120
Direct I/O count:          220     Peak virtual size:      376
Page faults:               773     Mounted volumes:          0
Charged CPU time: 0 00:02:27.34 Elapsed time: 0 05:23:44.76
```

Where the accounting information consists of the following:

- *Buffered I/O count* Amount of information transferred between the terminal and VAX.
- *Direct I/O count* Amount of information transferred between computer's main memory and the disk.
- *Page faults* The number of pages of information fetched from disk into main memory.
- *Charged CPU time* Period of time this process was running (i.e using the CPU). This is used as a measure of machine use, and therefore in some establishments an indication of the charge to be made for the use of the computer.
- *Peak working set size* The maximum amount of main memory used during this session.
- *Peak virtual size* The maximum amount of disk memory (paging file) the process occupied.
- *Mounted volumes* The number of times this processes mounted tapes, disks or other devices.
- *Elapsed time* Amount of time the user was connected (i.e. the amount of time from log on to log off).

Chapter

3

Using the VAX/VMS Command Language—DCL

3.1 Introduction

VAX/VMS is an interactive operating system: users type in commands, the computer performs that command and then waits for the next command. Commands are instructions to the operating system to tell it to perform various functions. If the command is not a valid one, and there are over 200 valid commands in VAX/VMS, then VMS responds with an error message which gives a hint as to why the command was rejected. For example, if VMS believes you may have misspelt a valid command, then an error message is generated, suggesting that you may like to check the spelling or that the command you typed was not in the VMS vocabulary. After each instruction has been executed (or rejected), VMS prints a prompt and waits indefinitely for the next command. The prompt generated is by default the dollar sign ($), although the user can modify this to be any character or string, as shown in Chapter 2.

The form VMS commands take is specified in DCL, the Digital Command Language. As with any computer language, DCL specifies a series of rules and syntax, which are then used to build up valid command lines. Unlike programming languages, such as FORTRAN and Pascal, DCL is able to assist you in inputting a command line by displaying possible options for the next part of an incomplete command line. Its ability to prompt for and suggest possible responses, combined with user commands made up from phrases in English, make it a user-friendly operating system.

Commands can be typed in a combination of uppercase and lowercase characters; DCL automatically converts, before execution, all characters to uppercase. The words, usually called fields of VMS commands, have to be separated by at least one space. Command qualifiers used to specify options to the command must be preceded by a slash (/).

3.2 DCL Commands and their Structure

We shall now describe the structure of a VAX/VMS command line, as specified by DCL:

$	This is the prompt displayed by DCL when it is ready to receive the next command.
Command	Specifies which command is to be executed.
Parameter	This field tells the command which item to use. There may be more than one parameter to a single command.
Qualifier	Usually preceded by a slash (/), qualifiers are sometimes called "switches". They are used to specify various options selected to use with a command. Although it is good practice to place the qualifier at the end of the command line, they can, in fact, be placed anywhere on the line.
Value	Usually preceded by an equals sign (=), values act as parameters to the qualifier. Values can be a VMS keywords (a word which is valid to use with the command), a file name, a character string, or a number value.

Let us now look at a some valid DCL commands, and identify their various components. A brief description of the computer's response to these commands is given later.

```
$ show users

     VAX/VMS Interactive Users
      22-MAR-1989 08:47:56.18

     Total number of interactive users = 4
Username       Process Name     PID        Terminal
$OPER          OPERATORS        00001876   OPA0:
$OPER          John Smith       00001A7F   TXA4:
FRED           * Hello *        00001880   LTA1186 LTA1186:
RAY            RAY              00001A81   RTA1:
```

This executes the SHOW command with the parameter USERS to produce a list of all people currently logged on to the computer (the exact output of this command depends on the version of VAX/VMS, see Section 3.3). Examples of other valid parameters for the SHOW command are: SYSTEM (for a list of all processes on the system), QUOTA (displays user's disk quota usage), and QUEUE (shows either batch or print queue jobs).

```
$ show system

VAX/VMS V5.0 on node MOLE 22-MAR-1989 08:48:01.51 Uptime 5 14:11:09

Pid      Process Name State Pri   I/O         CPU      Page flts Ph.Mem
00000201 SWAPPER      HIB   16       0 0 00:03:55.70        0       0
00000204 ERRFMT       HIB   12    4764 0 00:00:30.99       76     124
00000205 OPCOM        HIB   11    3035 0 00:00:18.30      415     176
00000206 JOBCONTROL   HIB    9    7523 0 00:05:41.75      258     505
0000020F SYMBIONT_006 HIB    9     578 0 00:00:07.95     6403      76
00000210 NETACP       HIB   10   27519 0 00:06:25.10      250     458
00000211 EVL          HIB    6     992 0 00:00:43.32    30546      70
00000212 REMACP       HIB   10     929 0 00:00:05.70       80      75
00000219 DBMS MONITOR LEF   15    5270 0 00:00:43.12    16726      62
00001876 $OPER        CUR   24   12027 0 00:29:04.00     6974     779
00001877 SYMBIONT_014 HIB    6     694 0 00:00:18.46     5211     246
00001A7F RAJ          LEF    9     605 0 00:00:05.08     1354     218
00001880 Buzby Bird   HIB    8     299 0 00:00:02.69      883     375
00001A81 RAY          CUR   14     190 0 00:00:02.75      969     371

$ show quota

User [12,5] has 19786 blocks used, 1214 available,
of 21000 authorized and permitted overdraft of 500 blocks on DUA2
```

If the computer contains a queue for a printer, the default name for that queue is SYS$PRINT. We display the queue on the screen, again by using the SHOW command and by specifying the QUEUE parameter in conjunction with the SYS$PRINT qualifier.

```
$ show queue sys$print

Terminal queue SYS$PRINT, on _TXA2:, mounted form DEFAULT
〈Main System Printer〉

  Jobname          Username      Entry  Blocks  Status
  -------          --------      -----  ------  ------
  DEC10            RAY             338       3  Printing
```

This only shows information about any files of your own in the print queue and excludes files entered into the queue by other users. The example above shows that the file entered into the queue by username RAY has reached the front of the queue and is currently being printed.

If we wish to see information on all the other files waiting to be printed, we use the /ALL qualifier. Notice that the file that has reached the top of the queue is currently being printed.

```
$ show queue sys$print/all

Terminal queue SYS$PRINT, on _TXA2:, mounted form DEFAULT
<Main System Printer>

  Jobname           Username        Entry  Blocks  Status
  -------           --------        -----  ------  ------
  HEADER            SULEMA            586       1  Printing
  DB2               JOSEPH            950       2  Pending
  ARRAYTEST         QLUEC             128       2  Pending
  DEC10             RAY               338       3  Pending
  VISA              KHWAJA            604       4  Pending
  CREDSTO           BASHIRA           699       4  Pending
  C                 YEUNGB            905       4  Pending
```

Finally, to produce detailed information on all the files waiting to be printed in the queue, the qualifier /FULL is used.

```
$ show queue sys$print/full

Terminal queue SYS$PRINT, on _TXA2:, mounted form DEFAULT
<Main System Printer>
/BASE_PRIORITY=4/DEFAULT=(FEED,FLAG,FORM=DEFAULT)/NOENABLE_GENERIC
Lowercase/OWNER=[AUSTAFXN,SYSTEM]/PROCESSOR=PCLFLAG/PROTECTION=
(S:E,O:D,G:R,W:RW)

  Jobname      Username      Entry  Blocks  Status
  -------      --------      -----  ------  ------
  DEC10        RAY            338       3   Pending

Submitted 22-MAR-1989 09:44 /FORM=DEFAULT /PRIORITY=100
File: _DUA2:[CCSROOT.RAY]DEC10.TXT;3
```

By using the /FULL and /ALL qualifiers together, the above information is given for each file in the queue.

Output produced by the SHOW QUEUE command is discussed in greater detail in Chapter 9.

To save typing, all DCL commands can be abbreviated to a least significant number of characters at which they still retain their uniqueness. For example:

```
$ show queue sys$print
```

can be typed as

```
$ sh que sys$print
```

Notice that the queue name must be specified in full, otherwise VMS tries to display the contents of a queue named SYS$PRI or whatever we abbreviated it to. SHOW cannot be abbreviated any further than SH. For example, typing the character "S" makes the command no longer unambiguous, as S could also mean SET as well as SHOW. To avoid any confusion, we will always give the unabridged versions of DCL commands.

We have seen how commands lines can be built and how we can restrict the amount of typing we need to do. What happens if we are uncertain about the full specification of a command? We can make use of DCL to prompt for the next field. Again to illustrate this, we will use the SHOW QUEUE SYS-$PRINT command. If we need to produce a listing of the printer queue, but are not sure of the order of the command, we could either consult the VMS HELP facility, or get DCL to prompt us for the next field. For example, we know that we need to show a queue, therefore we type in SHOW and press the ⟨Return⟩ key, VMS now asks us which item we would like to show. We do not want to show the system (SHOW SYSTEM) or users (SHOW USERS), but a queue, so we type QUEUE and press the ⟨Return⟩ key. There may be several queues on the computer, so VMS will respond, to ask us which queue we wish to see. We now specify the name of the default print queue SYS$PRINT and press ⟨Return⟩. DCL then combines the fields we have previously input to produce the command line, in this case:

SHOW + QUEUE + SYS$PRINT = SHOW QUEUE SYS$PRINT

The actual process of building up the command line is as follows:

```
$ show
_What: queue
_Queue: sys$print

Terminal queue SYS$PRINT, on _TXA2:, mounted form DEFAULT
⟨Main System Printer⟩

  Jobname          Username        Entry  Blocks  Status
  -------          --------        -----  ------  ------
  DEC10            RAY               338       3  Pending
```

DCL commands can become quite long—they can have up to 128 fields and each of these fields may contain up to 128 characters. The whole command line must not exceed 1024 characters (this includes the expansion of symbols and lexicals; these are explained in Chapter 13). Since the majority of terminals have a screen width of 80 characters, how do we input lengthy command lines? There are two ways: we can use DCL prompting, as used in the previous example, to split the command over several lines; or we can use the minus sign (−) and then the ⟨Return⟩ key, to move to the next line without the command being executed. Let us look at another example of the former, the DCL prompting, and this time use the COPY command to copy a file to another user's disk area. COPY takes two parameters, the first is the full location of the original file, the second is the full location of the file's destination (in fact it is not necessary to specify the full file location, but we will deal with this further in Chapter 7). Thus using DCL to prompt, we get:

```
$ copy

_from: dua0:[computercenter.programmers.mike]prog.for

_to: dua0:[computercentre.programmers.ray.fortran]prog.for
```

or we can place a minus sign at the end of the current line, as shown below, which suppresses the ⟨Return⟩ and stops the incomplete command from being executed. Instead, it generates a new line. This time, we shall split the previous command into smaller sections. The command line can be broken at any point, it does not even have to be between words.

```
$ copy-

_$ dua0:[computercentre.programmers.ray.fortran]-

_$ prog.for dua0:[computercentre.programmers.mike]-

_$ prog.for
```

The complete command will not be executed until the last ⟨Return⟩ is pressed. Notice also how VMS modifies the prompt by placing an underscore character in front of the dollar sign, indicating that the command line is incomplete and has not yet been executed. When extending commands in this way over certain lines, ensure that the continuation sign is placed up against the last word in each line, since if there is a gap, a space will be inserted in the command line and this will produce an error message—"invalid number of parameters".

DCL commands can be placed in a file, to form a *command procedure*. These procedures, which are effectively programs written in the DCL language, in much the same way as one would write any other program in a high level language, such as BASIC or FORTRAN, can then be run to perform desired tasks. A series of command procedures can be built up, to help automate many of the tasks we may wish to perform on the system. We shall look at command procedures and the various statements that provide tests and flow control within these procedures in Chapter 14.

3.3 Some Useful DCL Commands

3.3.1 The SHOW command

The SHOW command is useful for new users to get acquainted with the computer, and for the more experienced user to monitor what the computer is doing. We will now look at various parameters we can use with the SHOW command and examine the response from the computer. To start, we will look at a command we have already used as an example in this chapter: SHOW USERS.

```
$ show users

          VAX/VMS Interactive Users
           16-JAN-1989 14:58:50.98
   Total number of interactive users = 6

Username      Process Name     PID       Terminal
BOB           Rigsby           0000204C  LTA1226      LTA1226:
BRENDA        BRENDA           00002416  LTA1416      LTA1416:
MALCOLM       Malcolm          0000207C  LTA1258      LTA1258:
MARCUS        - m a r c u s -  00001A6F  LTA1252
RAY           Ray Pretty       000024A5  LTA1380
WOODS         WOODS            000022EF  LTA1484      LTA1484:
```

The first few lines of the output display the date, the time, and the total number of users on the system. The rest of the output is a list in alphabetical order, sorted on username of all users currently logged into the system. Following the username is the process name. If this is not set by the user, then by default it is set to be the same as the username. PID is Process IDentification; this hexadecimal number is unique for each process running on the system and it is assigned by VMS on start of process execution. The terminal field specifies the line number on which the user's terminal is connected to the computer. Briefly, numbers beginning with LT are connections from terminal servers and connect over the network into the computer. Numbers starting with RT are connections from users on another computer in the network (using the DECnet command SET HOST), and TX connections are terminals wired directly into the computer.

The major change to VAX/VMS for users in release 5.2 of the operating system is a difference in the output generated from the SHOW USER command. We shall briefly look at this before continuing to look at other commands.

Executing the command SHOW USERS on a system running VMS V5.2 generates the following output:

```
$ show users

     VAX/VMS User Processes at 16-JAN-1989 14:58:50.98
   Total number of users = 5, number of processes = 9

Username      Interactive  Subprocess   Batch
BOB                1
BRENDA             1
MALCOLM            1            2
OPERATOR           3
SYSMGR             -            -         1
```

This shows that there are five separate accounts logged into the system, although the operators have logged into the OPERATOR account in three separate locations. Therefore, the system is currently executing six interactive processes. From the MALCOLM account two subprocesses are currently being activated, and the SYSMGR account is current running a program in the batch queue (notice that you do not need to be logged in to do this). The SPAWN and SUBMIT commands which enable us to run subprocesses are explained in Chapters 8 and 9 respectively.

To obtain more detailed information add the FULL qualifier:

```
$ show users/full

     VAX/VMS User Processes at 8-OCT-1989 01:15:12.87
   Total number of users = 5, number of processes = 9

Username  Process Name    PID       Terminal
BOB       Rigsby          00002504  LTA1226   (SERVER1/PORT1)
BRENDA    BRENDA          00001023  LTA1416   (SERVER2/PORT5)
MALCOLM   Malcolm         0000212D  TXA2:
OPERATOR  Op1             0000022F  LTA1354   (SYSTEM1/PORT5)
OPERATOR  Op2             0000023F  RTA1:     (OTTER::SUPPORT)
OPERATOR  Op3             0000025F  LTA1374   (SYSTEM1/PORT7)
SYSMGR    The Boss        00000120  LTA1221   (PROGS_1/PORT6)
```

This provides the user with information similar to the pre-version 5.2 command. The column on the right gives the name of the terminal server, and the socket on that server to which the user's terminal is connected for those accessing the computer via the network. User MALCOLM is directly connected (hence TXA2:) and OPERATOR (process name: Op2) has used the SET HOST command from the computer OTTER to log in to this machine from the user account SUPPORT.

Another useful command to provide user information is SHOW PROCESS:

```
$ show process

16-JAN-1989 14:59:32.50    TXA3:              User: RAY
Pid: 00002858   Proc. name: Ray Pretty    UIC: [12,5]
Priority:    4   Default file spec: DUA2:[RAY]
Devices allocated: TXA3:
```

This command shows details of our account and current process. The first line states the date, the time, the terminal number we are using, and our username. The second line shows the process identification allocated to our process when we logged in, the process name that we have previously modified (see SET COMMANDS below), and the UIC allocated to our account by the System Manager when our account was created. The fourth line states that we have a base priority of 4—the default for a VMS account. The operating system according to circumstances may need to increase or decrease this value during our terminal session. We can see this change in priority levels by using the ⟨Ctrl⟩T command. The default file specification is the name of the disk area assigned to our account. In this case, DUA2 is the name of the disk and RAY the name of the area on that disk. We have one device allocated to us and that is the terminal we are using. The terminal is connected into the computer via line TXA3:. If we want to use a tape drive, or a personal printer, for example, then we would need to allocate those devices to our process and they would also appear in the list.

With release 5.2 of VMS the format has been altered to provide a more descriptive summary:

```
$ show process

16-JAN-1989 14:59:32.50     User: RAY     Process ID:    00002858
                            Node: WOLF    Process name: "Ray Pretty"
Terminal:             LTA251:(NCSC6/NCSC6-1)
User Identifier:      [12,5]
Base Priority:        4
Default file spec:    DUA2:[RAY]
Devices allocated:    WOLF$LTA251:
```

To obtain a list of the disk devices connected to the computer, we execute the SHOW DEVICE command and specify DUA as the device type:

```
$ show device dua

Device      Device        Error    Volume          Free  Trans Mnt
Name        Status        Count    Label         Blocks  Count Cnt
DUA0:       Mounted           0    SYSTEM         53832    188   1
DUA1:       Mounted           0    APPS           87300     72   1
DUA2:       Mounted           0    USER1          55281     49   1
DUA3:       Mounted           0    USER2         534954      1   1
```

Since we did not state the full name of a specific device when we entered the command, we have therefore been given a complete list of the devices that have the device name DUA in common. This is a list of all the disks in use. We observe that this computer has a total of four disks. Further, from the previous command, SHOW PROCESS, we know that our files are stored on DUA2, with the label USER1. Also, we can guess by its label that the fourth disk, DUA3, has also been allocated to store users' files. Device DUA0 contains files that go to make up the VAX/VMS system itself. The "free blocks" value specifies the total amount of free space on each device. We can see that all disks are working satisfactorily and have not generated any errors.

If the computer you are using is part of a network, you can issue the following command to see which of the other machines are connected:

```
$ show network

VAX/VMS Network status for local node 1.5 MOLE on 16-JAN-1989 15:02

   Node           Links  Cost  Hops   Next Hop to Node
 1.5    MOLE          4     0     0   (Local)     -> 1.5    MOLE
 1.3    OTTER         1     4     1   BNA-0       -> 1.3    OTTER
 1.4    STOAT         3     4     1   BNA-0       -> 1.4    STOAT
 1.6    FERRET        0     4     1   BNA-0       -> 1.6    FERRET
 1.7    WEASEL        0     4     1   BNA-0       -> 1.7    WEASEL
 1.8    MOUSE         0     4     1   BNA-0       -> 1.8    MOUSE
              Total of 6 nodes.
```

The above is an example of the connect of six computers on an Ethernet-based DECnet network. Each computer on the network is connected directly to a single Ethernet cable. A computer connected to a network is called a node. Each node is given a unique number and name. All the computers in this network have the names of animals. The link field shows how many "virtual" connections exist between computers. Virtual connections are software connections, along a physical "wire" connection. DECnet creates a new virtual connection when either someone uses the SET HOST command to log in to a second computer, while remaining logged into the original one, or when a user wishes to copy files between computers. We can deduce from the information above, that one user is connected between OTTER (one link) and MOLE (one of the four links) computers, and three users are connected between STOAT (three links) and MOLE (three of the four links). The cost of connection between computers is used by DECnet as a guide to efficiency. For instance, if there were two separate possible connections between two computers, DECnet would choose the one with the least cost. In the network shown here, every computer has a single connection to the Ethernet. The connections between any pair are as efficient as connections between any other pair. Each computer can be reached by simply using the SET HOST command and then logging in. This gives a hop of value 1 between computers. That is, each computer is seen as being one step (i.e. one hop) away from the others. In some computer networks you may need to log in to one computer before logging in to a second (the computers would then be two or more hops apart). Since we are currently logged into MOLE, MOLE has a hop value of zero. BNA-0 is the name of the device that connects the computer to the Ethernet. Some computers in a network may produce a line near the top of the listing, stating that one of the computers in the network is a "routing node". This computer is one that has been configured to act as a "bridge" between two or more separate networks. A diagram of the network is shown in Figure 3.1.

The SHOW TERMINAL and SHOW QUOTA commands have been covered in the previous chapter. The SHOW QUEUE command is dealt with in Chapter 9.

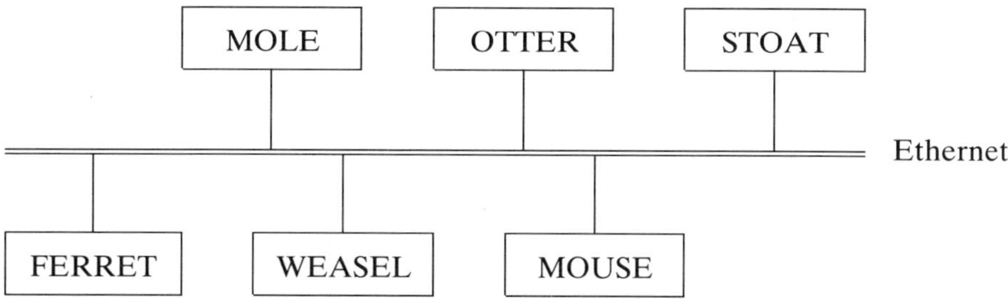

Fig. 3-1 An Ethernet-based DECnet network.

3.3.2 Redirecting output from the screen

It is possible with many DCL commands to redirect the output generated by a command into a file, instead of displaying it on the screen. This is done using the /OUTPUT=filename qualifier, where "filename" is the name of the file that is to contain the listing. Because of the importance of being able to obtain an output, this subject is discussed in detail in Chapter 4, with a description of the various available techniques. The following example creates a listing of the names of all the files in the default directory, which includes the date of creation of each file and its current size. The complete listing is then stored in a file—MYDIR.DAT. To display the information, use the TYPE command.

```
$ directory/date/size/output=mydir.dat

$ type mydir.dat

Directory USER0:[REBECCA]

DCL_SLIDE.TEX;1             2  20-AUG-1987 10:29:52.92
IBM_POSTER.TEX;5            2   9-MAR-1988 14:18:48.01
JANET.DVI;1                44  29-MAR-1988 09:59:33.42
JANET.LIS;1                 1  29-MAR-1988 09:59:29.57
JANET.LN3;1               182  29-MAR-1988 10:00:10.18
JANET.TEX;47               42  29-MAR-1988 09:59:16.63
TABLE5.OSI;1                2  26-MAY-1988 09:18:09.88

Total of 7 files, 275 blocks.
```

3.3.3 Editing DCL commands

With the release of VAX/VMS version 4.0, a feature was introduced that allows the user to recall and edit previously typed commands. The last 20 commands entered can be returned to the screen and used again. Incorporated in the facility is a simple inbuilt line editor, so commands can be corrected or modified and re-executed. For example, if we mis-type the SHOW USERS command as SHOW USERD, we get an error message from VMS:

```
$ show userd

%DCL-W-IVKEYW, unrecognized keyword - check validity and spelling
/USERD/
```

Pressing the up-arrow key, or typing ⟨Ctrl⟩B, causes the command to reappear on the screen, with the cursor placed at the end of the command line. Pressing the delete key then erases the "D" that we originally mistyped, and by the typing "S" we have the valid command. Press ⟨Return⟩ to execute it:

```
$ show users

         VAX/VMS Interactive Users
          26-JAN-1989 10:12:50.98
   Total number of interactive users = 3

Username      Process Name     PID        Terminal
BOB           Rigsby           0000204C   TXA1:
BRENDA        BRENDA           00002416   TXA3:
DAVIS         * Reception *    00002416   TXA5:
```

Table 3-1 The line editing commands

Key	Action
Delete	Deletes character to the left of the cursor.
⟨Ctrl⟩A, F14	Toggles between insert and overstrike modes. In overstrike mode existing characters are overwritten. In insert mode all existing characters, to the right of the cursor, are moved right one space.
⟨Ctrl⟩D, ←	Moves cursor one space to the left.
⟨Ctrl⟩E	Moves cursor to the end of the current line.
⟨Ctrl⟩F →	Moves cursor one space to the right.
⟨Ctrl⟩H, F12, ⟨Backspace⟩	Moves the cursor to the start of the current line.
⟨Ctrl⟩I, Tab	Moves the cursor one tab stop to the right. A tab is usually eight spaces.
⟨Ctrl⟩J, F13, Linefeed	Deletes the word on the left of the cursor.
⟨Ctrl⟩K	Forwards the entire line to the next TAB stop.
⟨Ctrl⟩R	Rewrites the command line on the screen. The cursor is left in the same position. This is useful for reviewing edited lines on a hardcopy terminal.
⟨Ctrl⟩U	Deletes the entire line.

By using the command recall facility, we have thus saved ourselves typing the entire command again. By repeatedly pressing the up-arrow key (↑) or by repeated use of ⟨Ctrl⟩B we can cycle through the last 20 commands we typed, and then by pressing the ⟨Return⟩ key re-execute them. This can save a great deal of time when using lengthy commands. If we wish to search forwards through the command list, we use the down-arrow key (↓) of course, we must search back through the list before we can search forwards.

We have seen a simple example of line editing, now we shall look at this in greater detail. Table 3-1 gives a list of the major line-editing commands.

Before we start to use these editing codes, the terminal must be correctly set up. To ensure the terminal settings are correct, issue the commands:

```
$ set terminal/inquire

$ set terminal/line_editing
```

There are two methods of recalling previous commands. The first is as shown above, by pressing the up-arrow and down-arrow keys to find the command we wish to re-execute, or edit and re-execute. The second is by first recalling a complete list of the commands and then selecting the one we wish to use. To produce a list of the last commands used—of which VMS stores up to 20—we therefore issue the command:

```
$ recall/all

 1 type ray.lis
 2 deassign sys$output
 3 help pascal
 4 directory/date/size [.tex]
 5 assign ray.lis sys$output
 6 type tex_dir.dat
 7 directory/date/size/output=tex_dir.dat [.tex]
 8 show queue sys$print
 9 show network
10 show device dua
11 show process
12 copy fred.dat john.dat
```

Here we have typed 12 commands since logging in.

We can look through the list, and then retrieve the command in the following ways:

```
$ recall 8

$ show queue sys$print

Terminal queue SYS$PRINT, on _TXA2:, mounted form DEFAULT
<Main System Printer>
```

or

```
$ recall show

$ show process

22-MAR-1989 09:00:27.85   RTA1:            User: RAY
Pid: 00001A81    Proc. name: RAY          UIC: [12,5]
Priority:    4   Default file spec: PCL$CCSROOT:[RAY]
Devices allocated: RTA1:
```

Referring to the above command, the RECALL facility searches backwards through the list, starting from the last command, number 12 in this instance, until it finds a match for the parameter following the RECALL command, in this case SHOW. It then displays this command on the screen. Notice that if the list contains more than one SHOW command, then the most recent one will be retrieved. Once retrieved, pressing ⟨Return⟩ executes the command.

To edit either of the above retrieved commands into new commands we are currently inputting, we use the line-editing keys. In the examples that follow, the position of the cursor is shown as an up-arrow (↑).

If we made a mistake with the syntax of DCL and typed in, for instance, the command "SHOW SYS$PRINT QUEUE" instead of "SHOW QUEUE SYS$PRINT", we could edit the line as follows:

```
$ show sys$print queue

%DCL-W-IVKEYW, unrecognized keyword - check validity and spelling
/SYS$PRINT/
```

Error from VMS.

```
$ recall show
```

⟨Ctrl⟩B or ↑ to recall the command (after this point do not press ⟨Return⟩ until you are ready to execute the edited command).

```
$ show sys$print queue
                     ↑
```

Type ← six times to move cursor six characters to the left.

```
$ show sys$print queue
                ↑
```

⟨Ctrl⟩J twice to delete word. Note that the first ⟨Ctrl⟩J only deletes up to $.

```
$ show queue
       ↑
```

⟨Ctrl⟩E to move to end of line.

```
$ show queue
            ↑
```

Press ⟨Space⟩ and type SYS$PRINT.

```
$ show queue sys$print
                     ↑
```

Finally press the ⟨Return⟩ key to execute.

Another example, this time with a mistyped SHOW USERS command.

```
$ shopusers

%DCL-W-IVVERB, unrecognized command verb - check validity
and spelling
/SHOPUSERS/
```

Error from VMS.

```
$ <Ctrl>B
```
Recall command.

```
$ shopusers
          ↑
```
Press ⟨Backspace⟩ to go to beginning

```
$ shopusers
  ↑
```
Press → three times, to go to P.

```
$ shopusers
     ↑
```
Terminal in overstrike mode, so press W.

```
$ showusers
     ↑
```
Press ⟨Ctrl⟩A, to use insert mode.

```
$ showusers
     ↑
```
Press spacebar.

```
$ show users
      ↑
```
Press ⟨Return⟩, to execute.

Notice that when the editing is completed and we wish to execute the command, we can press the ⟨Return⟩ key with the cursor at any location along the line, it need not be at the end.

3.3.4 Programming the function keys

It is possible to program the keyboard function keys so that when pressed, they execute a predefined command. This facility saves the time and effort of retyping or recalling frequently used DCL commands. Function keys available for programming are labeled PF1, PF2, PF3 and PF4 on VT100-type terminal keyboards. On VT200 or VT300 keyboards these are PF17, PF18, PF19 and PF20. It should be noted that editors and some of the other VMS utilities, while they are being run, temporarily reprogram these keys with their own functions. When exited, however, the keys revert back to their original DCL programs. The programming of function keys is sometimes referred to as mapping. To map function keys, use the DEFINE command in conjunction with the key qualifier, followed by the key name and finally the command itself in double quotes. Thus to program the function key PF1 on a VT100:

```
$ define/key pf1 "show users"

%DCL-I-DEFKEY, DEFAULT key PF1 has been defined
```

then by pressing the ⟨PF1⟩ key:

```
$ 〈PF1〉
$ show users

          VAX/VMS Interactive Users
           22-MAR-1989 09:01:12.59
   Total number of interactive users = 3

Username       Process Name    PID        Terminal
$OPER          $OPER           00001876   OPA0:
$OPER          BR              00001883   TXA5:
RAY            RAY             00001A81   RTA1:
```

After we press the ⟨PF1⟩ key, the command SHOW USERS appears on the current command line. The characters "pf1" do not appear on the screen.

After the command appears on the screen, we still need to press the ⟨Return⟩ key. This enables us to modify, if we wish, that command. In the example below, we add the username RAY to the end of the command line, to produce a list of all users with the username RAY on the system:

```
$ 〈PF1〉
$ show users ray

          VAX/VMS Interactive Users
           22-MAR-1989 09:01:12.59
   Total number of interactive users = 3

Username       Process Name    PID        Terminal
RAY            RAY             00001A81   RTA1:
```

To execute the command instantly, without the need to press ⟨Return⟩, we can use the /TERMINATE qualifier.

We will now program key PF2.

```
$ define/key/terminate pf2 "show quota"

%DCL-I-DEFKEY, DEFAULT key PF2 has been defined

$ 〈PF2〉
$ show quota

  User [12,5] has 19800 blocks used, 1200 available,
  of 21000 authorized and permitted overdraft of 500 blocks on DUA0:
```

By using the SHOW KEY command we can obtain the key definitions:

```
$ show key pf1

DEFAULT keypad definitions:
  PF1 = "show users"
```

or, for all keys:

```
$ show key/all

DEFAULT keypad definitions:
  PF1 = "show users"
  PF2 = "show quota"
```

We can erase the key definitions by using the delete key command:

```
$ delete/key pf1
%DCL-I-DELKEY, DEFAULT key PF1 has been deleted
```

3.4 The Help Library

3.4.1 Introduction to help

VAX/VMS has a built-in HELP facility. HELP not only contains a list of all the possible VMS commands, but also examples on how to use them. Any DIGITAL software that the computer has installed which is in addition to the basic system, such as some of the programming languages, also has information stored in the help system. The HELP facility is known as the "help library". The fact that subjects are grouped together makes it easier to locate the help you require, and browsing through help is also made easy. Updating the information contained in the help file is usually the responsibility of the system manager. The file that contains all the help information is called HELPLIB.HLB in the SYS$HELP directory.

Help is organized in a hierarchy. At the root is a list of the main topics and help on the HELP command itself. At the next level are subtopics, which are entities associated with the topics mentioned at the root level. The third level contains information, subtopics, on the topics in the second level, and so on. At the bottom level, many subjects conclude by showing example commands with an accompanying explanation. Topic names may be abbreviated to the least number of characters that still make them unique from the others in the list.

3.4.2 Using help

An example of using help

To run HELP, type:

```
$ help

  Information available:
  8086_68000_C          :=        =         @         ACCOUNTING ADVICE
  AI         ALLOCATE   ANALYZE   APPEND    ASSIGN    ATTACH     AUTOGEN
```

```
  BACKUP     BASIC      BULLETIN   CAL        CALL       CANCEL     Case
  CC         CDD        CDDL       CDDV       CLOSE      COBOL      CONNECT
  CONTINUE   CONVERT    COPY       CPROLOG    CREATE     DATATRIEVE DBMS
  DBO        DDL        DEASSIGN   DEBUG      DECK       Default_Printer
  DEFINE     DELETE     DEPOSIT    DIFFERENCES           DIRECTORY
  DISKQUOTA  DISMOUNT   DML        DMU        DUMP       EDIT       ELLA
  ENCRYPT    Environment           EOD        EOJ        EPS        Errors
  EVE        EXAMINE    EXCHANGE   EXIT       FDL        FMS        FORTRAN
  GIMMS      GOSUB      GOTO       GRAPHICS   HELP       Hints      IF
  INITIALIZE            INIT_EDT   INQUIRE    INSTALL    Instructions
  JANET_on_VMS          JOB        Kermit     LATCP      Lexicals   LIBRARY
  LICENSE    Line_editing          LINK       LOGIN      LOGOUT     LSEDIT
  MACRO      MAIL       Mail_at_PCL           MAKE       MERGE      MESSAGE
  Microlabs  MINITAB    MODULA     MONITOR    MOUNT      NCP        News
  OCCAM      ON         OPEN       ORACLE     PASCAL     PASSWORD   PATCH
  PHONE      PLI        PLOT       PRINT      PURGE      QNAP2      Queues
  RDBVMS     RDML       RDO        READ       RECALL     RECOVER    RENAME
  REPLY      REQUEST    RETURN     RMS        RMU        ROOM
  RTL_Routines          RUN        RUNOFF     SEARCH     SET        SHOW
  SOFT       SORT       SPAWN      Specify    SPICE2     SPICE_Graphics
  STAF2      START      STOP       SUBMIT     Symbol_Assign
  SYNCHRONIZE           SYSGEN     SYSMAN     System_Services       TFF
  TSA        TYPE       UMapIT     UNIX_Utilities        UNLOCK
  V50_NewFeatures       WAIT       Wells_St   WRITE

  Additional help libraries available (type @name for topics):

  Comp_Centre

Topic?

$
```

The system concludes by asking for a choice of topic (press ⟨Return⟩ to return to VMS level as shown here).

The list of topics shown in the above example reflects the software available on the system, and thus varies from computer to computer. The system manager may also add further topics to the help library and remove others. We have shown the complete list to illustrate the wide range of topics available. The line before last, "Comp_Centre", gives the name of an additional help library, which in this instance contains information for use by Computer Centre Staff.

If your terminal has been previously set to the correct type, a screen of text will be displayed at a time. To continue to the next screen, press the ⟨Return⟩ key. Help displays a list of topics contained in the library and then prompts you to choose one. This is useful if you are searching for a command to perform some function, but are unsure of the complete specification of the command, or even if such a command exists at all. If a likely topic appears on the list, you can carry on searching deeper into that topic and, eventually, locate the command. If, however, you do not see a likely command, then pressing the ⟨Return⟩ key will exit at this point (see above example where ⟨Return⟩ was pressed at the "Topic?" prompt). Alternatively, if we know the type of information we are seeking, we can add that as a parameter to the help command.

```
$ help show

SHOW

Displays information about the current status of the process, the
system, or devices in the system.

 Format:

   SHOW option


Additional information available:

  ACCOUNTING ACL         AUDIT        BROADCAST  CLUSTER    CPU        DEFAULT
  DEVICES    ENTRY       ERROR        INTRUSION  KEY        LICENSE    LOGICAL
  MAGTAPE    MEMORY      NETWORK      PRINTER    PROCESS    PROTECTION QUEUE
  QUOTA      RMS_DEFAULT              STATUS     SYMBOL     SYSTEM     TERMINAL
  TIME       TRANSLATION              USERS      WORKING_SET

SHOW Subtopic?
```

This presents a list of all the possible show commands and then prompts us to choose one. The parameter we pass to help, SHOW in the above example, is known as a topic. If we are interested in information on the SHOW QUEUE command, then QUEUE becomes a subtopic, which can again be used to pinpoint the information required:

```
$ help show queue

SHOW

 QUEUE

  Displays information about queues and jobs that are currently in
  queues.

  o Display characteristic names and numbers that are available on
    queues (see /CHARACTERISTIC).
  o Display form names and numbers that are available on queues
    (see /FORM).

   Format:

     SHOW QUEUE [queue-name]

   Additional information available:

   Parameters Command_Qualifiers
   /ALL_ENTRIES       /BATCH    /BRIEF    /BY_JOB_STATUS   /DEVICE
   /FILES             /FULL     /GENERIC  /OUTPUT          /SUMMARY
   /CHARACTERISTIC    /FORM

SHOW QUEUE Subtopic?
```

And next, for help on using the /FULL qualifier:

```
$ help show queue /full

SHOW

 QUEUE

 /FULL

 Displays full information about all queues, and about any jobs
 in the queue that are owned by the current process. The
 information on jobs includes the full file specification, date
 and time of submission, and all settings that were specified for
 the job.

 Information about a queue includes the queue name and type and
 all settings that have been set for the queue. Use this
 qualifier to find out which characteristics and forms have been
 set for all queues or for the queues specified.

 If you use wildcard characters in the queue name parameter,
 information about all queues that match the queue name will be
 displayed.
```

All the examples shown above assume that you know what you are looking for and the structure of the command itself.

If you need help to build the command line, then instead of going straight to the information in help, let help guide you by prompting. This is shown in the following example:

```
$ help

  Information available:

   8086_68000_C          :=          =          @          ACCOUNTING ADVICE
  AI          ALLOCATE   ANALYZE     APPEND     ASSIGN     ATTACH     AUTOGEN
  .
  .
  .
  SYNCHRONIZE            SYSGEN      SYSMAN     System_Services       TFF
  TSA         TYPE       UMapIT      UNIX_Utilities         UNLOCK
  V50_NewFeatures        WAIT        Wells_St   WRITE

  Additional help libraries available (type @name for topics):

  Comp_Centre

Topic? show

SHOW

Displays information about the current status of the process, the
system, or devices in the system.
```

```
 Format:

  SHOW option

Additional information available:

  ACCOUNTING ACL         AUDIT      BROADCAST  CLUSTER    CPU        DEFAULT
  DEVICES    ENTRY       ERROR      INTRUSION  KEY        LICENSE    LOGICAL
  MAGTAPE    MEMORY      NETWORK    PRINTER    PROCESS    PROTECTION QUEUE
  QUOTA      RMS_DEFAULT            STATUS     SYMBOL     SYSTEM     TERMINAL
  TIME       TRANSLATION            USERS      WORKING_SET

SHOW Subtopic? queue

 QUEUE

  Displays information about queues and jobs that are currently in
  queues.

  o Display characteristic names and numbers that are available on
    queues (see /CHARACTERISTIC).
  o Display form names and numbers that are available on queues
    (see /FORM).

    Format:

      SHOW QUEUE [queue-name]

    Additional information available:

    Parameters Command_Qualifiers
    /ALL_ENTRIES       /BATCH    /BRIEF    /BY_JOB_STATUS   /DEVICE
    /FILES             /FULL     /GENERIC  /OUTPUT          /SUMMARY
    /CHARACTERISTIC    /FORM

SHOW QUEUE Subtopic? /full

 /FULL

  Displays full information about all queues, and about any jobs
  in the queue that are owned by the current process.
```

And so on. Obviously this method takes longer, but it provides more information and is generally more helpful to the less experienced user. To return back to the level of help above the current help page, press the ⟨Return⟩ key when prompted for topic/subtopic.

To show the path we have taken down the hierarchy to locate this information, we can draw a section of the help tree diagram as shown in Figure 3-2.

3.4.3 Help and wildcards

Although we will not give an example of the output (there would be too much to show here), typing an asterix (*) to any prompt displays information on all the topics in the list.

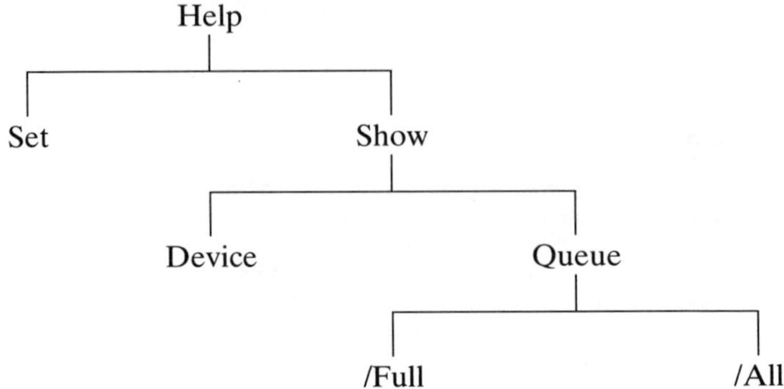

Fig. 3-2 The tree structure of the help library.

Typing, as before:

```
$ help

  Information available:

  8086_68000_C         :=        =        @          ACCOUNTING ADVICE
  .
  .
  .
  V50_NewFeatures      WAIT      Wells_St   WRITE

  Additional help libraries available (type @name for topics):

  Comp_Centre

Topic?
```

You are then invited to choose one of the topics above. Typing "*" at the "topic" prompt will display first level information on all the subjects in the list.

3.4.4 Help commands

Typing a question mark (?) redisplays either the previous page of help, or the main topics if you are on the first level. To exit at either stage type ⟨Ctrl⟩Z, which causes an immediate exit, or press the ⟨Return⟩ key repeatedly, to traverse back up the help tree structure and exit.

3.4.5 Using other help libraries

The system may contain other help libraries. To search these, you can use an "at" symbol (@), followed by the name of the file to be searched for help. For example, we can look in the library named COMP_CENTRE:

```
$ help @comp_centre

Information available:

Ascii_table        BULLETIN    CRON      HELP      JANET_lists
Laser_Printer      Mailing_lists         OPS       ORACLE        PROGS
SWING              SYS         TEX       This_Library            VAXC

Additional help libraries available (type @name for topics):

  Comp_Centre

Topic?
```

The topic concerning "ops" is accessed by the command:

```
$ help @comp_centre ops

OPS

The information contained in the library is to be used as a guide
by the operations team.

 For fuller information read the VMS ops manual and the
 "VMS guide to System Management and Daily Operations".

 Additional information available:

 Menu_system            Directory_layout        Location_of_files      Backup
 Disks      Listings    Case        Accounts    Tapes        Queues    Console
 Stop       Commands    Notice      Alarms      Halting_mole

OPS Subtopic?
```

In the example shown above, the help library COMP_CENTRE has been specifically created for the use of Computer Centre Staff. It has been protected by the System Manager, so as to prevent access by users outside that department. The computer operators have their own section in COMP_CENTRE help, which contains information to assist them with their everyday tasks.

Another example of a help library may be one that contains information relating to the specific equipment in use, such as the various types of printers. In the example below, this information is stored in the SPECIFICHELP library:

```
$ help @specifichelp printers
```

causes help to search a library called SPECIFICHELP.HLB which the System Manager has placed in the SYS$HELP directory, to give users help on printers.

Help libraries may exist to provide information available to all users on items specific to a particular computer, or to provide restricted help, which is only available to certain users.

To use another help library, instead of the default, (SYS$HELP: HELPLIB.HLB), the /LIBRARY qualifier has to be used:

```
$ help /library = sys$help:opshelp.hlb tapes
```

The directory SYS$HELP and the help library extension .HLB are the defaults, so alternatively we only need type:

```
$ help /library = opshelp tapes
```

3.4.6 Redirecting the output from help into a file

Instead of displaying text from help on to the screen, we can direct it into a file, which can afterwards be printed on a lineprinter. This is useful for obtaining a permanent record of commands and their various switches, as well as information relating to the usage of software languages. The subject of redirecting output is discussed in detail in Chapter 4.

A useful reference manual can be built up from the output of the Help facility. In this case, the repeated information and the various menus would be deleted using the system's editor EVE.

To obtain the required output it is best first to set the terminal type to UNKNOWN. This will prevent problems when printing due to any screen control sequences, such as "clear screen", for instance, appearing in the finished text. Alternatively the control characters may be edited out of the file before printing. To set the terminal type to UNKNOWN, enter:

```
$ set terminal/type=unknown
```

Before we run HELP, we need to know the subject we require in the HELP menu. For instance, to run HELP and to place information on Pascal in a file named PASCAL_HELP.TXT, we use the following command:

```
$ help/output=pascal_help.txt pascal
```

We can then print the file in one of two ways. The first prints the file and retains a copy of the file in the present directory. The second deletes the file from the current directory after printing:

```
$ print pascal_help.txt
 Job PASCAL_HELP (queue SYS$PRINT, entry 330) started on SYS$PRINT
```

or

```
$ print/delete pascal_help.txt
Job PASCAL_HELP (queue SYS$PRINT, entry 331) started on SYS$PRINT
```

The file will contain help on Pascal. For example, the printout will be similar to the small section shown here:

```
PASCAL

 VAX PASCAL is an extended implementation of the PASCAL language
 that has been developed for use under the VAX/VMS operating
 system.

 The command, PASCAL, invokes the VAX PASCAL compiler to compile
 one or more source programs.

    Format:

        PASCAL file-spec[,...]

  Additional information available:

  Parameters                           Qualifiers
  /ANALYSIS_DATA[=file-spec]       D=/NOANALYSIS_DATA
  /CHECK[=(option[,...])]          D=/CHECK=BOUNDS
  /CROSS_REFERENCE                 D=/NOCROSS_REFERENCE
 .
 .
 .
 .
 Compilation_Units                     Attributes
  Miscellaneous
  Release_Notes
```

If you have previously reset the terminal type, after obtaining the output reset the terminal to its original setting with the command:

```
$ set terminal/inquire
```

We will see how it is possible to create your own libraries and add items into the help library in Chapter 12.

Chapter

4

Obtaining Output

4.1 Introduction

Most work on computers is done on visual display unit (VDU) terminals, which consist of a screen and keyboard. This type of terminal has no facilities for producing output onto paper. Although this is not a problem for most of the time—since VDU terminals can, generally, operate at higher speeds than a printer—there are occasions when we do need to obtain a permanent record of the output, and we therefore need to find a method of reproducing the screen image on paper. To achieve this, some of the following methods can be used:

1. Hardcopy terminal. This is essentially a printer with a keyboard, and is similar in appearance to a typewriter. It has several disadvantages:

   (a) Everything is written to paper. This can prove wasteful because menus and other temporary and repeated information are printed. There is no selectivity for the output.
   (b) Slow speed compared to VDU.
   (c) Cannot run procedures that perform screen control. For example, screen editors such as EVE and the VAX/VMS MONITOR utility.
   (d) May be expensive, in addition to the cost of paper and ribbons.

2. A printer attached to the terminal. This is an added expense and the terminal must be fitted with a suitable output to drive the printer. In some instances quite complicated key sequences are needed to switch the printer on or off.
3. Placing the output into a file, which is then printed on a system printer. This

is the simplest technique, and is the method that we shall investigate in this chapter.

Of course methods 1 and 2 above have many advantages, such as security, high-quality output (depending on the printer), and convenient and fast access to the output produced. However, they have two disadvantages: firstly, we need physical access to a printer; and secondly, the file cannot be edited to exclude irrelevant information, whereas the output in a file can be readily edited using a suitable editor, such as EVE.

4.2 Output from VAX/VMS

On VAX/VMS there are three methods of obtaining output:

- The /OUTPUT qualifier.
- The ASSIGN command.
- The SET HOST command.

Each of these works in a slightly different way, as is shown below.

4.2.1 The /OUTPUT qualifier

This qualifier is available for use with most VAX/VMS commands. Its action is to output the response from a DCL, i.e. a VAX/VMS command, into a file, instead of displaying it on the screen.

The example below produces a directory listing of all the files in the current directory and writes the information to a file called MY_DIRECTORY.LIS:

```
$ directory/output=my_directory.lis

$

$ type my_directory.lis

  Directory PCL$CCSROOT:[RAY]

  ACC2.COM;3        ADD.C;2           ADD.EXE;2        ADD.EXE;1
  ADD.LIS;1         ADD.OBJ;3         ADD.OBJ;2        ADD.OBJ;1
  AFTER.TXT;1       BEFORE.TXT;1      BRENDA.DIR;1     DEC10.TXT;9

  Total of 12 files.

$ print my_directory.lis

Job MY_DIRECTORY (queue SYS$PRINT, entry 32) started on SYS$PRINT
```

We use the TYPE command to display the contents on the screen. The last command places the file into the printer queue.

If we had mistyped the DIRECTORY command, the output file would not have been created and we would receive an error message of the form:

```
$ dickrectory/output=my_dir.lis

%DCL-W-IVVERB, unrecognized command - check validity and spelling
/DICKRECTORY/
```

The /OUTPUT qualifier will only direct the output from the current command into the file. Thereafter output is directed once again back to the screen.

By using the /OUTPUT qualifier we can obtain listed output from the help library. These files can then be bound together, to form a personal help document (see Chapter 3).

4.2.2 The ASSIGN command

There are times when it would be useful to create a log file, which is a record of the result of the actions of more than one command. To do this, we use the ASSIGN command. When we log in to the system, several logical names are created for our use. One of these is SYS$OUTPUT. SYS$OUTPUT is special in that it takes as its assignment the device, or filename, to which the output is to be directed. When we log in, SYS$OUTPUT is assigned by default to the screen (defined as “tt:”). If instead we wish to send the output to a file, we reassign SYS$OUTPUT to be a file name. The example that follows shows the equivalence string, the destination of SYS$OUTPUT before and after reassignment. Once the reassignment has been made, thereafter everything is written into a file, including the SHOW LOGICAL SYS$OUTPUT command which follows the reassignment and any error messages.

```
$ show logical sys$output         Default setting.

  "SYS$OUTPUT" = "_RTA3:" (LNM$PROCESS_TABLE)

$ assign dir.lis sys$output       Reassign it to DIR.LIS.

$ show logical sys$output         Check it is correct.

$ show default                    Show current directory.

$ directory                       Directory of files.
```

```
$ deassign sys$output             Reassign to SYS$OUTPUT.

$ show logical sys$output         Check it is correct.

  "SYS$OUTPUT" = "_RTA3:" (LNM$PROCESS TABLE)

$ type dir.lis                    Type log file.

"SYS$OUTPUT" = "_DUA2:" (LNM$PROCESS_TABLE)

DUA2:[RAY]

Directory DUA2:[RAY]

ACC2.COM;3        ADD.C;2           ADD.EXE;2         ADD.EXE;1
ADD.LIS;1         ADD.OBJ;3         ADD.OBJ;2         ADD.OBJ;1
AFTER.TXT;1       BEFORE.TXT;1      BRENDA.DIR;1      DEC10.TXT;9

Total of 12 files.
```

All commands executed between the ASSIGN and DEASSIGN commands have their output directed to the file DIR.LIS. Since only the output is directed to the file, there is no record of the actual commands we typed to obtain the output. For new users of the system, who wish to log their terminal sessions for later analysis, this may present a problem.

It should be noted that when the ASSIGN command is used, everything that is normally written to the screen is also written in the same format to a file. This has the drawback that it includes escape sequences and special characters, for updating, redrawing and refreshing the screen. Such characters cannot be printed and should be edited out before printing the file. Alternatively, the terminal can be set to device type UNKNOWN or to type HARDCOPY. This causes VAX/VMS to "believe" it is sending characters to an elementary terminal or lineprinter and therefore does not send any of the escape sequences which those devices are not expected to be able to cope with. Remember, after logging has been completed, to set your terminal back to the correct type (use the command SET TERMINAL/INQUIRE), especially if you wish subsequently to run a screen editor. Therefore, to recap:

```
$ set terminal/device=unknown

$ assign ray.lis sys$output       Where RAY.LIS is logfile

                          session logged to file

$ deassign sys$output             Reassign to SYS$OUTPUT.

$ set terminal/inquire
```

4.2.3 The SET HOST/LOG command

This is probably the most complete method of logging a terminal session into a file. Unfortunately, however, this command is only available on systems that use DECnet—a networking system that allows several VAXs to communicate.

Using DECnet it is possible to gain access to any other computer in the network by using the SET HOST command (i.e. SET HOST PANDA will connect you to the VAX named PANDA). This makes a connection to the named computer and allows you to log in. We can also "set host" to the node (a "node" is a VAX in the network) we are on. If we were currently logged into a computer called MOLE, we can establish a second session, by typing "SET HOST MOLE" and log in a second time. This would have the effect of creating another terminal session "on top" of the existing one. If we do not know the name of the computer we are using, we can use the command SET HOST 0, which effectively performs the same function.

To log the complete terminal session, we connect to another computer, or reconnect to the computer we are currently using, by specifying the /LOG qualifier to the SET HOST command. The following commands log you on to a computer called WOMBAT and log the terminal session. Since no log file name was specified, all the output is stored in the default file SETHOST.LOG.

```
$ set host wombat/log

     Welcome to Wombat running VAX/VMS V5.0

Username:
.
.
.
$ logout
```

Now to review the log session give the command:

```
$ type sethost.log

               Welcome to Wombat running VAX/VMS V5.0

Username:
.
.
.
$ logout

$
```

As with the ASSIGN command, escape sequences may be generated in the file—to avoid this, use the SET TERMINAL/DEVICE=UNKNOWN command at the beginning of the session. The next example does this and creates a log of the Pascal help library on the current computer. In this example we specify the file name HELP_PASCAL.LIS as the name of the log file.

```
$

$ set host 0/log=help_pascal.lis          Start log session.

       Welcome to Mole running VAX/VMS V5.0

Username:
.
.
.
$ set terminal/device=unknown             Stop control characters.

$ help pascal                             List Pascal library.

$ logout                                  End log session.

   RAY          logged out at 23-MAY-1989 10:21:07.17
  %REM-S-END, control returned to node _MOLE::

$ print help_pascal.lis                   Print log file.

Job HELP_PASCAL (queue SYS$PRINT, entry 66) started on SYS$PRINT
```

Unlike the ASSIGN command, both the output from the computer and the input from the keyboard are written to the file.

Chapter

5

A First Visit to the Editor EVE

5.1 Introduction

EVE is short for Extensible Vax Editor. VAXTPU, commonly known as TPU (Text Processing Utility), provides a programmable, text editing facility. EVE itself has been written using TPU.

In this chapter the fundamentals of using a text editor are introduced, together with a description of a set of commands that should be sufficient to make a start on using the VMS editor EVE.

Further and more advanced operations, e.g. to delete blocks of text, are discussed in Chapter 6.

5.2 What Is an Editor?

The editor is a program that allows text manipulation to be carried out according to its own set of rules.

The purpose of an editor is to accept input from the terminal into a named file, i.e. the creation of a new file, and to allow the revision and modification of an existing file. The file can be a text, such as, for example, an article, or the source code of a program. Whatever the content of the file, it should have a name that reflects its purpose.

The editor is often the most widely used tool on a computer system. It evolved from the analysis of users' requirements to help them perform diverse tasks associated with producing a lexically acceptable format of the file.

5.3 Requirements of an Editor

1. Preserve the current state during a system crash or disconnection of the terminal from the system. (Save.)
2. Present the existing file for inspection.
3. Note any modifications one wishes to make.
4. On instruction, to make the modifications indicated at step 3 permanent, i.e. create a replacement version of the initial text.
5. Carry out repeatedly operations 3 and 4 until the user is satisfied that all the modifications are completed.

When any alterations to the file have been made VMS allocates on exit from the editor, the next highest version number to the file and places it in the directory along with the previous version. By default, starting with a new file, the new file becomes the latest version and thus has a version number one greater than the original.

Thus the command:

```
dir t*
```

produces a display of all the files whose name begins with "t" in the current directory:

```
$ dir t*

  Directory DISK1:[MIKE]

  TEMP.TXT;4

  Total of 1 file.
```

After completion of an editing session, the command produces the result:

```
$ dir t*

  Directory DISK1:[MIKE]

  TEMP.TXT;5                TEMP.TXT;4

  Total of 2 files.
```

Showing that the original version is preserved, together with the latest edited version.

5.4 Entering EVE

EVE is entered by typing:

```
$ edit/tpu filename.ext
```

where FILENAME.EXT is the name of the file we wish to create or edit. Notice that we type EDIT/TPU to run the editor, and not EVE (although we could set up the symbol EVE :== EDIT/TPU, in our LOGIN.COM file to make this the case).

For example, to edit the file SORT.PAS, type:

```
$ edit/tpu sort.pas
```

FILENAME is the name of the file you wish to work with. If the file already exists, then EVE reads the contents of the file into a working storage area known as a "buffer." EVE will display, starting from the beginning of the file, as much of this file as will fit onto the screen. The screen is therefore acting as a "window" into the buffer.

If the file does not exist, then EVE creates a new and empty buffer for you (Figure 5-1). If EVE does this when you are trying to edit an existing file, then this means that you have probably spelt the filename incorrectly.

Example

The command

```
$ edit/tpu diary.dat
```

will enter you into the file DIARY.DAT, allowing you to proceed with an editing session on this file.

5.5 The EVE Status Line

As can be seen in Figure 5-1, there is a "status line" near the bottom of your screen. This will initially indicate the following:

Buffer	Name of the current editing buffer.
Insert	Shows that insert mode is currently selected. This means that any characters that you enter are inserted at the current cursor position.
Overstrike	This is the alternative operation to insert, where the characters at the cursor position are replaced with the characters typed in at the keyboard.

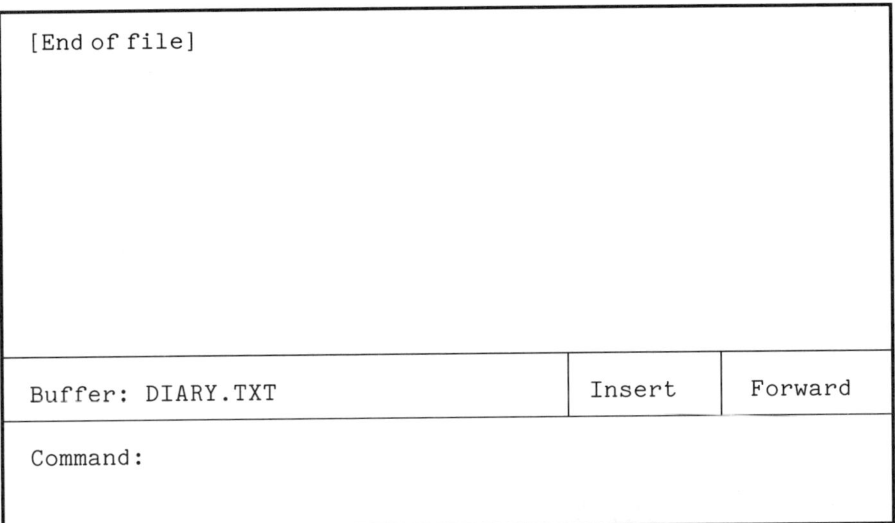

Fig. 5-1 Screen display on creation of a new, empty file.

Forward — Moving the cursor to the next word, or searching for a string (a sequence of characters), moves the cursor forward from its current position.

Reverse — This is the alternative to forward. Here movement is backwards towards the beginning of the file.

5.6 EVE Keyboard Layouts and Keypad Commands

EVE can be controlled either from the keypad or from the keyboard by typing control characters. However, after gaining familiarity with EVE, one finds it more convenient to use a combination of these methods.

The layout of the keypad keys depends upon which terminal type you are using. The keypad layouts for the VT100 and VT200 series terminals are given in Figures 5-2 and 5-3, together with the control key commands.

If your terminal is not one of the authentic Digital VT100 or VT200 series, then it is likely that it emulates one, i.e. it behaves as if it were of that type. Your VDU manual should provide you with this information.

5.7 Entering EVE Commands

To enter EVE commands from the keyboard, first press the ⟨Do⟩ key(or key ⟨PF4⟩ on VT100 terminals) and then press the appropriate command sequence. The command is ended by pressing the ⟨Return⟩ key.

↑	↓	←	→

⟨BKSPACE⟩ – Start of Line
⟨Ctrl⟩B – Recall
⟨Ctrl⟩E – End of Line
⟨Ctrl⟩R – Remember
⟨Ctrl⟩U – Erase To Start Line
⟨Ctrl⟩V – Quote
⟨Ctrl⟩W – Refresh
⟨Ctrl⟩Z – Exit

Use the Do key to enter advanced commands.

Find	Help	Forward Reverse	Do
Select	Remove	Insert Here	Move by Line
	↑		Erase Word
←	↓	→	Insert Overst
Next Screen		Prev Screen	

Fig. 5-2 EVE keypad for VT100 series terminals.

For example, to enter the QUIT command, which exits from EVE without writing the contents of buffers to the disk, the following sequence of keys would be pressed:

1. Press the ⟨Do⟩ key.
2. Type QUIT.
3. Press the ⟨Return⟩ key.

EVE commands may be abbreviated to the smallest unique initial string. If an abbreviation is not unique, EVE displays the possible choices and prompts for the command name.

Remember that under the EVE protocol, EVE is either in “insert” or in “overstrike” mode. Thus the complete operation consists of the following steps:

1. First, create a window.
2. Second, position the cursor at the required position.
3. Select either “insert” or “overstrike” modes.
4. On completion of the above give the desired EVE command.
5. Leave the session using the EXIT command if you are satisfied with the changes you have made. Alternatively, if you decide to abandon the editing session without any alterations, then use the QUIT command.

5.8 Getting Help

The HELP keypad command enables you to access help information about the other keypad commands. To exit from HELP, press the ⟨Return⟩ key.

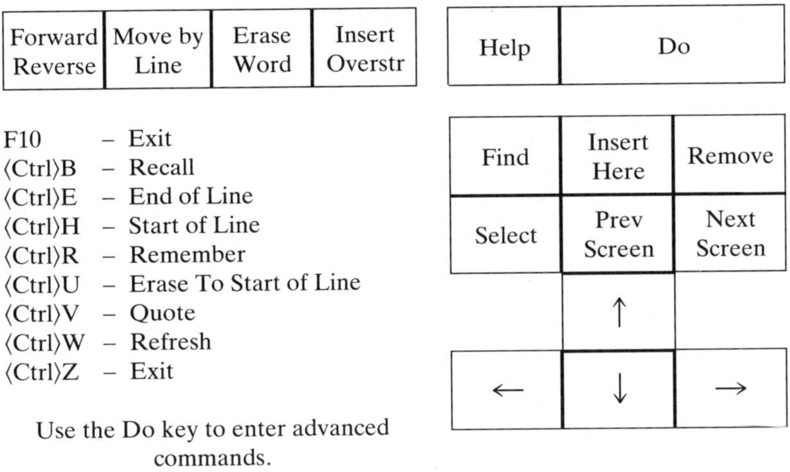

Forward Reverse	Move by Line	Erase Word	Insert Overstr

Help	Do

F10 – Exit
⟨Ctrl⟩B – Recall
⟨Ctrl⟩E – End of Line
⟨Ctrl⟩H – Start of Line
⟨Ctrl⟩R – Remember
⟨Ctrl⟩U – Erase To Start of Line
⟨Ctrl⟩V – Quote
⟨Ctrl⟩W – Refresh
⟨Ctrl⟩Z – Exit

Use the Do key to enter advanced commands.

Find	Insert Here	Remove
Select	Prev Screen	Next Screen
	↑	
←	↓	→

Fig. 5-3 EVE keypad for VT200 series terminals.

To get information on more advanced EVE commands, use the HELP command:

1. Press the ⟨Do⟩ key.
2. Type HELP.
3. Press the ⟨Return⟩ key.

The HELP command then provides you with a list of all the EVE commands. Type the name of the command of interest, or to see the list of commands again press the question mark (?) key. In order to leave the HELP command, press the ⟨Return⟩ key.

You can ask for help on a particular command in a single step. For example:

```
help top
```

provides help on the TOP command, which can be used to move the cursor to the top of the file being edited.

5.9 Insert and Overstrike Modes

This keypad command changes the current mode of the buffer. The current mode is displayed on the status line at the bottom of the window. Its status is either of the two possible modes—insert or overstrike—according to its last setting.

In insert mode, the characters typed are inserted to the left of the current cursor position. In overstrike mode, the character at the current cursor position is replaced by typing in a new character.

The ⟨Insert/Overstrike⟩ key invokes this command.

5.9.1 Inserting new text and replacing text

Inserting new text is simple. Ensure that insert mode is displayed on the status line, then typed text is inserted at the cursor position by typing the appropriate characters. To change from overstrike mode to insert mode, press the ⟨Insert/Overstrike⟩ key.

If overstrike mode is selected the status line displays OVERSTRIKE and the character typed replaces that at the cursor position. The cursor moves to the next space on the right, ready to replace that character in turn and so on until the overstrike mode is cancelled.

5.10 Changing Direction

The current direction affects the way that the FIND, MOVE BY LINE, and MOVE BY WORD commands work.

CHANGE DIRECTION changes the current direction of the buffer. The current direction is displayed as either FORWARD or REVERSE on the status line at the bottom of the window.

The ⟨Forward/Reverse⟩ key invokes this command. By judicious use of this key, one can rapidly scan through the buffer and carry out alterations randomly in different sections of the buffer.

5.10.1 Forward

When the direction is forward:

⟨Find⟩	searches forward in the buffer.
⟨Move by Line⟩	moves to the end of the current line.
⟨Move by Word⟩	moves to the start of the next word.

5.10.2 Reverse

When the direction is reverse:

⟨Find⟩	searches backward in the buffer.
⟨Move by Line⟩	moves to the start of the current line.
⟨Move by Word⟩	moves to the start of the previous word.

5.11 Moving the Cursor

The cursor is moved by using the four arrow keys: up (↑), down (↓), right (→), and left (←).

The following key operations allow you to move the cursor to the start and to the end of the current line:

⟨Ctrl⟩E	Move to end of line.
⟨Backspace⟩	Move to start of line.

More advanced actions are carried out by using the following keypad commands:

⟨Top⟩	Top of file.
⟨Bottom⟩	End of file.
⟨Move by Word⟩	Next word.
⟨Next Screen⟩	Next screen.
⟨Previous Screen⟩	Previous screen.
⟨Find⟩	Next occurrence of a string.

The ⟨Move by Word⟩ and ⟨Find⟩ keys operate in the direction specified on the status line. You can select the direction by using the ⟨Forward/Reverse⟩ keypad command and "toggle" by repeatedly pressing the forward/reverse direction.

5.12 Simple Deletion of Text

The ⟨Delete⟩ key is used to delete individual characters.

5.12.1 The ⟨Delete⟩ key

Pressing the ⟨Delete⟩ key erases the character to the left of the current cursor position. As with the delete command, the action of the ⟨Delete⟩ key depends upon whether insert or overstrike mode is currently active:

- *Insert mode* In insert mode, after deletion the rest of the line moves left one space to close up the space vacated.
- *Overstrike mode* In overstrike mode, the character to the left of the cursor position is replaced by a space; the rest of the line remains in the same place on the screen, i.e. the character has been replaced with a blank space.

When the cursor is at the start of a line, the RETURN at the end of the preceding line is deleted. The text on the next line is joined to the right of the text in the current line. Note that this action can be used to join subsequent lines.

5.12.2 Erase line

This command erases all the characters from the current cursor position to the end of the current line. It then appends the next line to the current line.

5.12.3 Restore

This command reinserts the text last erased as a consequence of using one of the following commands: ERASE WORD, ERASE LINE, ERASE PREVIOUS WORD, and ERASE START OF LINE. The text is reinserted regardless of whether the current mode is insert or overstrike.

5.13 Leaving EVE

There are several methods of leaving the EVE editor. The most commonly used method is to press the ⟨PF4⟩ key, then type either EXIT or QUIT. Below we look at both of these with alternative ways of specifying the commands.

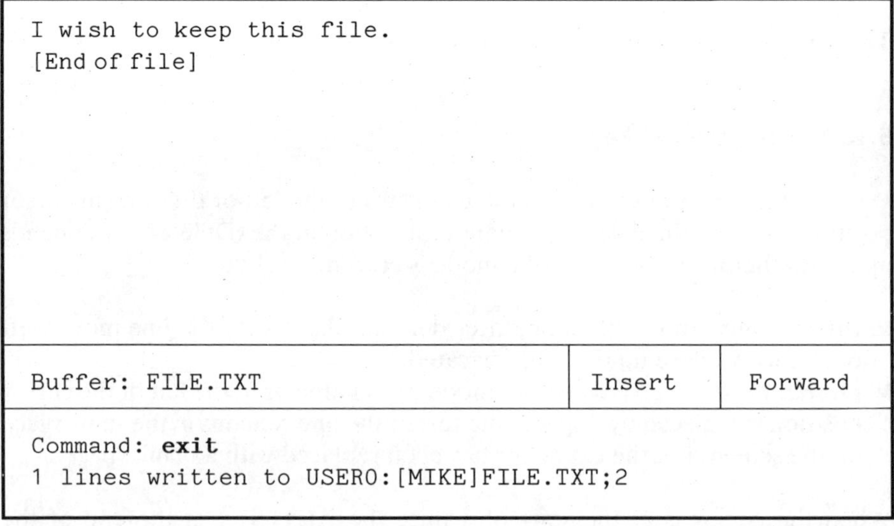

Fig. 5-4 Exiting from EVE and saving the edited file.

5.13.1 The EXIT command

The EXIT command causes you to leave the EVE editor, saving your current buffer. EXIT will also ask you if you want to save each of your other modified buffers (Figure 5-4).

Referring to Figure 5-4, pressing the ⟨PF4⟩ key, and typing EXIT when prompted with "Command:", causes the file to be saved to disk. The file will be given the name FILE.TXT, as shown, and have a version number one greater than any existing files with the same name.

Typing ⟨Ctrl⟩Z also invokes the ⟨EXIT⟩ command, which also saves the current buffer, as does the EXIT key on VT200 series terminals.

5.13.2 The QUIT command

You can use the QUIT command, to leave the EVE editor without creating any new files (Figure 5-5). You can also use the WRITE FILE command to write the current buffer to a new file name (see Chapter 6).

With reference to Figure 5-5, pressing the ⟨PF4⟩ key places the cursor at the "Command:" prompt. We then type QUIT. Before terminating the editing session, EVE will question our actions by displaying the message "Buffer modifications will not be saved, continue quitting (Y or N)?" If we do not wish to save the file we type Y, or to save the file and resume our editing session we type N.

```
I DO NOT wish to keep this file. It contains mistooks.
[End of file]

Buffer: RUBBISH.TXT                        Insert       Forward

Command: quit
Buffer mods. will not be saved, continue quitting (Y or N)?
```

Fig. 5-5 Exiting from EVE without saving the edited file.

The QUIT operation is very useful if you realize that you have made a mess of the file during the current editing session. In such cases it is often easier to use QUIT, which leaves the editor preserving only those changes that you have made before the last WRITE operation.

Chapter

6

A Second Visit to the Editor EVE

6.1 Introduction

In Chapter 5 we looked at simple EVE commands, such as character and line insertion and deletion, cursor movement, and entering and exiting the editor. In this chapter we shall look at the more powerful EVE commands, allowing such features as text substitution, text cut-and-paste commands, and use of the learn protocol. Learn enables us to "teach" the editor a sequence of keystrokes that it can then repeat whenever they are needed.

This chapter refers to the keyboard diagrams for VT100 and VT200 terminals, shown in Figures 5-2 and 5-3, respectively. Some of these keys, which have been directly assigned to perform commands, have already been discussed earlier in Chapter 5. The others we review below.

We start by introducing the use of a qualifier, which we can use when we run EVE to perform "disaster recovery" of a file in the event of machine failure.

In this chapter the features described, such as cut-and-paste, using different techniques of multiple windows and buffers, are particularly powerful and efficient at carrying out diverse operations. However, at first sight these operations appear to be complicated. Because of this, the step-by-step operations are described exactly as one has to carry them out. To gain familiarity, we suggest that before carrying out operations on a large file you either create simple text files and test the described processes, or that you type in and carry out the example processes given in this chapter.

6.2 The /RECOVER Qualifier

If while you are editing a file, the computer crashes, i.e stops working, or the connection between your terminal and the computer is lost, you may still be able to recover the alterations you have made to your file during the editing session. To do this, run EVE with the /RECOVER qualifier. For example:

```
$ edit/tpu/recover file.txt
```

where FILE.TXT is the name of the file you were last editing. EVE should then update the file by "playing back" the last editing session on the screen. After the recovery has been completed, the cursor is placed at the same location that it occupied when the disconnection occurred. The user can then continue with the editing session. In some instances it may not be possible to retrieve all the alterations made to a file and the last few alterations may be lost; this depends on when the editor last automatically saved the edited file to the "journal".

6.3 The EVE Keypad

In this section we shall describe the function of various keypad keys. One key in particular, ⟨PF4⟩, deserves special attention since it allows us to type commands directly to EVE. Its use and selected EVE commands are reviewed in Section 6.4.

6.3.1 The Find key

The ⟨Find⟩ key enables us to search for and locate a text string, or any sequence of characters, in a file. Pressing the ⟨Find⟩ key causes the cursor to move to the command line at the bottom of the screen. We then type in the series of characters, or a single character, that we wish to search the file for. If the string we are searching for contains spaces or tabs, then the complete string should be placed between quotation marks (" "). Once located, the characters in the text will be highlighted, i.e. shown in bold text, and the cursor is positioned on the first character of the sequence. The string and the file can then be edited as normal. Moving the cursor off the highlighted string causes it to revert to its normal intensity.

If the search string is in lowercase, the search is not case sensitive. However, it is case sensitive when the search string is typed in a mixture of upper- and lowercase characters. For example, if we input a search string that consists of lowercase characters only, then EVE would try and find the following strings:

Search string ray
Matches ray, RAY, Ray, RAy, raY, rAY, rAy, RaY

If we type in the search string in a mixture of uppercase and lowercase characters, EVE will try to match the cases of the two strings exactly.

Search string Ray
Matches Ray

After searching for the first occurrence of a string in a file, we can subsequently search for the next occurrence of the same string by pressing ⟨Find⟩ twice.

The search takes place in the direction indicated by the status line on the bottom of the screen. Use the ⟨Direction⟩ key to toggle between forward and reverse scanning of the file.

If an occurrence of the string is found in the opposite direction to which we are searching, the editor informs us of this and enquires if we would like the cursor to be moved to that position.

Let us conclude with an example: to search in the simple C program shown in Figure 6-1 for the string "hello world". In the example, the bottom line of the text contains the string "[End of file]". This is not part of the text of the file, but it is used by the editor to indicate the location of the bottom of the file.

1. First we press the ⟨Find⟩ key, which causes the cursor to move to the bottom of the screen and prompt for input by displaying "Forward Find:".

```
/* A simple C program */

main()
{
printf ("This program prints hello world on the screen.");   (3)
}
[End of file]

Buffer: HELLO.C                    Insert      Forward

Foward Find: "hello world"                                   (2)
```

Fig. 6-1 Screen display with steps marked for find operation.

2. We then type in the string to search for, in this case, "hello world". The string needs to be enclosed in quotation marks since it contains a space character. We then press ⟨Return⟩.
3. The editor then searches forwards through the text for the first occurrence of the text. When located, the string is highlighted and the cursor placed on the first character of the string as shown in Figure 6-1.

6.3.2 The Select, Remove, and Insert keys

Introduction

These keys are usually used in conjunction with each other. They allow you to perform three functions:

- Delete a section of the text.
- Move text from one place to another.
- Copy text from one place to another.

The operations to perform each of these functions are similar, and therefore we shall cover them here together.

Deleting, moving and copying text

First we have to select the text we need to copy, remove, or delete. To do this, we move the cursor to the start of the text and press the ⟨Select⟩ key. We then move the cursor to the end of the text to be selected. If we choose to select the text "bottom to top" instead of "top to bottom", the selected data will still appear in the correct order when it is retrieved, i.e. it is not reversed. When selecting text that ends in a specific character sequence, we can use the ⟨Find⟩ key to search for that sequence and move the cursor there. If we decide that we have chosen the wrong text, pressing ⟨Select⟩ a second time will cancel the previous selection.

The selected text appears in block mode.

At the end of the selection, we press the ⟨Remove⟩ key. The text is then deleted from the screen and the screen accordingly redrawn. The text however has not been completely deleted, but is stored in an internal buffer. It is this buffer that is used in the next action. The content of this buffer is then used for pasting into a location, or it is cut and then thrown away. Hence the name: cut-and-paste operations.

The next action depends on whether we wish to delete, move, or copy the text. The procedure for each of the three possibilities is outlined below.

Deleting text

To delete the text permanently, do not press the ⟨Insert Here⟩ key, but allow the buffer to be overwritten on the subsequent use of the ⟨Select⟩ and ⟨Remove⟩ keys by the next text copied into the buffer.

Moving text

To move the text, i.e. to transfer it from one place to another, position the cursor at the location in the file where you want the text to appear and press the ⟨Insert Here⟩ key.

Copying text

To copy the text, press the ⟨Insert Here⟩ key immediately after pressing the ⟨Remove⟩ key and before moving the cursor to the new location. This operation replaces the text back into its original position. Then move the cursor to the new location and press ⟨Insert Here⟩. By repeating this sequence, a selected piece of text can be inserted into several different parts of the file.

An example of deleting a block of text

In the following example we shall delete the first three lines of the text. The sequence of operations is shown below and is indicated in Figure 6-2a:

1. Move cursor to the start of the text you wish to delete (i.e. the "T" of "This").
2. Press the ⟨Select⟩ key.
3. Press the ⟨Down arrow⟩ key three times, to move to the start of the line "The end." The selected text appears in reverse video (dark characters in a light block).
4. Press ⟨Remove⟩ to delete the current selected text and to place it in the paste buffer.
5. The text is stored in the paste buffer but will be overwritten by any further use of the ⟨Select⟩ and ⟨Remove⟩ keys.

The final text is shown in Figure 6-2b.

```
This is a text file which contains instructions on how        (1)
to delete a piece of text from this file.
                                                              (3)
The end.
Move is not the same as copy. Copy leaves a copy of the
text in its original location.

[End of file]

Buffer: TEXT.TXT                    Insert       Forward
```

Fig. 6-2a Screen display before text deletion.

```
The end.
Move is not the same as copy. Copy leaves a copy of the
text in its original location.

[End of file]

Buffer: TEXT.TXT                    Insert       Forward
```

Fig. 6-2b Screen display after deletion operation is completed.

```
This is a text file which contains instructions on how          (1)
to move a piece of text from one part of the file to
another.
                                                                (3)
The end.
Move is not the same as copy. Copy leaves a copy of the text
in its original location.

[End of file]

Buffer: TEXT.TXT                          Insert    Forward
```

Fig. 6-3a Screen display before the text is repositioned.

```
The end.
Move is not the same as copy. Copy leaves a copy of the
text in its original location.
This is a text file which contains instructions on how
to move a piece of text from one part of the file to
another.

[End of file]

Buffer: TEXT.TXT                          Insert    Forward
```

Fig. 6-3b Screen display after moving a section of text.

An example of moving a block of text

In the following example, we shall move the first three lines of text to the bottom of the file (see Figure 6-3a). The sequence of operations is as follows:

1. Move cursor to the start of the text you wish to move (i.e. the "T" of "This").
2. Press the ⟨Select⟩ key.
3. Press the ⟨Down arrow⟩ key three times to move to the start of the line "The end." The selected text appears in reverse video.
4. Press ⟨Remove⟩ to delete the current selected text and place it in the paste buffer.
5. Press ⟨Do⟩ and type BOTTOM to move to the bottom of the screen.
6. Press ⟨Insert Here⟩. The text is inserted at the bottom of the screen.

The final text is shown in Figure 6-3b.

An example of copying a block of text

The procedure for coping text is very similar to that for moving text. The only difference is that we press the key ⟨Insert Here⟩ once before moving the cursor to reinsert the text into its original location. In the following example we shall copy the first three lines of text to the bottom of the file (see Figure 6-4a). The sequence of operations is as follows:

1. Move cursor to the start of the text you wish to move (i.e. the "T" of "This").
2. Press the ⟨Select⟩ key.
3. Press the ⟨Down arrow⟩ key three times to move to the start of the line "The end." The selected text appears in reverse video.
4. Press ⟨Remove⟩ to delete the current selected text and to place it in the paste buffer.
5. Press ⟨Insert Here⟩ to place the text back into its original location.
6. Press ⟨Do⟩ and type BOTTOM to move to the bottom of the screen.
7. Press ⟨Insert Here⟩. The text is now inserted at the bottom of the screen.

The final text is shown in Figure 6-4b.

6.4 Entering EVE Commands

The ⟨Do⟩ key is used when typing commands directly to the editor. We can use it to activate some of the commands already covered and some of the more

```
This is a text file which contains instructions on how      (1)
to move a piece of text from one part of the file to
another.
                                                            (3)
The end.
Move is not the same as copy. Copy leaves a copy of the text
in its original location.
[End of file]

Buffer: TEXT.TXT                         Insert    Forward
```

Fig. 6-4a Screen display before a section of text is copied.

```
This is a text file which contains instructions on how
to move a piece of text from one part of the file to
another.
The end.
Move is not the same as copy. Copy leaves a copy of the
text in its original location.
This is a text file which contains instructions on how
to move a piece of text from one part of the file to
another.
[End of file]

Buffer: TEXT.TXT                         Insert    Forward
```

Fig. 6-4b Screen display after text has been copied.

powerful new commands introduced below. To perform the FIND command, which is directly equivalent to pressing the ⟨Find⟩ key, either of the next two series of keystrokes are used:

```
⟨Find⟩
hello ⟨Return⟩
```

or

```
⟨Do⟩
find hello ⟨Return⟩
```

They both search for the string "hello", although the first method marginally saves on typing.

6.4.1 The EVE command—WILDCARD FIND

Pressing the ⟨Do⟩ key and typing FIND, followed by the name of the search, causes the string to perform the same function as pressing the ⟨Find⟩ key and typing the name of the search string. There is however, a more powerful use for the former method.

Pressing ⟨Do⟩ and typing WILDCARD FIND followed by the search string initiates the process of matching wildcards, such as asterisks (*) and the percentage sign (%), to locate strings in a file. The wildcard characters are used in much the same way they would be to describe file names (see Section 7.3.4).

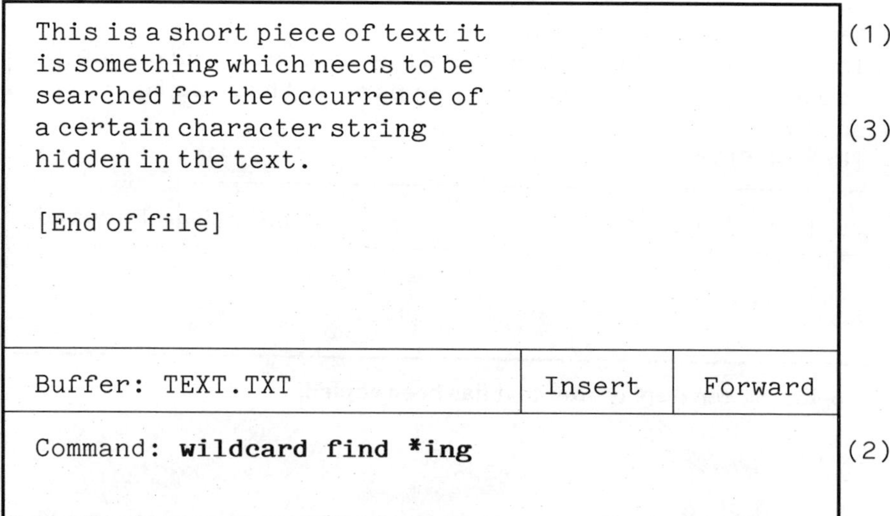

Fig. 6-5 An example of using a wildcard.

In any case, an asterisk matches a string of characters of any length, while the percentage matches exactly one character.

In the following example we shall search for a string ending in "ing" (see Figure 6-5). The procedure is:

1. Place the cursor at the top of the file (and not just the screen).
2. Press the ⟨Do⟩ key and type WILDCARD FIND *ING on the command line, and press ⟨Return⟩.
3. The cursor moves to the start of the first line that ends with "ing".

In the above example, the cursor will be placed at the beginning of line 4. Note that WILDCARD FIND matches the line and not a single word with similar characteristics. In the example above, WILDCARD FIND will locate a line ending in "ing", and not the first word ending in "ing" ("something" in line 2), in contrast with the FIND command. This is because WILDCARD FIND ignores spaces and considers each line as being a single string. Therefore if you are looking for a word that finishes with "ing", you have to use FIND. The distinction between the two operations should be noted.

6.4.2 The EVE command—REPLACE

This command is similar to the FIND command in that it searches for a specified string. Unlike FIND however, it then prompts the user to change the string that has been searched for with another user-specified string. To use the command, perform the following key sequences:

⟨Do⟩

```
command: replace string1 string2
```

which will cause a search for "string1". When located, the EVE editor will prompt the user on the type of action to take. The choices are as follows:

- *Yes* Type Y (Yes) to replace "string1" with "string2". EVE will then automatically continue to search in the selected direction (either forward or reverse) for any other occurrences of the string. If any are found, the editor will prompt with:

  ```
  Replace? Type Yes, No, All, Last, or Quit:
  ```

  If the string does not exist in the current direction of searching, but it is located in the opposite direction, EVE will prompt with either of the following messages as appropriate:

  ```
  Found in reverse direction. Go there? [Y]
  ```

or

```
Found in forward direction. Go there? [Y]
```

- *No* Type N to leave this string unchanged and continue searching for the next string (as for "yes" above).
- *All* Type A to continue searching through the file and automatically replace all occurrences of "string1" with "string2". After all the strings have been modified EVE may still ask:

  ```
  Found in forward direction. Go there? [Y]
  ```

  or

  ```
  Found in reverse direction. Go there? [Y]
  ```

  This will occur if the search string "string1" contains a character sequence also found in "string2". For example, if we are searching for "ing" and replacing it with "sing", then once modified the replacement string still contains the search string (i.e. "ing").
- *Last* Type L to change "string1" to "string2" and end the search for any more occurrences of "string1".
- *Quit* Type Q to stop searching for any more occurrences of the string. Do not change this current occurrence.

When using the REPLACE command with text that contains spaces, the strings must be placed between quotation marks.

Let us consider the following example (Figure 6-6), which searches for the string "hello" and replaces it with the string "goodbye".

1 Press the ⟨Do⟩ key. This takes the cursor to the command line at the bottom of the screen. Type in the command REPLACE HELLO GOODBYE and press ⟨Return⟩. Notice that since neither the search nor the replacement strings contain space characters, we do not need to enclose either of them in quotation marks.

2. EVE then finds the first occurrence of the search string (highlights the string in bold type) and then prompts in the command window with:

   ```
   Replace? Type Yes, No, All, Last, or Quit:
   ```

3 Since this is the only occurrence in the file, we type L for Last. EVE replaces "hello" with "goodbye" and exits from the replace command. In this instance we could have equally well have typed R for replace.

```
/* A simple C program */

main()
{
printf ("This program prints [hello] world on the screen.);      (2)
}
[End of file]

Buffer: HELLO.C                    Insert      Forward

Command: replace hello goodbye                                    (1)
Replace? Type Yes, No, All, Last, or Quit:
```

Fig. 6-6 Screen display for REPLACE string operation.

6.4.3 The EVE command—INCLUDE FILE

In EVE there is a command that allows you to insert the contents of another file at any selected place in the file you are currently editing. It allows one, while editing "file1" to include "file2" into the editing buffer, thus giving a new buffer with the content of "file1" + "file2". This operation is done using the INCLUDE FILE command.

The command is of the form INCLUDE FILE filename, where the filename can be the name of any file in the current directory, or for files resident in other directories, the complete file description (e.g. USER0:[RAY.TEST] EXAMPLE.PROG).

To demonstrate this, suppose we wish to insert the contents of FILE2.DAT into the middle of a document FILE1.TXT.

If FILE1.TXT contains the text:

```
Dear Leslie,

This is the data you required from the experiment we
conducted.

Hope this is of some use.

                                    Ray
```

```
Dear Leslie,

This is the data you required from the experiment we
conducted.                                                    (1)

Hope this is of some use.
                                        Ray
[End of file]

Buffer: FILE1.TXT                   | Insert   | Forward

Command: include file file2.dat                               (2)
```

Fig. 6-7a Screen display of FILE1.TXT.

```
Dear Leslie,

This is the data you required from the experiment we
conducted.
                Temperature          Pressure                 (3)
                   20 C              34 m/kg
                   40 C              54 m/kg
                   60 C              65 m/kg
                   80 C              78 m/kg

Hope this is of some use.
                                        Ray
[End of file]

Buffer: FILE1.TXT                   | Insert   | Forward

Command: include file file2.dat
```

Fig. 6-7b Screen display of FILE1.TXT with FILE2.DAT inserted.

and FILE2.DAT contains the data:

```
Temperature          Pressure

     20 C             34 m/kg
     40 C             54 m/kg
     60 C             65 m/kg
     80 C             78 m/kg
```

Then the following actions, need to be taken (see Figure 6-7a):

1. First, we run EVE to edit FILE1.TXT and we move the cursor to the position in the file where we want to include the contents of the second file (FILE2.DAT).
2. We then press the ⟨Do⟩ key, which takes us to the command line. Next, we type in the command INCLUDE FILE FILE2.DAT and press ⟨Return⟩.
3. The contents of FILE2.DAT are then copied into FILE1.TXT.
4. Press ⟨Do⟩ and type EXIT to finish editing.

The results of this file inclusion operation is shown in Figure 6-7b.

6.4.4 The EVE command—LEARN

A very powerful feature of EVE is its ability to remember and to repeat a given series of keystrokes. This is useful for repeating a series of EVE commands several times, such as, for instance, the removal of a column of characters that occupy, say, the first three characters of each line.

First we need to "teach" the editor the series of commands it will need. To do this, we press the ⟨Do⟩ key and then type in LEARN. The status line along the bottom of the screen then reads "Press keystrokes to be learned. Press CTRL/R to remember these keystrokes". We first edit the file, using the key sequences to be stored by the LEARN command and then, when finished, we type ⟨Ctrl⟩R. EVE next generates the message: "Press the key that you want to use to see what was just learned". Pressing any key then designates that key as the one to store the sequence. You will then be informed that the sequence has been learnt by the message "Key sequence remembered". From this point on, each time that key is pressed, the learnt key sequence will be repeated. For this reason, it is best not to choose a commonly used keypad key, such as for example the ⟨Screen up⟩ key; a good choice would perhaps be keypad ⟨4⟩, which is not normally defined by default.

In the next example we show how we could use LEARN to edit a file.

Suppose in the file below we would like to place each sentence on a new line, separated from the previous sentence with a blank line. We type the necessary commands into LEARN and then replay them at each full stop.

The file SENTENCE.TXT contains some text:

```
Start. This is a text file. It comprises of separate
sentences. These sentences need to be put on separate lines.
A blank line must separate each sentence. The end.
```

The following actions are taken:

1. Edit the file by typing EDIT/TPU SENTENCE.TXT.
2. Press ⟨Do⟩ to move the cursor to the command line.
3. Type LEARN and then press ⟨Return⟩. EVE displays the message:

   ```
   Press keystrokes to be learned. Press CTRL/R to remember these keystrokes.
   ```

4. Type in the key sequences to be learnt. In this case:

⟨Find⟩ .	Search for full stop. Press ⟨Return⟩.
→	Move right one space.
→	Move right a second time.
⟨Delete⟩	Delete space following ".”
⟨Return⟩	Move text to new line.
⟨Return⟩	Insert blank line.
⟨Ctrl⟩R	Finished.

   Typing ⟨Ctrl⟩R at the end informs EVE (a) that you have finished typing in the sequence to be learnt and (b) that EVE should remember that sequence. EVE then responds with the message:

   ```
   Press the key that you want to use to see what was just learned.
   ```

   Press a key, in this case, since keypad ⟨4⟩ has not been defined by default, we shall press this key.
5. EVE responds with:

   ```
   Key sequence remembered.
   ```

6. Press the key, keypad ⟨4⟩ each time, to repeatedly perform the key sequence that has been learnt.
7. The edited file is shown below:

   ```
   Start.

   This is a text file.

   It comprises of separate sentences.
   ```

```
These sentences need to be put on separate lines.

A blank line must separate each sentence.

The end.
```

6.4.5 The EVE command—REPEAT

REPEAT can be used together with LEARN to repeat several times a sequence that has been learnt. To use REPEAT, press the ⟨Do⟩ key and type REPEAT at the command line. EVE then prompts for the key that is to be repeated to be pressed, and then for the number of times that key action is to be performed.

Although the key to be repeated is usually one that has been mapped to an EVE command, in fact we can use any character key. Pressing a character key results in that character appearing the specified number of times on the screen.

To demonstrate the use of the REPEAT operation, we shall combine the use of the REPEAT and LEARN keys, for the example given in the Section 6.4.4. To perform the key sequence that has been learnt, we previously pressed the key keypad ⟨4⟩ repeatedly—a total of five times, one for each of the remaining full stops. Alternatively we use here the REPEAT command and carry out the following actions:

1. Press ⟨Do⟩ and type REPEAT to run the REPEAT command.
2. Press ⟨4⟩ on the keypad to indicate which key is to be repeated.
3. Press ⟨5⟩, i.e. the number of times to repeat the operation.

In a second example, we use REPEAT to move down through the text five screens:

1. Press ⟨Do⟩ key and type REPEAT followed by the number of times the command is to be repeated, i.e. REPEAT 5
2. EVE prompts with: "Press key to be repeated".
3. Press ⟨Next Screen⟩.

6.4.6 The EVE command—SPAWN

This command is discussed fully in Chapter 8; however, for completeness we give a brief review of its application to editing. To finish editing a file, instead of using EXIT, we can use the command SPAWN. This is useful if we wish to return after a short while to continue editing the same file, since it is quicker to re-enter the editor via this process than to start the process with EDIT/TPU. This is particularly useful during program development, where it is necessary temporarily to exit from the editor, in order to compile, link, and run the program.

To exit from the editor, by spawning a subprocess, type:

```
⟨Do⟩

command: spawn
```

and to return to the editor type:

```
$ logout
```

i.e. you have now terminated the spawned process, and you are once again back in the editor.

If while editing you run out of disk space, EVE will not let you EXIT and save the file. You will be allowed to exit if you use the QUIT command; however, your current editing session will be lost. To overcome this, you can use SPAWN temporarily to exit from the editor, to free disk space—by either deleting or purging files in your directory area—and then return to the editor to EXIT normally and save the file.

6.4.7 The EVE commands—MARK and GOTO

The MARK command is useful for marking a location in a large file, to which we return using the GOTO command. A location can be marked with a label-name consisting of alphanumeric characters, i.e. any combination of characters and numbers.

In the example below, we show how to MARK, during editing, a location in a file and subsequently return there by using the GOTO command (see Figure 6-8). The procedure is in two stages; the first stage is to mark the text:

1. Move the cursor to the location you wish to mark. This need not be the start of a new line. Here we have chosen the "h" of the word "here".
2. Press the ⟨Do⟩ key and type MARK at the command line. Press the ⟨Return⟩ key.
3. The "command" prompt is now replaced by a new prompt "Mark name:". At this point type in the name you have chosen for your label, e.g. pos_1. Press ⟨Return⟩.
4. The text is now marked. The position of the marker is not shown on the screen.

The second stage follows later on, when it is required to move the cursor from its current position to the marked location. For this we use GOTO:

1. Press the ⟨Do⟩ key and type "GO TO label", where label is the "mark name"

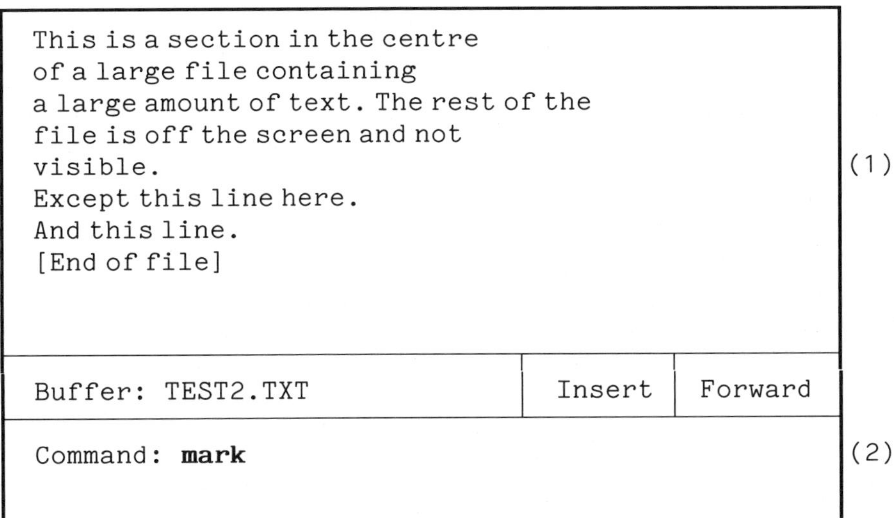

Fig. 6-8 Screen display during MARK and GOTO operation.

you previously typed. In this example, we would need to type GO TO POS_1.

2. The cursor is now moved to the marked point in the file, i.e. the "h" of "here".

By specifying different label names, this technique can be used to mark several locations in the file.

6.4.8 The EVE text formatting commands

It is possible to do simple text formatting in EVE by using the commands listed below. What follows is a brief list, which should be sufficient for less demanding applications. Additional commands can be found by using HELP, from within EVE. Each one of the commands must be preceded by pressing the ⟨Do⟩ key.

CAPITALIZE WORD	Capitalizes current word. Also works for text highlighted by the use of the ⟨Find⟩ or ⟨Select⟩ keys. This command makes the first character of a word uppercase.
CENTER LINE	Centers the line currently containing the cursor.
FILL	Adjusts the current paragraph, or selected range, so that each line consists of the maximum number of words.

FILL PARAGRAPH	As above, but for paragraph only.
FILL RANGE	As "Fill" but for text in current range or current FIND range.
INSERT PAGE BREAK	Place a form feed (shown as a small "FF") at the current cursor position. Typing ⟨Ctrl⟩L performs the same function.
UPPERCASE WORD	Converts current word or selected text (highlighted by the FIND or SELECT command) into uppercase.
LOWERCASE WORD	Opposite to "Uppercase Word".
SET LEFT MARGIN n	Sets the position of the lefthand side of the text on the screen to an integer value "n". The left margin must be less than the right margin by an integer greater than 0. The default setting is 1.
SET RIGHT MARGIN n	Sets the position of the limit on the right hand side of the text to an integer value "n". The right margin typically has a default value of 79 (terminal screens are generally 80 characters wide). The right margin must have a value which is greater than that of the left margin.
SET TABS AT n	Specify the position of the columns. The default is every eighth character.
SET TAB SPACES	Pressing ⟨Tab⟩ inserts the appropriate number of spaces into the file, instead of a tab character.
SET TAB MOVEMENT	Causes tab to move the cursor to the next tab location, but does not insert spaces.
SET TABS EVERY n	Sets the interval between each tab stop to a given size "n".
SET TABS VISIBLE	Tabs are displayed as visible characters on the screen.
SET TABS INVISIBLE	Tabs are not displayed as visible characters on the screen. This is the default.
SET WIDTH n	Sets the screen width. The default is 80. Specifying "n" as a value greater than 80 causes the screen to go to 132 character mode.
SET WRAP	Words are automatically wrapped at the right margin without the need to press ⟨Return⟩. This is the default (i.e. it generates new lines).
SET NOWRAP	Disables word wrapping.
SHIFT RIGHT n	Moves the window on the file over to the right a specified number of columns, specifed by "n". Allows you to view text currently off the

	righthand side of the screen. Does not alter the text.
SHIFT LEFT n	Moves the window on the file left a specified number of columns. Can only be used after a "shift right" instruction.

6.4.9 The EVE command—DCL

It is possible to run DCL commands from EVE by executing the following sequence:

1. Press the ⟨Do⟩ key.
2. Type DCL into the command window followed by the name of the command. For example, DCL DICTIONARY to perform the VMS directory command.
3. The message "Creating DCL subprocess..." appears at the bottom of the screen.
4. An additional window that contains the output from the DCL command is now created at the bottom of the screen.

It is now possible to transfer data from the bottom window, containing the DCL command, to the top window containing the file we are currently editing. The process for doing this is described in Section 6.7.

To execute more than one DCL command, either repeat the above procedure, or SPAWN a process from EVE, as described in Section 6.4.6.

6.4.10 The EVE commands to define keys

It is possible to define keys in the EVE editor in much the same way as it is in DCL (for key defining operations in DCL, see Chapter 3). There are two general methods of saving the key definitions into a file, and these are shown in the next two sections. The essential difference between the use of a "section file" and an "initialization file" is that a "section file" can be constantly added to, by saving any key defined *during* the editing session, whereas with the "initialization file" commands to define the keys must be typed in using an editor (or the CREATE command).

To define a key:

1. Press the ⟨Do⟩ key, to move to the command window.
2. Command: **define key** ⟨Return⟩.
3. Type in the command you wish to assign to a key. Press ⟨Return⟩, i.e. BOTTOM ⟨Return⟩.
4. Press the key to be remapped to that particular EVE command.

Any keys that have been defined only remain defined for the duration of the editing session, and must be redefined for any subsequent sessions. However, by defining the key definitions in either a startup file or by saving them to a "section file" (see below), we can avoid the need for repeated redefinitions.

Saving key definitions in a section file

To save key definitions into a section file, so that they are available during subsequent editing sessions, the following sequence is used:

1. Press the ⟨Do⟩ key, to move to the command window.
2. Command: **save extended eve savekey**
   where SAVEKEY is the name of the file into which the definitions are saved. Any file name can be chosen; the default file extension is TPU$SECTION.

After defining additional keys, either in this or any future editing session, by repeating the above command the section file can be expanded to include a comprehensive list of key definitions.

To run EVE and to load this file, type:

```
$ edit/tpu/section=user0:[student]savekey.tpu$section letter.txt
```

where USER0:[STUDENT]SAVEKEY.TPU$SECTION is the section file and LETTER.TXT is the file we wish to edit.

We use a symbol (Chapter 13) defined in our LOGIN.COM file to abbreviate this command. For example, placing the following line into our LOGIN.COM file:

```
$ eve :== edit/tpu/section=user0:[student]savekey.tpu$section
```

would mean that we just need to type:

```
$ eve letter.txt
```

to use the section file when we edit the file LETTER.TXT.

Defining keys in an initialization file

It is useful when defining keys to place them into an initialization file. This file consists of a list of EVE commands to be executed each time the editor is run.

For example, we could create a file called SETUP.COM that contains the following commands:

```
define key=Ctrl/D erase line
! Define KeyPad 4 key
define key=kp4 bottom
set left margin 10
set right margin 78
overstrike mode
```

To activate this file while in EVE we press the ⟨Do⟩ key and then type:

```
command: @setup.com
```

Alternatively EVE will always look to see which file name has been assigned to the logical name EVE$INIT. Each time the editor is run this file will then be automatically executed. To define this logical name, place a line similar to the following in your LOGIN.COM file:

```
$ define eve$init dua0:[ray]setup.com
```

where SETUP.COM is the name of the EVE initialization file in the directory DUA0:[RAY].

6.5 Accessing Buffers

6.5.1 Introduction

Throughout this chapter, we have referred to the text we are editing as a "file". Although this is true, what EVE actually creates is a buffer to store that file. Thus when we run the editor, EVE copies the file we wish to edit off the disk and stores it in memory, in a store called a buffer. When we finish editing and type EXIT that buffer is copied back to disk. If, however, we finish by typing QUIT then the edited file is not copied back to the disk, but deleted from memory leaving the file unchanged.

When we start editing a file, EVE places the file into a buffer. This buffer is represented on the terminal screen as a window. The main part of the EVE screen can be considered as a window onto the buffer.

An analogy would be a person looking at a page of a newspaper through a magnifying glass. Here the magnifying glass represents the window and the newspaper page the buffer containing the file. Although we cannot see the page in its entirety through the magnifying glass, we can move the lens over the page in order to read sections. The same applies to EVE—we can move the window on the buffer, using the PAGE UP, PAGE DOWN, SHIFT LEFT and SHIFT

RIGHT commands, but unless the file—and therefore the buffer—is small, we are unable to see all the text on the screen at any one time.

Let us take this analogy one step further. If we wanted to read another page of the newspaper, we would need to select the page and then move the magnifying glass to that page. In EVE it is possible to perform a similar function. We are able to move the window onto another buffer (containing a separate file), and switch between the two buffers. Only one buffer is in the window at any one time, i.e. in comparison to our analogy we read only one page of the newspaper at any one time.

EVE thus allows us to edit two or more files in the same editing session and provides facilities to switch between those two files.

We now review below the EVE commands that we need to use to create, delete, and store files in these buffers.

6.5.2 The EVE buffer commands

All these commands are initiated by first pressing the ⟨Do⟩ key and then entering the command on the command line. Note that in each case an argument must be included, as shown in the example.

BUFFER	Moves the specified buffer into the current window. The cursor is placed at the location it last occupied in that file. If the buffer does not already exist, a new buffer is created. For example, BUFFER hello.txt—loads buffer, called "hello.txt", into the current window.
DELETE BUFFER	Deletes the contents of the buffer specified. For example, DELETE hello.txt—deletes the contents of the buffer "hello.txt" (similar to using the QUIT command to exit from EVE).
GET FILE	Creates a new buffer and loads the contents of the file specified, into that buffer. This buffer is then placed into the current window. If the file does not exist, EVE creates a new empty file. Specifying the same name as an existing buffer, i.e. you have already created a buffer for that file, loads that buffer into the current window. For example, GET FILE test.for—loads file "test.for" into a buffer and places it

	into the current window. For information: when we run EVE and specify a filename, it is this command that EVE automatically performs in order to load the file into the editor.
GO TO	Causes the cursor to go to a named location in the buffer that was previously identified by using the MARK command. Note, however, that if the location exists in another buffer, which is not currently being edited, then that buffer will be loaded into the current window.
SHOW	Displays information relating to the buffers you have created in this editing session. If you have created more than one buffer, then press for information on any of the others the ⟨Do⟩ key. To return to editing, press any other key.
SHOW BUFFERS	Provides a list of the buffers currently being edited. Use the arrow keys and press the ⟨Select⟩ key to view the contents of the buffers. To delete a buffer, press the ⟨Remove⟩ key.
SHOW SYSTEM BUFFERS	As above, but shows the system buffers that were created by EVE. Do not delete any system buffers as they are integral to the functioning of the editor.
WRITE FILE	Saves a buffer to disk. If no file name is specified EVE uses the buffer name. If the buffer was originally created with the BUFFER command, EVE will prompt for a file name. This command can be seen to be similar to using EXIT to finish an editing session.

The name of the current buffer is shown at the bottom of the main window.

The small window at the bottom of the screen, in which we type the EVE commands and in which EVE displays any messages, is known as the MESSAGE window. All error or information messages scroll through this window. In order to display these messages in the main window, press ⟨Do⟩ and type BUFFER MESSAGES. You are now able to view in full any of the messages that scrolled out of the message window. To return to editing mode, press ⟨Do⟩ and type BUFFER followed by the name of the buffer you were editing (i.e. BUFFER hello.txt).

6.5.3 Copying text between two files in EVE

We shall now describe how we can use buffers in EVE to copy a section of one file into another file. In Section 6.4.3 we used the INCLUDE FILE command to place the complete contents of one file into another. Now we shall perform a similar operation, but this time by using buffers. We shall use the same example we used for demonstrating the INCLUDE FILE command, except that now we shall not copy the table headings. Remember that inside the editor, files and buffers can be considered as effectively being the same entity.

Assume therefore that FILE1.TXT contains the following text:

```
Dear Leslie,

This is the data you required from the experiment we
conducted.

Hope this is of some use.

                                        Ray
```

and FILE2.DAT contains the following data:

```
              Temperature          Pressure

                 20 C              34 m/kg
                 40 C              54 m/kg
                 60 C              65 m/kg
                 80 C              78 m/kg
```

To carry out the copying process, we need to go through the following steps. First we need to run EVE and load the first file into a buffer. This is done by typing the VMS command:

```
$ edit/tpu file1.txt
```

alternatively we could have typed:

```
$ edit/tpu
```

to run the editor, and then press:

⟨Do⟩

to move to the command line, and finally type:

```
command: get file file1.txt
```

to load the file into a buffer called FILE1.TXT. The contents of this buffer will be displayed in the window.

The appearance of the screen is shown in Figure 6-9a.

Next, we need to load the other file, FILE2.DAT, into a second buffer. We do this by pressing the ⟨Do⟩ key and entering the GET FILE command, as below:

```
⟨Do⟩
```

EVE then moves the cursor to the command window

```
command: get file file2.dat
```

The file is loaded into a buffer, which is then displayed in the window as shown in Figure 6-9b. The cursor is at the start of the file. Since we wish to copy all the data, but not the table headings (i.e. not the line that states "Temperature Pressure"), we need to move the cursor down the file, past this line. We use the down-arrow key to move the cursor from position (1) to position (2) in Figure 6-9b. Now we are in a position to select the text. Press the following keys:

```
⟨Select⟩
```

then move the cursor to the bottom of the file (use the down-arrow key). The text appears in inverse video.

```
⟨Remove⟩
```

The text is now extracted from the file and stored in the INSERT HERE buffer. Now we need to recall the FILE1.TXT buffer. To do this:

```
⟨Do⟩
```

moves the cursor to the command window, then type

```
command: buffer file1.txt
```

Next move the cursor to the appropriate location in the file and press

```
⟨Insert Here⟩
```

The contents of the INSERT HERE buffer are then written into the FILE1.TXT buffer.

To exit:

```
⟨Do⟩
```

```
command: exit
```

Eve then asks if you wish to save any other modified buffers (in this instance

```
Dear Leslie,

This is the data you required from the experiment we
conducted.

Hope this is of some use.
                                          Ray
[End of file]


Buffer: FILE1.TXT                  | Insert  | Forward
```

Fig. 6-9a Screen display of FILE1.TXT.

```
                Temperature       Pressure             (1)
_                                                      (2)
                   20 C            34 m/kg
                   40 C            54 m/kg
                   60 C            65 m/kg
                   80 C            78 m/kg
[End of file]


Buffer: FILE2.DAT                 | Insert | Forward
```

Fig. 6-9b Screen display of FILE2.DAT.

FILE2.DAT). Since we might wish to keep FILE2.DAT in its original form, we reply here NO. As a consequence FILE2.DAT is retained in its original form.

6.6 Using Windows

So far we have seen how we can load buffers into the EVE window. Now we shall discuss how we can split the existing window in order to create another window(s). This technique enables us to have more than one buffer visible on the screen at any one time, and to view simultaneously more than one section of the same file.

Before we present an example, let us review the window commands:

SPLIT WINDOW	Splits the current window into two or more smaller windows. The cursor resides in the original window. For example, SPLIT WINDOW splits the window into two segments, SPLIT WINDOW 3 splits the window into three segments, and so on.
TWO WINDOWS	Same as SPLIT WINDOW (or SPLIT WINDOW 2) command.
NEXT WINDOW	Moves cursor into another (or next) window.
PREVIOUS WINDOW	Moves cursor into another (or preceding) window.
ONE WINDOW	Reverts back to a single window.
DELETE WINDOW	Deletes the window in which the cursor is currently present.
ENLARGE WINDOW	Increases the size of the current window by the specified number of lines. The adjacent window shrinks accordingly. For example, ENLARGE WINDOW 3 enlarges the current window by three lines, causing the adjacent window to shrink by three lines.
SHRINK WINDOW	Opposite to the ENLARGE WINDOW command.

6.6.1 Single file editing using windows

If we are editing a large file and we wish to move text from one part of the file into another, we can create two windows onto the same file (see Figure 6-10), and then move the cursor, using the cursor movement keys, in one of the windows in order to view a different section of the file. We can then select and

```
This is Long_File.txt
It is a Very long file, and is quite boring.
In fact it is so boring, that you are lucky
to be able to read only a small part of it.
It just seems to go on, and on, and on....
seemingly for ever. Aren't you glad the rest
will not be in the window......
```

Buffer: LONG_FILE.TXT	Insert	Forward

```
This is Long_File.txt
It is a Very long file, and is quite boring.
In fact it is so boring, that you are lucky
to be able to read only a small part of it.
It just seems to go on, and on, and on....
seemingly for ever. Aren't you glad the rest
will not be in the window......
```

Buffer: LONG_FILE.TXT	Insert	Forward

Fig. 6-10 Single-buffer/two-window display.

move the text to the other window and insert it at the desired position into the file.

To do this:

1. Type EDIT/TPU LONG_FILE.TXT, where LONG_FILE.TXT is the file you wish to edit.
2. Press the ⟨Do⟩ key and type the command TWO WINDOWS (or SPLIT WINDOWS). This splits the current window into two segments, each containing the same section of the buffer.
3. Move the cursor in the current window, to the location at which you wish to copy the text. You can locate the required location by various methods previously discussed, such as FIND or MARK/GOTO commands.
4. Press the ⟨Do⟩ key and type the command NEXT WINDOW to move the cursor into the other window.
5. Move the cursor to the text you wish to extract.
6. Press the ⟨Select⟩ key, and move the cursor to select the text you wish to place in the INSERT HERE buffer. Press the ⟨Remove⟩ key. Text is now removed from the current buffer and placed in the INSERT HERE buffer.

7. Press the ⟨Do⟩ key and type NEXT WINDOW to switch the cursor into the other window.
8. Locate the cursor and press the ⟨Insert Here⟩ key to copy the text from the INSERT HERE buffer into the current buffer.
9. Press the ⟨Do⟩ key and type ONE WINDOW to return to a single window display.

Note that when editing a single buffer using two windows, the text is changed simultaneously in both windows. This can be clearly seen by creating two windows and editing the text in one, and watching the alterations also appear in the other window.

6.6.2 Editing two files using two windows

In the previous section we have seen how we can create two windows onto the same buffer. Now we shall consider how to create two windows which contain two separate buffers (see Figure 6-11 below). This method is particulary useful for copying sections of text between different files.

```
Dear Leslie,

This is the data you required from the experiment we
conducted.

Hope this is of some use.
                                   Ray
[End of file]
-----------------------------------------------------------
Buffer: FILE1.TXT                  | Insert   | Forward
-----------------------------------------------------------
             Temperature           Pressure
_
                20 C               34 m/kg
                40 C               54 m/kg
                60 C               65 m/kg
                80 C               78 m/kg
[End of file]
-----------------------------------------------------------
Buffer: FILE2.DAT                  | Insert   | Forward
-----------------------------------------------------------
```

Fig. 6-11 Two-window/two-buffer display.

To do this:

1. Type EDIT/TPU FILE1.TXT, where FILE1.TXT is the file you wish to edit.
2. Press the ⟨Do⟩ key and type the command TWO WINDOWS (or SPLIT WINDOWS). This splits the current window into two segments, each containing the same section of the current buffer.
3. Press the ⟨Do⟩ key and type GET FILE FILE2.DAT to load the second file into a buffer, where FILE2.DAT is the filename of the second file.
4. The current window now contains the content of buffer FILE2.DAT. We can now use the ⟨Select⟩ and ⟨Remove⟩ keys to place the text we wish to move into the other buffer, called the INSERT HERE buffer.
5. Press the ⟨Do⟩ key, and type NEXT WINDOW to move the cursor into the other buffer.
6. First move the text to the correct location and then press ⟨Insert Here⟩ to insert the text into the file.
7. Press the ⟨Do⟩ key, and type EXIT to finish.

6.7 Incorporating Text Created by DCL Commands into a File

We have seen how we can run DCL commands from EVE by:

1. Pressing the ⟨Do⟩ key.
2. Typing DCL, followed by the command we wish to execute, (i.e. DCL DIRECTORY).

A window is then created at the bottom of the screen containing the output from the DCL command.

Now that we have looked at buffers and windows, we shall consider how to copy text from the DCL buffer into a specified file.

After performing stages 1 and 2 above:

3. Move the cursor by pressing the ⟨Do⟩ key and typing NEXT WINDOW from the current window into the DCL window.
4. Use the ⟨Select⟩ and ⟨Remove⟩ keys, to extract the text from the DCL buffer and to place it into the INSERT HERE buffer.
5. Move the cursor from the DCL window, back to the main window, by pressing the ⟨Do⟩ key and typing NEXT WINDOW.
6. Move the cursor to the location in the text at where the text is to be inserted and press ⟨Insert Here⟩.
7. Press the ⟨Do⟩ key and type EXIT to finish.

Chapter

7

Files and Directories

7.1 Introduction

The meaning of the term files might be compared with a specification of the attributes of a book. The main attributes of a book are the following:

1. It has a title.
2. It is bound by a beginning and an end.
3. Between the beginning and the end a book has a content that is divided into subunits—the pages. The length of its contents might be zero, or may be very large up to an allowed maximum length.
4. The book is organized for clarity, into chapters or subunits that may have different lengths and possibly different types of contents, e.g. text and diagrams.
5. The book is created, i.e. it is written, and subsequently might be read repeatedly by authorized users according to ownership and the class of privileges attributed to various classes of potential users.

An examination of the properties of computer files and directories shows that the attributes described above for a book can almost be applied as a direct description for the organization of computer systems.

Considering each attribute in turn, we note the first major difference. A user's directory (known as a directory file) is a dynamic entity, it is created under the authority of the Computer Systems Manager (the supervisor). The ownership is assigned to a particular user. At the same time, certain attributes are specified. These attributes are described in more detail later in the chapter.

Thus the file is assigned the following properties:

1. System identification name.
2. Facilities to enter and exit from the file.
3. Authority to read the content (r).
4. Authority to write—i.e. create or alter—the content (w).
5. Authority to execute the executable code in the file (e).
6. Authority to delete the file (d).

The permission for 3–6 is allocated to four classes of user, namely:

- *Owner* The owner is given full rights, i.e. rwed, except for subdirectories. Subdirectories are protected by the system from accidental deletion when they are not empty, i.e. when they contain one or more files. The properties of subdirectories are described in Section 7.5.
- *System* The System Manager has full rights over any user file (rwed).
- *Group* Members of the same group are often given the right to read or execute (re) but not to alter or delete. Creation and assignment to group membership is undertaken by the System Manager only.
- *World* All the remaining users are classed under the generic name world. These users are generally given no rights to another user's files.

The owner of a file has authority to decrease or increase the protection of his or her files for all the above classes of user (with the exception of system).

Of course, absolute equivalent owner privilege over the user's directory is allocated by disclosure of the LOGIN password. This does not necessarily mean that the user owns all the files in that directory.

The first file created during the setting up of a user's account by the System Manager is given a special name—the *home directory* of the username. The owner, by virtue of the privileges received, is in a position to create his or her own directories. These directories must be created from inside the user's main or home directory. This enables user's to build a hierarchial subdirectory structure according to their individual requirements.

These subdirectories may be further organized to house certain logically related entities. For example, a subdirectory may be created to store all source programs, or mail files. Subdirectories provide a method of storing files in ordered groups, making files easy to locate.

We have started by introducing the attributes of a book and their relation to computer files. The creation and organization of special files led to the recognition of a unique group of files—the home directory and its various subdirectories.

One special point to note about directories is that they are supervised by the system programs. Their integrity and preservation is carried out under the control of the VAX/VMS operating system.

Following the above description, we can now differentiate between directories and files, with the directories being considered to be the table of contents listing chapter headings.

The contents of directories are housed in files with specific names and attributes created under different conditions appropriate for their use. These files are given the file extension .DIR, and are created automatically whenever we create a subdirectory. Thus they might be provided via systems management with a content of our own software or they might be externally supplied (commercial) software. In addition to these, the user, by using an editor, can create a source code program, which on execution carries out a specified task. Furthermore, there is an interaction between users in sending to, or copying files from each other (see Section 7.6.5) which is controlled by the owner of the file.

7.2 File Characteristics (Classification)

Files are usually classified, according to their content and method of organization, into two main classes, which can subsequently be subdivided further.

The first main group of files might consist of textual information composed of individual characters (of letters, digits, and some special characters). Such a file is called a text file and is stored in a translated form, according to the ASCII (American Standard Code for Information Interchange) character code in the system's memory (or on disk or on tape).

The content of this file can be inspected by a number of different techniques:

1. It can be displayed on the VDU from beginning to end by giving the command TYPE (file specification) (see Section 7.6.3).
2. It can be inspected and modified by using the system editor, such as EVE (see Chapters 5 and 6).
3. It can be sent to a printer connected to the main computer system (see Chapter 9), or it can be printed at a printer connected to the VDU. The local printer is first activated into the printing mode by sending a control code. After the printing is completed, it is necessary to send a second control code to stop the printer.
4. Finally, it can be written into another file for permanent retention (see COPY—Section 7.6.5). In this context, it should be mentioned that the VDU is really only a special file, where the content is displayed in a nonpermanent form (see also Section 4.2.3).

The second main group of files are stored in a machine-readable form called binary format. These files cannot be inspected directly and they need the execution of special programs (e.g. see DUMP—Section 7.6.4) to allow their inspection.

Care must be taken not to attempt to read one of these binary files directly, since the display can modify the set-up mode of the terminal with its consequent suspension of execution. Attempting to print a binary file can also result in strange effects—such as ejecting large volumes of paper!

If your VDU should become inoperable in this way you could try the following method:

1. Resetting your VDU (exactly how you do this depends upon the VDU you are using); or if this fails
2. Switch the power supply off for a period of at least a minute and then switch it on again.

Either of these two actions could result in your being disconnected from the computer system, in which case you will need to login again.

The message is thus clear:

- Avoid displaying or printing of binary files.
- An aid in identifying binary files is to assign them a clearly recognizable file type (see Section 7.3.2). The DIRECTORY command (see Section 7.4) also enables you to distinguish between text and binary files.

We shall describe various aspects of file operation and their characteristics in Section 7.6.

A word of warning: it is important to adhere to the format shown, in particular to blank spaces (if any) between "words". Further, ensure that a command is always terminated with a carriage return, ⟨Return⟩.

7.3 File Specifications and Naming Conventions

A file is referred to by its filename, type, and version number:

```
filename.type;version number
```

or

```
filename.type.version number
```

For example:

```
BUBBLE.PAS;3
```

has

Filename	BUBBLE
Type	PAS
Version number	3

Here are some more examples:

```
myprog.for;2
stats.dat.1
DO.COM;4
```

No distinction is made between uppercase and lowercase names.

7.3.1 Filenames

A filename can consist of up to 39 letters and digits in addition to the dollar sign ($) and underscore (_) characters. It is a good idea not to use the dollar sign as it is to be found widely in VAX/VMS names used for other purposes. Furthermore, the first character must be a letter in the range a–z or a digit. It is a good idea to use meaningful names, which bear some relation to the content or purpose of the file.

7.3.2 File types

The same rules apply for the name of a file type as those for a file name. The file type is often used, and should be selected to indicate the type of contents of the file.

For example, it would be assumed that the file

BUBBLE.PAS;7	contains Pascal source code,
BUBBLE.OBJ;4	is an object file, and
BUBBLE.EXE;2	is an executable program.

The more common conventions for files containing source code are shown in Table 7-1. A list of file types and their usage is given in Appendix A.

7.3.3 Version numbers

It is possible to have more than one generation of the same file; the precise number of generations that you are allowed is determined locally by your System Manager and can vary from one upwards.

To distinguish between different versions of the same file, a version number

Table 7-1 Source file types and source languages

File type	Referring to the source language
ADA	Ada
BAS	BASIC
C	C
COB	COBOL
FOR	FORTRAN
PAS	Pascal
EXE	executable program
OBJ	object file
COM	command procedure
DAT	data file
MAI	MAIL message file
TXT	text file

is used. This version number ranges from 1 to 32 767 and it is incremented each time that you modify a file (e.g. with an editor).

Sometimes when you issue a command that takes a filename as parameter, if you omit the version number, VAX/VMS assumes that you wish to use the latest version (the file with the highest version number). This is the case when wishing to display the contents of a file using the TYPE command. In other cases, e.g. when you wish to delete a file with the DELETE command, VMS protocols insist that you supply a version number or numbers.

Let us now look at some examples:

```
$ directory
```

displays the titles of the files and subdirectories existing in the particular directory. For example:

```
$ directory

Directory DISK1:[MIKE]

HELLO.EXE;1    HELLO.OBJ;3    HELLO.OBJ;2    HELLO.PAS;4
HELLO.PAS;3    HELLO.PAS;2

Total of 6 files.
```

The DIRECTORY command gives us the name of the current directory, in this case DISK1:[MIKE], followed by a list of the files in this directory. DISK1 is the "volume" label (i.e. the name) of the disk device on which the directory is held; more details are given in Section 7.4.

We can display the contents of the file HELLO.PAS by using the TYPE command. Unless we specify a version number VMS protocols dictates that the file with the highest version number is used.

```
$ type hello.pas

program hello(input, output);
begin
 writeln('Hello world')
end.

$
```

To delete a file we use the DELETE command and we must specify a version number, or alternatively indicate that we want to consider all version numbers by using the asterisk wildcard character (*), which is discussed in the following section.

```
$ delete hello.exe

%DELETE-E-DELVER, explicit version number or wild card required
```

Here the VAX/VMS operating system displays an error message informing us that we need to provide a version number for the file to be deleted or use a wildcard.

We could delete version number 1 of the file HELLO.EXE by:

```
$ delete hello.exe;1
```

and also delete all versions of the file HELLO.OBJ by:

```
$ delete hello.obj;*
```

The DIRECTORY command now shows us the current state of our directory after performing these deletions.

```
$ directory

Directory DISK1:[MIKE]

HELLO.PAS;4          HELLO.PAS;3          HELLO.PAS;2

Total of 3 files.
```

7.3.4 Wildcards

Sometimes you may want to refer to a group of files collectively by a common feature of their filenames. This can be done by using wildcards. For example, we could produce a directory listing of all Pascal source files by giving the command:

```
$ directory *.pas
```

Similarly, to delete all object files we use the command:

```
$ delete *.obj;*
```

The term wildcard describes a character with special properties. It is used, as shown below, to specify a group of characters that fall within a group of related characters.

There are two types of wildcard the asterisk (*) and the percent sign (%). These wildcard characters can be used for file names, types, and version numbers:

- `*` matches any string of characters (including a string of length zero)
- `%` matches exactly one character

You need to be careful when using wildcards. For example:

```
$ delete *.*;*
```

will delete all your files in your current directory! However, all may not be lost and it is worth throwing yourself at the mercy of your System Manager who should regularly make backup copies of files on the system. It is possible, therefore, that only files created or changes made to files during the current day are lost.

The combination of wildcards for files together with command qualifiers can be very powerful. For example:

```
$ delete *.*;*/exclude=*.pas/before=YESTERDAY
```

will delete all files in the current directory that are dated before yesterday and are not Pascal source files.

7.4 Directories

All files reside in directories. Your System Manager will have created a directory for you when your account was created. You can find the name of your current directory by typing:

```
$ show default
```

For example:

```
$ show default

DISK1:[MIKE]
```

Here the directory name is shown to be [MIKE] and it resides on the disk device called DISK1. It is quite likely that the device name will be something other than DISK1 at your site.

You can find the name of the disk devices attached to your VAX as shown in the example below where the letter "d" specifies all devices whose name begins with "d". This will include all disk devices. Similarly, the use of the letter "mu" will specify all devices that have "mu" as their first two characters.

```
$ show devices d

Device    Device         Error     Volume          Free     Trans Mnt
Name      Status         Count     Label           Blocks   Count Cnt
DUA0:     Mounted            0     SYSTEM          12772    177    1
DUA1:     Mounted            0     DISK1           18756     18    1
DUA2:     Mounted            0     DISK2           10804     40    1
```

7.5 Subdirectories

The main directory has been created for you by the System Manager. Any other directory created by you is called a subdirectory.

Subdirectories are useful for organizing your work. For example, you could create a subdirectory to hold all your Pascal programs and a subdirectory to hold your C programs. You might additionally create sudirectories from within the Pascal subdirectory to hold your coursework and project files (see Figure 7-1). A further example showing the creation of each subdirectory is shown in Figure 7-2 (p. 107).

Referencing of subdirectories can be absolute or relative. You can specify a subdirectory either by its position relative to your current directory or by an absolute name.

Using square brackets provides a shorthand way of specifying the current directory. If your current directory is DISK1:[MIKE], then you could refer to the subdirectory DISK1:[MIKE.PASCAL] by [.PASCAL], or [MIKE.PASCAL], or DISK1:[MIKE.PASCAL].

If you want to refer to a file that is not in your current directory, then you should prefix the filename by the directory name.

Note that it is important to use square brackets—parentheses or braces do not work.

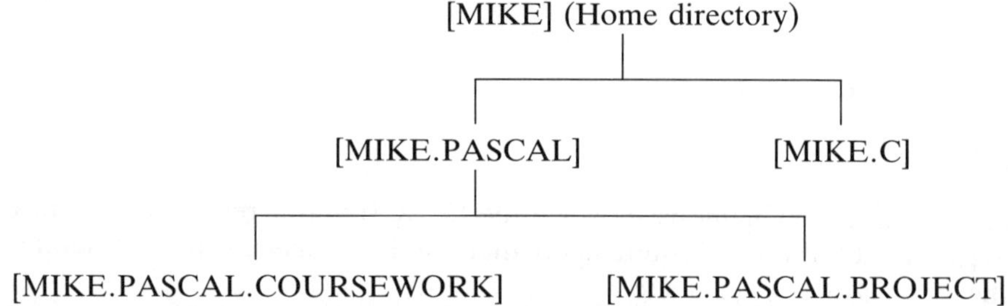

Fig. 7-1 The hierarchy of a subdirectory structure.

Example

```
$ delete [mike.pascal]bubble.pas;2
```

Deletes the file BUBBLE.PAS with version number 2 in the directory [MIKE.PASCAL].

7.5.1 Subdirectory names

Subdirectories are represented as files and as such you can choose any valid filename for a subdirectory name.

7.5.2 Creating a subdirectory

Subdirectories are created by the CREATE/DIRECTORY command. Examples of subdirectory structure are summarized in Figure 7-1 (see also Section 7.5.3).

Examples

```
$ set default [mike]
$ create/directory [.pascal]
$ create/directory [.c]
```

Creates the subdirectories [MIKE.PASCAL] and [MIKE.C] as offshoots from the current directory. They are represented as files PASCAL.DIR and C.DIR in the current directory [MIKE]. The command

```
$ create/directory [mike.pascal.coursework]
```

creates the subdirectory [MIKE.PASCAL.COURSEWORK], while

```
$ create/directory [.pascal.project]
```

creates a subdirectory relative to the current directory.

Giving the above commands results in the creation of the directory structure shown in Figure 7-1.

7.5.3 Wildcards for directories only

VAX/VMS also uses special wildcard characters, which can only be used when working with directories:

... (3 full stops)	refers to all subdirectories below a directory or subdirectory.
- (hyphen)	refers to the directory or subdirectory immediately above the current directory or subdirectory. The one above is sometimes known as the "parent" directory of the current directory.

The following examples will help to illustrate the use of these wildcards. We refer to the subdirectory structure created with the commands given in Section 7.5.2; their corresponding hierarchy is shown in Figure 7-1.

1. [DIR MIKE...]
   Produces a directory listing of all the files in directory [MIKE] and all subdirectories below [MIKE]. Note that the complete subdirectory structure is traversed, thus resulting in a great deal of information, as shown in the example.

```
$ show default

DISK1:[MIKE]

$ dir [mike...]

Directory DISK1:[MIKE]

C.DIR;1         EX1.LOG;2      EX1.LOG;1       HELLO.PAS;4
HELLO.PAS;3     HELLO.PAS;2    PASCAL.DIR;1

Total of 7 files.


Directory DISK1:[MIKE.C]

SORT.C;1              WCOUNT.C;1

Total of 2 files.
```

```
Directory DISK1:[MIKE.PASCAL]

COURSEWORK.DIR;1     PROJECT.DIR;1

Total of 2 files.


Directory DISK1:[MIKE.PASCAL.COURSEWORK]

CW11MAY.PAS;1        CW25MAY.PAS;1

Total of 2 files.


Directory DISK1:[MIKE.PASCAL.PROJECT]

CPATH.PAS;1

Total of 1 file.
```

With the final summary message:

```
Grand total of 5 directories, 14 files.
```

2. DIR [-]
   Produces a directory listing of the parent directory. The first command moves us to the PROJECT subdirectory (see Figure 7-1).

```
$ set def [.pascal.project]

$ show default

DISK1:[MIKE.PASCAL.PROJECT]

$ dir [-]

Directory DISK1:[MIKE.PASCAL]

COURSEWORK.DIR;1     PROJECT.DIR;1

Total of 2 files.
```

3. $ DIR [--]*.PAS
   Produces a directory listing of all Pascal source files in the directory two levels above the current directory. This can be extrapolated further so that [----] refers to the directory four levels (i.e. 4 × -) above the current directory.

```
$ dir [--]*.pas

Directory DISK1:[MIKE]

HELLO.PAS;4          HELLO.PAS;3          HELLO.PAS;2

Total of 3 files.
```

4. DIR [...]
Produces a directory listing of all files in the current directory and below (compare with example 1). The first command moves up one level.

```
$ set def [-]

$ show default

DISK1:[MIKE.PASCAL]

$ dir [...]

Directory DISK1:[MIKE.PASCAL]

COURSEWORK.DIR;1     PROJECT.DIR;1

Total of 2 files.


Directory DISK1:[MIKE.PASCAL.COURSEWORK]

CW11MAY.PAS;1        CW25MAY.PAS;1

Total of 2 files.


Directory DISK1:[MIKE.PASCAL.PROJECT]

CPATH.PAS;1

Total of 1 file.


Grand total of 3 directories, 5 files.
```

7.5.4 Changing directories

You can change your current directory by using the SET DEFAULT command together with the appropriate directory specifications as shown by the examples below.

Examples

```
$ show default

DISK1:[MIKE]
```

To enter a subdirectory two levels below the current directory (see Figure 7-1) and then display the new current directory the following commands are used:

```
$ set default [.pascal.project]

$ show default

DISK1:[MIKE.PASCAL.PROJECT]
```

The next sequence of commands move you up one level from the current directory and verifies this:

```
$ set default [-]

$ show default

DISK1:[MIKE.PASCAL]
```

A convenient way of referring to your home directory is through the logical name SYS$LOGIN. So for example:

```
$ show translation sys$login

SYS$LOGIN = "DISK1:[MIKE]" (LNM$JOB_80C58B0)
```

shows the translation of the logical name SYS$LOGIN and thus identifies the name of the home directory.

In some cases it is very convenient to return to the home directory by giving the command:

```
$ set default sys$login
```

and to confirm its validity the following command is given:

```
$ show default

DISK1:[MIKE]
```

which shows the current directory to be the home directory.

7.5.5 Deleting subdirectories

Before you can delete a subfile directory all files in that subdirectory (including further subdirectories) must be deleted or moved to another directory. In addition, the protection of the subdirectory must be modified to allow deletion by its owner. VAX/VMS does not grant the owner delete privilege by default as a protective measure against acidental deletion. Subdirectories are deleted in the same way as a normal file, by using the DELETE command. Trying to delete a subdirectory that has not first been deprotected to allow deletion by the user results in the error message:

```
$ delete test.dir;1

%DELETE-W-FILNOTDEL, error deleting USER0:[RAY]TEST1.DIR;1
-RMS-E-PRV, insufficient privilege or file protection violation
```

We therefore first need to delete the contents of the subdirectory. This can be done in one of two ways, depending on whether the subdirectory contains any subsequent directories. To delete files from a subdirectory we can use the command:

```
$ delete [.test]*.*;*
```

This will delete all the files but not any subdirectories resident in TEST.DIR. To delete these, we would need to set our default directory from the current level into TEST (SET DEFAULT [.TEST]) and then execute the DELETE command again, this time with the name of the subdirectory contained in the TEST subdirectory. This process would need to be continued for each subsequent subdirectory.

Alternatively we could use the command:

```
$ delete [.test...]*.*;*/log
```

to delete all the files in the subdirectory TEST and in any subdirectories below test ("..." means this directory, i.e. TEST, and any following subdirectories in that hierarchy). With these "global" DELETE commands it is advisable to use the /LOG switch to check on which files are being deleted. A typing mistake may result in files in the parent directory being deleted as well. Be careful!

Once we have used one of these methods to delete all the files, we can then start to delete the subdirectories. Normally subdirectories are protected against accidental deletion by default, so we may need to deprotect them. To do this check the protection, and if necessary use the SET FILE/PROTECTION command.

```
$ delete test.dir;1

  %DELETE-W-FILNOTDEL, error deleting PCL$CCSROOT:[RAY]TEST1.DIR;1
  -RMS-E-PRV, insufficient privilege or file protection violation

$ directory/protection test.dir;1
   Directory PCL$CCSROOT:[RAY]

  TEST1.DIR;1           (RWE,RWE,RE,)

  Total of 1 file.

$ set file/protection=(o:d) test.dir;1

$ delete test.dir;1
```

In this example the first attempt to delete TEST.DIR failed because of its protection, the next command checked the protection and it was noticed that the owner's privileges did not include delete. The next command altered the protection to give delete privilege to the owner (o = owner : d = delete). The directory was then successfully deleted.

This series of commands needs to be carried out for each subdirectory in the hierarchy. You would need to start at the lowest subdirectory and work up towards the parent directory, changing the protection and deleting the subdirectory as you work your way towards the top.

The following example below illustrates this technique. Suppose we have the directory structure shown in Figure 7-2. We shall now delete the entire directory structure below our default directory (USER0:[RAY]). First we need to be in the default directory. Then we can delete all the files contained in USER0:[RAY.TEST] and the two subdirectories below that. Now we can move to USER0:[RAY.TEST], change the protection on both subdirectories, and delete them. Finally we return to the default directory and delete the TEST subdirectory. In each instance, VMS responds with the $ prompt, indicating that it is ready for the next command. However, note the response when the /LOG qualifier is used.

```
$ set default user0:[ray]

$ delete [test...]*.*;*/log

  %DELETE-W-FILNOTDEL, error deleting USER0:[RAY.TEST]C.DIR;1
  -RMS-E-MKD, ACP could not mark file for deletion
  -SYSTEM-F-NOPRIV, no privilege for attempted operation

  %DELETE-W-FILNOTDEL, error deleting USER0:[RAY.TEST]FOR.DIR;1
  -RMS-E-MKD, ACP could not mark file for deletion
  -SYSTEM-F-NOPRIV, no privilege for attempted operation

  %DELETE-I-FILDEL, USER0:[RAY.TEST.C]RAY3.LOG;1 deleted (6 blocks)
  %DELETE-I-FILDEL, USER0:[RAY.TEST.C]RAY4.LOG;2 deleted (6 blocks)
```

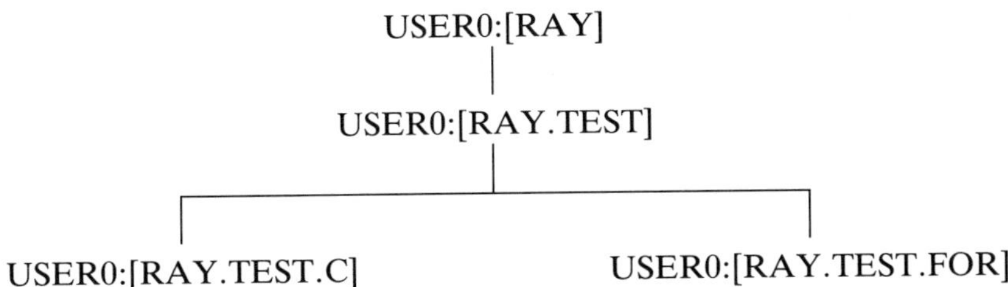

Fig. 7-2 Subdirectory traversal for delete operation.

```
  %DELETE-I-FILDEL, USERO:[RAY.TEST.FOR]ADD.C;11 deleted (3 blocks)
  %DELETE-I-FILDEL, USERO:[RAY.TEST.FOR]A.FOR;34 deleted (3 blocks)
  %DELETE-I-FILDEL, USERO:[RAY.TEST.FOR]A.DAT;14 deleted (3 blocks)

  %DELETE-I-TOTAL, 5 files deleted (21 blocks)

$ set default [.test]

$ set file/protection=(o:d) c.dir;1,for.dir;1/log

  %SET-I-PROTECTED, USERO:[RAY.TEST]C.DIR;1 file protection
  changed to S:RWE,O:D,G:RE,W:

  %SET-I-PROTECTED, USERO:[RAY.TEST]FOR.DIR;1 file protection
  changed to S:RWE,O:D,G:RE,W:

$ delete c.dir;1,for.dir;1/log

  %DELETE-I-FILDEL, USERO:[RAY.TEST]C.DIR;1 deleted (3 blocks)
  %DELETE-I-FILDEL, USERO:[RAY.TEST]FOR.DIR;1 deleted (3 blocks)

$ set default [-]

$ set file/prot=(o:d) test.dir;1/log

  %SET-I-PROTECTED, USERO:[RAY]TEST.DIR;1 file protection
  changed to S:RWE,O:D,G:RE,W:

$ delete test.dir;1/log

  %DELETE-I-FILDEL, USERO:[RAY]TEST.DIR;1 deleted (3 blocks)
```

7.6 File Manipulation Commands

7.6.1 CREATE

The simplest way to create a file is to use the CREATE file command. Note, however, that this is suitable only for very brief files.

The characters you type in are entered into the file until the end of file is indicated by typing ⟨Ctrl⟩Z. For example:

```
$ create appointments.dat

5/11/88 14:00 Dentist          Input text.
6/11/88 Course Work Due
^Z                             ⟨Ctrl⟩Z typed. End of input, file is closed.
```

An obvious disadvantage of using CREATE for anything other than very small files is that there is no way of editing what you have typed. For this purpose we use the text editor EVE (see Chapter 5).

7.6.2 DIRECTORY

This command provides information about a file or group of files in a directory.

Examples

1. `$ directory`

   Lists all the files in the current directory.

2. `$ dir [...]`

   Lists files in the current directory and all directories below this.

Directory qualifiers and their use

Qualifiers were introduced in Chapter 3 and here we only give some examples of their usage as appropriate for this section. Qualifiers can be used to modify the amount of detail that is obtained. You can obtain information on how to use the DIRECTORY command and the qualifiers it can take by using the VMS HELP facility:

```
$ help directory
```

The sections which follow give a few examples of their use.

The /FULL qualifier

For example:

```
$ directory/full [mike.c]
```

provides detailed information on each file in the directory [MIKE.C]. This includes the size, owner, protection, creation date, and lots more useful information. You should note that in the following example we show only the output corresponding to one file.

```
$ directory/full [.c]

Directory DISK1:[MIKE.C]

SORT.C;2                       File ID:  (19449,5,0)
Size:             9/12          Owner:     [12,3]
Created:  27-MAY-1988 09:06    Revised:  27-MAY-1988 09:07 (2)
Expires:   <None specified>    Backup:    <No backup recorded>
File organization:  Sequential
File attributes:    Allocation: 4,Extend: 0,Global buffer count:0
                    Version limit: 3
Record format:      Variable length, maximum 159 bytes
Record attributes:  Carriage return carriage control
Journaling enabled: None
File protection:    System:RWED, Owner:RWED, Group:RWE, World:
Access Cntrl List:  None
```

The /TOTAL qualifier

This qualifier produces summary information giving the total number of files in the current directory but suppresses information about individual files. For example:

```
$ directory/total
Directory DISK1:[MIKE]

Total of 9 files.
```

The /SIZE qualifier

This qualifier lists the files in the parent directory together with their file sizes in VAX/VMS blocks (1 block = 512 bytes, a byte is 1 character). For example:

```
$ set def [.pascal]

$ show default

DISK1:[MIKE.PASCAL]
$ directory/size [-]
Directory DISK1:[MIKE]

C.DIR;1                     1
COUNT.C;3                   6
COUNT.C;2                   2
```

```
EX1.LOG;3                  2
HELLO.PAS;4                1
PASCAL.DIR;1               1
SORT.C;1                   2

Total of 7 files, 15 blocks.
```

The /SIZE qualifier in combination with other qualifiers

The /SIZE qualifier can be used in combination with other qualifiers. For example, $ DIRECTORY/SIZE/TOTAL [MIKE.PASCAL...]_*.PAS lists the total number of Pascal source files and the sum of their sizes in the directory [MIKE.PASCAL] and all subdirectories below this.

```
$ directory/total/size [...]

Directory DISK1:[MIKE]

Total of 5 files, 19 blocks.

Directory DISK1:[MIKE.PASCAL]

Total of 2 files, 2 blocks.

Directory DISK1:[MIKE.PASCAL.COURSEWORK]

Total of 2 files, 0 blocks.

Grand total of 3 directories, 9 files, 21 blocks.
```

The /OUTPUT qualifier

This qualifier lists the files in a directory and creates a file to record the information. For example, $ DIRECTORY/OUTPUT=C.LOG [MIKE.C] lists the files in the directory [MIKE.C] and also creates a file C.LOG in the current directory containing this information. The contents of this file can then be displayed by giving the command TYPE C.LOG, or the file can be sent to the default system printer by giving the command PRINT C.LOG/DELETE/COPIES=2. This set of qualifiers causes two copies to be printed, after which the file is deleted.

Note that we can specify any particular file specification in place of C.LOG. Thus MAY_18.LOG, 18MAY.LOG, 18_MAY.LOG would all be equally applicable and valid.

As usual, one selects meaningful file names and it is a convention to use the file type. LOG to refer to any file that contains the log of an activity—in this case the activity of executing the DIRECTORY command.

7.6.3 The TYPE command

The TYPE command displays the contents of a text file or a group of text files.

```
$ type wc.for
```

displays the contents of the file WC.FOR, which by VMS naming conventions should correspond to FORTRAN source code.

For files of any length, it is useful to pause between each screenful of text. The /PAGE qualifier allows this, pausing at the end of each page until the ⟨Return⟩ key is pressed.

```
$ type wc.for/page
```

A group of files can be specified by using wildcards. For example:

```
$ type *.pas
```

displays the contents of all Pascal programs, while

```
$ type *.pas/page
```

pauses at the end of each page, waiting for the ⟨Return⟩ key to be pressed. If we wished to stop looking at the current file and progress to the next file then we should type ⟨Ctrl⟩Z instead of ⟨Return⟩.

If we are not using the /PAGE qualifier, then the following actions can be used when displaying a group of files:

1. ⟨Ctrl⟩O abandons displaying the current file and goes on to the next.
2. ⟨Ctrl⟩Y interrupts the display of the current file. Typing CONTINUE continues displaying files from where the interruption took place; typing STOP abandons the execution of the TYPE command.

7.6.4 The DUMP command

DUMP displays or prints the contents of a file, or a group of files, in ASCII, decimal, hexadecimal, or octal representation. It is used for inspecting the contents of non-text (non-ASCII) files which cannot be looked at with the TYPE command or a text editor.

The representation can be selected by one of the following qualifiers:

- /DECIMAL (base 10, i.e. digits 0, 1, 2, . . ., 9)
- /OCTAL (base 8, i.e. digits 0, 1, 2, . . ., 7)
- /HEXADECIMAL (base 16, i.e. 0, 1, 2, . . ., 9, A, B, C, D, E, F)

In addition you can specify whether a file is to be dumped in terms of blocks (1 VAX/VMS block = 512 bytes) or records by using either the /BLOCKS or the /RECORDS qualifier.

The START and END options can be used to dump a selected part of a file. For example:

```
$ dump accounts.wks/records=(start:1,end:20)/octal/byte
```

Here the octal representation of records 1–20 of the file ACCOUNTS.WKS is displayed and formatted in bytes.

The alternative formats, or ways of grouping the data, are:

- BYTE
- WORD 2 bytes
- LONGWORD 4 bytes, which is the default format

It is often convenient to write the output from the DUMP program to a text file by using the /OUTPUT qualifier. The file can then be inspected by printing or by use of an editor such as EVE:

```
$ dump accounts.wks/byte/octal/output=accounts.txt
```

7.6.5 The COPY command

COPY creates a new file from one or more existing files. The COPY command is versatile and can be used to do the following:

1. Copy an input file to an output file:

   ```
   $ copy from.c to.c
   ```

2. Concatenate (i.e. join together) two or more input files into a single output file:

   ```
   $ copy *.dat join.dat
   ```

   By default, a wildcard character in an input file specification results in a single output file being created which consists of the concatenation of all the input files that match the file specification.
3. Copy a group of input files to a group of output files:

   ```
   $ copy *.dat *.doc/noconcatenate
   ```

   Here, NOCONCATENATE specifies that all *.DAT should not be

concatenated but that each file should be copied individually to a file of the same name but of type DOC. In this case, we have simply changed the file type.

Qualifiers to the COPY command

The power of the COPY command is increased by a number of qualifiers; a few of these are summarized below.

The /PROTECTION qualifier

The output file created by the COPY command inherits the protection associated with the input file. The PROTECTION qualifier can be used to override this protection. For example:

```
$ copy lib.c common.c/protection=(w:r)
```

allows world read access to the created file COMMON.C

The /REPLACE qualifier

Requests that if a file already exists with the same file specification (including version number) as that entered for the output file, the existing file is to be replaced, i.e. it is to be overwritten. The default is /NOREPLACE, in which case the COPY command creates a new version of the file with a version number that is one greater.

7.6.6 The DELETE command

The DELETE command can be used to delete one or more files. For example:

```
$ delete sort.pas;3
```

deletes the file SORT.PAS;3 from the default directory, while

```
$ delete *.bak;*
```

deletes all versions of files with the file type BAK from the current directory.

If more than one file specification is to be used, then these should be separated by commas or plus signs:

```
$ delete *.exe;*,*.obj;*,cworka.pas;3
```

deletes all files with type EXE or OBJ, and the file CWORKA.PAS with version number 3.

Many qualifiers can be used with the DELETE command. For a complete list type:

```
$ help delete
```

The example below demonstrates how the qualifiers can be combined with the DELETE command in order to delete files selectively.

```
$ delete/confirm/since=today [malcolm.testfiles]*.obj;*

DISK0:[MALCOLM.TESTFILES]AVERAG.OBJ;1, delete? [N]:  Y
DISK0:[MALCOLM.TESTFILES]SCANLINE.OBJ;4, delete? [N]:  N
DISK0:[MALCOLM.TESTFILES]SCANLINE.OBJ;3, delete? [N]:  N
DISK0:[MALCOLM.TESTFILES]SCANLINE.OBJ;2, delete? [N]:  N
DISK0:[MALCOLM.TESTFILES]WEATHER.OBJ;3, delete? [N]:  Y
```

The DELETE command above examines all versions of files with file type OBJ in the subdirectory [MALCOLM.TESTFILES], and locates those that were created or modified today. Before deleting each file, it requests confirmation that the file should be deleted. The default response, N (No), is given in square brackets, i.e. one can simply press ⟨Return⟩ to go to the next file.

7.6.7 The PURGE command

This command deletes all but the highest-numbered versions of selected files, which will generally be the most recent.

If a one or more file specifications are not provided, then all the files in the current directory are purged. For example:

```
$ purge
```

preserves one version of each file—that with the highest version number—in the current directory.

A useful qualifier is /KEEP, which retains a specified number of versions of a file. For example:

```
$ purge/keep=3 *.pas,*.c
```

deletes all but the three highest numbered versions of the files with file types PAS and C.

It may be useful for VAX/VMS to display the filenames of the files as it deletes them. To do this use the /LOG qualifier.

```
$ purge *.exe;/log
```

7.6.8 The RENAME command

The RENAME command changes the directory specification, file name, file type, or file version of an existing file or directory. For example:

```
$ rename sort.c bubble.c
```

creates the file BUBBLE.C;1 if the file BUBBLE.C does not already exist in the default directory. If the file currently exists with that version number, then the command gives the renamed file a version number one greater than the highest existing version.

```
$ purge
```

```
$ rename *.*;* *.*;*
```

leaves one version of each file in the current directory and renames each file to have a version number one.

```
$ rename [.test]*.*;* [.production]*.*;*
```

moves every file in the directory [.TEST] to directory [.PRODUCTION]. The file names, types, and version numbers are not changed.

7.6.9 The SEARCH command

The SEARCH command is used to search one or more files for a string (a sequence of characters) or a combination of strings.

SEARCH finds such occurrences and lists all the filenames (which were specified in the file specification list) where the string combinations exist together with the appropriate lines.

The format of the SEARCH command is:

`SEARCH` followed by *file-spec list* and then *search-string list*

The "file-spec list" specifies the filenames of one or more files to be searched. If there is more than one filename then these should be separated by commas. Wildcard characters (* and %) can be used in the file specification.

The "search-string list" specifies the string to be located. If the string specification contains lowercase letters or nonalphanumeric characters (such as spaces, #, etc.) then it should be enclosed between quotation marks.

Example

The following command searches the file CH1.TEX for the string DEFINE. The search matches both upper- and lowercase characters.

```
$ search ch1.tex define

#define ESC 27
#define clear() printf("%c[2J",ESC)
#define up(N) printf("%c[%dA",ESC,N)
```

The power of the SEARCH command is enhanced by a number of command qualifiers, and it is suggested that you use the VAX/VMS help facility to investigate these:

```
$ help search
```

SEARCH and its qualifiers

We give here a description of the /EXACT and /MATCH qualifiers together with examples of their use.

The /EXACT qualifier

The /EXACT qualifier controls whether the SEARCH command treats upper- and lowercase letters as equivalent.

Using the /EXACT qualifier is faster than using the default alternative, /NOEXACT, so if you are sure of the case you are looking for it is better to include the /EXACT qualifier. For example:

```
$ search/exact *.txt "database"
```

displays all records in all files with type. TXT in the current directory that contain the string "database" in lowercase.

The /MATCH qualifier

The MATCH qualifier is used to specify how the SEARCH command matches combinations of strings. This qualifier can take one of four options:

OR — A match occurs if a record contains *any* of the search strings.
AND — A match occurs if a record contains *all* of the search strings in a single record.
NOR — The negation of AND. A match occurs only if the record does not contain any of the search strings.
NAND — The negation of OR. A match occurs only if the record does not contain all of the search strings.

The following example will find all records in files, matching the file specification D_*.TXT in the current directory, which contains both "database" and "relational" and is insensitive to case.

```
$ search/match=and *.txt "database","relational"
```

It should be noted that this does not necessarily mean that SEARCH will find each occurrence of these two strings together in the same sentence as SEARCH works in chunks of records (records being terminated by a new line) and not sentences.

7.7 File and Directory Protection

Suppose a lecturer with username L wishes to allow a student with username S to copy a file, say ASSIGNMENT1.TXT, owned by L. The following conditions must be met:

1. The file protection associated with ASSIGNMENT1.TXT must allow read access to S. If for example, L and S are in the same group then L could give the command:

   ```
   $ set file assignment1.txt/protection=(g:r)
   ```

   which would give all users in the same group as L read access to the file. Alternatively, if L and S were not in the same group, then world read access would have to be given by L to the file:

   ```
   $ set file assignment1.txt/protection=(w:r)
   ```

2. It is necessary that S has execute access to the directory and all directories above that in which ASSIGNMENT.TXT resides. In addition, if S needed to use wildcards to give a file specification (e.g. to copy all files matching ASSIGNMENT*.TXT), then S would also need read access to the directory in which the files reside. If the files to be accessed are in the directory [DISK1:L.COURSEWORK], then

   ```
   $ set file disk1:[L]coursework.dir/protection=(w:r)
   ```

would allow read access to any user who had (at least) execute access to all directories above this.

A possible disadvantage with using this protection mechanism is that it is not possible to give access rights to an individual user—it must be to either the group to which the user belongs, or to the world (everyone). Access Control Lists (ACLs) allow access rights to be granted on a user or group basis.

7.7.1 Access Control Lists

An ACL is a list of Access Control Entries (ACEs) which, as the name suggests, control access to either files or to directories.

Here are some examples of using an ACL.

```
$ set file assignment.txt
_$ /acl=(identifier:[12,1],access:read+write)
```

allows read and write access to the file ASSIGNMENT.TXT to a process whose security identifier is [12,1]. This will correspond to the process that has this UIC. In this case the ACE is *added to the front of the ACL* for this file.

An assumption is made here that the user with UIC [12,1] has execute access to the directory in which ASSIGNMENT.TXT resides and also all directories above that in the directory tree structure.

```
$ set file assignment.txt-
_$ /acl=(identifier:[babs,*],access:read)/new
```

allows read access to any UIC in the group BABS. Again we have assumed here that the necessary directory protections exist and will continue to do so for the following examples.

The /NEW qualifier replaces the complete ACL with the associated ACE.

```
$ set file assignment.txt/acl/delete
```

deletes the ACL for the specified file.

Access rights are operated in the following way:

1. ACLs are searched for an appropriate ACE from the first ACE in the list. This first reference determines the access rights.
2. If there is no ACL for the file, or the ACL contains no relevant entry for the UIC or group to which the UIC belongs, then the access rights are determined by the protection set for the file with respect to group and world users.

ACLs can also be applied to directories, as illustrated in the following example.

```
$ set directory [l.coursework]/acl=(identifier:[12,3],access:read)
```

grants read access to the directory COURSEWORK.DIR with parent L.DIR to the process with UIC [12,3]. The assumption is made that process with UIC [12,3] has at least execute rights to all directories above COURSEWORK.-DIR.

You can check the security associated with any directory or file by the DIRECTORY/SECURITY command:

```
$ set directory [mike.pascal]-
_$ /acl=(identifier:[40,1],access:read+write)

$ directory/security [mike]pascal.dir

Directory PCL$CCSROOT:[MIKE]

PASCAL.DIR;1        [12,3]          (RWE,RWE,RWE,RE)
(IDENTIFIER=[40,1],ACCESS=READ+WRITE)

Total of 1 file.
```

7.8 Differences between Files

VAX/VMS has a facility for comparing the differences between two files. This is useful to locate any modifications made to a file, by comparing it with the previous version. Furthermore, if a file has been copied to another filename in the past, DIFFERENCE (frequently abbreviated to DIFF) can be used to compare the original file with the copy to see if both files are still identical. By default, the DIFFERENCE facility that displays both the line above and below, as well as the line that is different in both files. There are two parameters to the DIFFERENCE command: the first is the file specification of the primary file, and the second the file specification of the file to compare against the primary. For example, if we had a file called FILE1.DAT which contained the lines:

```
This file contains a few lines of text
so we can demonstrate the DIFFERENCE command.
First we shall copy this file and compare
the differences between the two, then we shall
alter the copy and re-compare.
```

We can copy that file to create a second identical file:

```
$ copy file1.dat file2.dat
```

Obviously FILE2.DAT is an exact copy of FILE1.DAT, so when we use DIFFERENCE to compare them, we find the contents of the files are identical:

```
$ difference file1.dat file2.dat

Number of difference sections found: 0
Number of difference records found: 0

DIFFERENCES /IGNORE=()/MERGED=1-
    PCL$CCSROOT:[RAY.TEST]FILE1.DAT;1-
    PCL$CCSROOT:[RAY.TEST]FILE2.DAT;1
```

If we edit line 4 in file FILE2.DAT so the first word becomes "for" (instead of "the") and we insert an extra "files" before the comma:

```
This file contains a few lines of text
so we can demonstrate the DIFFERENCE command.
First we shall copy this file and compare
for differences between the two files, then we shall
alter the copy and re-compare.
```

We now run the DIFFERENCE command to compare this file with the original:

```
$ difference file1.dat file2.dat

************
File PCL$CCSROOT:[RAY.TEST]FILE1.DAT;1
    4   the differences between the two, then we shall
    5   alter the copy and re-compare.
******
File PCL$CCSROOT:[RAY.TEST]FILE2.DAT;2
    4   for differences between the two files, then we shall
    5   alter the copy and re-compare.
************

Number of difference sections found: 1
Number of difference records found: 1

DIFFERENCES /IGNORE=()/MERGED=1-
    PCL$CCSROOT:[RAY.TEST]FILE1.DAT;1-
    PCL$CCSROOT:[RAY.TEST]FILE2.DAT;2
```

By default, DIFFERENCE compares the latest version of the files. If we want to see the modifications we have made to FILE2.DAT the last time we edited it, then by specifying a single filename, DIFFERENCE compares the latest version with the previous version of the file:

```
$ difference file2.dat

************
File PCL$CCSROOT:[RAY.TEST]FILE2.DAT;2
    4   for differences between the two files, then we shall
    5   alter the copy and re-compare.
******
File PCL$CCSROOT:[RAY.TEST]FILE2.DAT;1
    4   the differences between the two, then we shall
    5   alter the copy and re-compare.
************

Number of difference sections found: 1
Number of difference records found: 1

DIFFERENCES /IGNORE=()/MERGED=1-
    PCL$CCSROOT:[RAY.TEST]FILE2.DAT;2-
    PCL$CCSROOT:[RAY.TEST]FILE2.DAT;1
```

In this instance (since FILE2.DAT has been edited only once) we could equally well have typed:

```
$ difference file2.dat;2 file2.dat;1
```

Once it has found a line that is not the same in both files, DIFFERENCE assumes, after finding three successive lines that match, that the files are the same again. To override this default, use the /MATCH=n qualifier, where "n" is the number of lines that must match before the files can be said to be the same again. Instead of displaying a list of differences on the screen, they can be written to a file using the /OUTPUT=filename qualifier. Filename is the name of the file to which the nonmatching records are written. The following example compares file TEST1.TXT to TEST2.TXT and checks to see if five lines match before searching for the next difference. The output (containing the differences) is sent to a file called DIFFS.TXT:

```
$ difference file1.dat file2.dat /match=5 /output=diffs.txt
```

Then on typing DIFFS.TXT we have:

```
$ type diff.txt

************
File PCL$CCSROOT:[RAY.TEST]FILE1.DAT;1
    4   the differences between the two, then we shall
    5   alter the copy and re-compare.
******
File PCL$CCSROOT:[RAY.TEST]FILE2.DAT;2
    4   for differences between the two files, then we shall
    5   alter the copy and re-compare.
************
```

```
Number of difference sections found: 1
Number of difference records found: 1

DIFFERENCES /IGNORE=()/MATCH=5/MERGED=1/OUTPUT=DUA1:[RAY]DIFFS.TXT;1-
    PCL$CCSROOT:[RAY.TEST]FILE1.DAT;1-
    PCL$CCSROOT:[RAY.TEST]FILE2.DAT;2
```

7.9 The SORT Utility

VMS provides an extensive facility to sort records of up to 10 files into a single output file. Qualifiers are provided to cater for most likely requirements. A full description is given in the Help Sort facility. To obtain this information type:

```
$ help/output=sort.log sort *
```

There are certain requirements. If multiple input files are used, they must be separated in the specification by commas. Both the input and output files must have their types specified; the default type is .DAT. Sorting can be in ascending or descending order, as specified. The record and the file type for both the input and output files can also be specified, although there is a default value for each file if record and type are not specified. Workfiles for temporary operation need to be specified; again, up to 10 files can be specified. Sorting can be on a single primary key, or up to 255 preferential keys. The starting and terminating position of each key field must be specified. The /SPECIFICATION=file_spec qualifier allows all the qualifiers to be placed into a file. In its absence input from the keyboard is used.

The general format of the SORT command is:

```
$ sort/key=(position:AA,size:BB) input.lis output.lis
```

where AA is the column position of the start of the sort field, and BB is the length of that field. The input (unsorted) and output (sorted) files also need to be specified.

The following two examples access a file containing a list of employees' surnames with associated telephone extension(s). The first example sorts the file into alphabetical order, on employee's surname, and the second according to extension number. The input and output file are called respectively PHONE.DAT and SORTED_PHONE.DAT.

Example 1 Sorting on a single record

```
$ type phone.dat

smith  237
jones  345
zebra   27
```

```
black   72
apple  982
brown  472
white  121
green   42
green   21
green    4
yellow 496
yellow 222
```

```
$ sort/key=(position:1,size:6) phone.dat sorted_phone.dat
```

```
$ type sorted_phone.dat
```

```
apple  982
black   72
brown  472
green   42
green    4
green   21
jones  345
smith  237
white  121
yellow 222
yellow 496
zebra   27
```

In the example above we use the /KEY=(position,size) qualifier to specify a field on which to sort. We do this by specifying a start position for the field, in this instance column 1, and a size of the field, here a six-digit field is used. For example:

```
            yellow 222
            ↑    ↑ ↑ ↑
Positions:  1    6 8 10
```

Alternatively, we can specify the start position and field size of the employee's extension, and sort on that:

```
$ sort/key=(position:8,size:3) phone.dat sorted_phone2.dat
```

```
$ type sorted_phone2.dat
```

```
green    4
green   21
zebra   27
green   42
black   72
white  121
```

```
yellow 222
smith  237
jones  345
brown  472
yellow 496
apple  982
```

Example 2   Sorting on two records

In this example we use the /KEY=(position, size) qualifier twice to select two fields on which to sort. We first sort on the first key specified, and then, if the first key occurs more than once, on the second key.

Using the input file PHONE.DAT, we are able to sort first into surname order; in cases where the surname occurs more than once we can sort on the "secondary key" in order of extension for those surnames. The output file is PHONE_DIRECTORY.DAT.

```
$ type phone.dat

smith  237
jones  345
zebra   27
black   72
apple  982
brown  472
white  121
green   42
green   21
green    4
yellow 496
yellow 222


$ sort/key=(position:1,size:5)/key=(position:8,size:3)-
_$ phone.dat phone_directory.dat


$ type phone_directory.dat

apple  982
black   72
brown  472
green    4
green   21
green   42
jones  345
smith  237
white  121
yellow 222
yellow 496
zebra   27
```

Chapter

8

Process Creation—the SPAWN Command

8.1 Introduction

SPAWN allows you to create a subprocess (i.e. run a job) from the process that you are currently running. Remember that when you log in to the computer a process is created by VAX/VMS. This will be your current process, until you create a subprocess that then may become your current process. Therefore, even though you may be entering commands interactively, i.e. you are at the DCL level, you are still running a process.

The SPAWN command is very similar in operation to the SUBMIT command. The SUBMIT command is used to place a file in the BATCH queue (see Chapter 9). Both SPAWN and SUBMIT can execute processes in the "background", freeing the screen and keyboard for other work.

Processes are organized by VAX/VMS into a tree structure, called the "job tree". Each subprocess, sometimes known as a "child process", is attached by the "arm" of the tree to the originating process (the "parent process") that created it. If the parent process dies, e.g. if you log out of the system, then the child will also exit. Subprocesses are identified by the name of the parent followed by an underscore (_) and a unique integer. For example, if we have a process name of BUZBY for our main process, any subprocesses we create will be called BUZBY_1, BUZBY_2, and so on. If the processes BUZBY_1 and BUZBY_2 were created from the main process and we created a third process BUZBY_3 from BUZBY_1, the tree would have the structure shown in Figure 8-1. Each spawned process (child) is dependent on the presence of its parent.

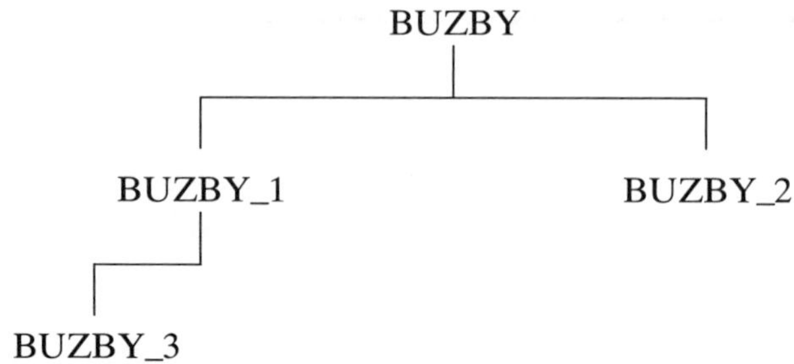

Fig. 8-1 The structure of the SPAWN job tree.

Subprocesses have the same privileges, logical name, and symbol tables as their parent.

8.2 Creating Subprocesses

There are two main ways of creating and using a subprocess: SPAWN and SPAWN/NOWAIT.

8.2.1 The SPAWN command

The SPAWN command is inbuilt in the VAX/VMS, i.e it is integral to DCL, and so VAX/VMS does not have to run a program to execute this command. Therefore, we can spawn "out" at any time from a current process, the "parent", interact with the subprocess, the "child", exit from the subprocess, and then return to the parent. On spawning a subprocess in this way the parent process activity is suspended, it is said to be "hibernating", until we return to it from the subprocess. Control is resumed from the same point at which it was suspended. A few illustrative examples are given below:

1. When running a program we can press the ⟨Ctrl⟩ and Y keys simultaneously to stop execution and return to the DCL prompt. We can then SPAWN a process, perform some commands, "exit" from the spawned process by typing LOGOUT, and then continue the original program by typing CONTINUE. In the example shown below, SPAWN starts the subprocess. DIRECTORY is a command to the subprocess, and LOGOUT terminates the subprocess:

```
          ----- Running Program -----

$ <Ctrl>Y

$ spawn

$ directory *.log

  Directory DUA0:[RAY]

  C6.LOG;1     C8.LOG;1     WHO.LOG;2   WHO.LOG;1

  Total of 4 files.

$ logout

$ continue

          ----- Resume running program -----
```

2. When you run the EVE screen editor, it takes a while for the process to be initiated. If you are debugging a program or command procedure and are constantly editing and running the code, the time it takes to enter and exit the editor may be quite significant. This can be overcome using the SPAWN command. Since SPAWN is a built in command, if you use it to exit from EVE, it will leave the code associated with the parent process in the computers main memory (normally when you exit EVE your file will be written to disk). Therefore when you re-enter EVE from the subprocess, there is no resulting time delay in reinitializing the editor and in waiting for the file to be copied from disk into main memory.

The example below demonstrates two things. First, how to spawn out of the EVE editor (remember the ⟨PF4⟩ key places you in command mode from screen mode). Secondly, the program example was selected such that it displays at each stage the process currently active. Therefore, we can see which process we are currently using. Unfortunately the difference in speed between initially running the editor with the EDIT/TPU WHAT_PROC.COM command and how quickly the process is restarted on returning (logging out) from the subprocess cannot be shown here. However, the user may like to run, for comparison, the process shown below. Figures 8-2a and b show the stages at which SPAWN is started and terminated.

Example

1. Enter EVE.

```
$ edit/tpu what_proc.com
```

2. Subprocess started.

```
$ @what_proc

The current processes are :-
23-MAY-1989 11:16:04.35                  User: RAY
Pid: 00002C90    Proc. name: RAY_1       UIC:  [12,5]
Priority:   4    Default file spec: PCL$CCSROOT:[RAY]

$

$ logout
  Process   RAY_1   logged   out   at   23-MAY-1989   11:16:11.38
```

3. Subprocess terminated, return to EVE.
4. Now exit “normally” and run the procedure a second time.

```
$ @what_proc

The current processes are :-
23-MAY-1989 11:16:04.35                  User: RAY
Pid: 00002C90    Proc. name: RAY         UIC:  [12,5]
Priority:   4    Default file spec: PCL$CCSROOT:[RAY]
```

When we use SPAWN to create a subprocess, control of the terminals, screen, and keyboard passes to the child process. Normally, any commands executed in that subprocess are independent of any other processes, including the parent one, on the system. However, any SET TERMINAL commands executed in the subprocess will affect the terminal characteristics on returning to the parent from the child process.

8.2.2 The SPAWN/NOWAIT command

Specifying the /NOWAIT qualifier with the SPAWN command enables you to work on the parent process while the subprocess works in the background. Since the parent process is not put into hibernation when the child process is started, the child process can be viewed as a “batch job” (Chapter 9). Note, however, that the child process is unable to accept any input from the keyboard. Furthermore, any job that can be run as a batch job can also be run as a subprocess using the SPAWN/NOWAIT command. Subprocesses that are run in this way are sometimes known as “background jobs”.

To run a command procedure called STATS.COM as a spawned process, we type the command:

```
$ spawn/nowait @stats

%DCL-S-SPAWNED, process RAY_1 spawned
```

```
$!  Program : WHAT_PROC.COM
$!  Program to show current processes
$!  This program is very simple it executes the DCL
$!  command — "show process"
$   write sys$output "The current processes are :—"
$   show process
[End of file]

Buffer:  WHAT_PROC.COM                   Insert      Forward

Command:  spawn
```

(a)

```
$!  Program : WHAT_PROC.COM
$!  Program to show current processes
$!  This program is very simple it executes the DCL
$!  command — "show process"
$   write sys$output "The current processes are :—"
$   show process
[End of file]

Buffer:  WHAT_PROC.COM                   Insert      Forward

Command:  exit
```

(b)

Fig. 8-2 Using SPAWN to exit from EVE temporarily.

this provides an alternative to the command:

```
$ submit stats.com

Job WHAT_PROC (queue SYS$BATCH, entry 674) pending
      pending status caused by queue stopped state
```

Note that there are two major differences between the SUBMIT and SPAWN/NOWAIT commands:

- Processes submitted to the batch queues are executed, by default, at priority level 3, whereas spawned processes operate at priority level 4. Therefore spawned processes run faster.
- Spawned processes are killed when the parent process dies. Thus all processes created with the SPAWN and SPAWN/NOWAIT commands are terminated when the user logs out. Therefore any programs that are still running will not be completed, and caution is therefore necessary before terminating the parent process. This is not the case with the SUBMIT command.

8.3 Useful Qualifiers

We have dealt with the two main types of spawn command—SPAWN and SPAWN/NOWAIT. Now we look briefly at some of the other qualifiers which we can use.

8.3.1 The /OUTPUT qualifier

When using SPAWN/NOWAIT, both processes are running concurrently, and it is possible that both of them might attempt to write, at the same time, to the terminal screen. To avoid confusion, the output of the subprocesses can be redirected to a file. This is done using the /OUTPUT qualifier. For example, the command

```
$ spawn/nowait/output=result.log calibrate.com

%DCL-S-SPAWNED, process RAY_1 spawned
```

runs CALIBRATE.COM in the background, writing all the output to RESULT.LOG. As a point of interest, we could have equally well run the procedure as a batch job:

```
$ submit/output=result.log calibrate.com
```

8.3.2 The /PROCESS qualifier

We can use the /PROCESS qualifier to choose a different process name than those assigned by default. If your parent process name were FROG, then the first subprocess we created would be, by default, FROG_1. By using the /PROCESS qualifier we can specify another name for the subprocess. The following example renames the subprocess to TADPOLE, instead of the default FROG_1:

```
$ spawn/process=tadpole

%DCL-S-SPAWNED, process TADPOLE spawned
%DCL-S-ATTACHED, terminal now attached to process TADPOLE
```

Note that all process names must be unique.

8.3.3 The /NOLOGICAL NAME and /NOSYMBOL qualifiers

In creating a subprocess, a copy of the logical name tables and symbol tables are created for the use of that subprocess. The production of these tables occupies quite a large proportion of the time it takes to create the subprocess itself. Consequently, to save time and effort, if you do not need to use logical names or symbols within your subprocess, use the /NOLOGICAL_NAMES and /NOSYMBOL qualifiers.

Example

```
$ spawn/nological_names/nosymbol @what_proc

%DCL-S-SPAWNED, process RAY_1 spawned
%DCL-S-ATTACHED, terminal now attached to process RAY_1
```

8.4 Attaching to Processes

So far we have exited from child processes by logging them out with the command LOGOUT. But we can also pass control back from a subprocess to the parent by using the ATTACH command. Let us examine the differences between the two methods.

By using the LOGOUT command the child process is deleted, along with any other processes that were created by it. Control is subsequently returned to the parent process. However, by using the ATTACH command we can transfer control from one process to another without having to delete the first process. The process that initiates the ATTACH command is put into hibernation until control is passed back to it. Specifying ATTACH provides an easy mechanism to "switch" between child and parent processes.

In the following example we create a subprocess using the SPAWN command and then, after running SHOW PROCESS, we switch from the child back to the parent process and display the characteristics of the parent process. Finally we reattach to the child and LOGOUT, to delete the process. To help clarify the process with which we are communicating, we have changed the prompts (default is $).

```
$ set prompt = "parent> "

parent>

parent> spawn

%DCL-S-SPAWNED, process RAY_1 spawned
%DCL-S-ATTACHED, terminal now attached to process RAY_1

$ set prompt = "child>"

child>

child> show process

23-MAY-1989 11:22:21.67                         User: RAY
Pid: 0000289D    Proc. name: RAY_1              UIC: [12,5]
Priority:    4   Default file spec: PCL$CCSROOT:[RAY]

child> attach ray

%DCL-S-RETURNED, control returned to process RAY


parent>

parent> show process

23-MAY-1989 11:22:37.68    RTA2:                User: RAY
Pid: 00002C8F    Proc. name: RAY                UIC: [12,5]
Priority:    4   Default file spec: PCL$CCSROOT:[RAY]
Devices allocated: RTA2:

parent> attach ray_1

%DCL-S-RETURNED, control returned to process RAY_1

child> logout

Process RAY_1 logged out at 23-MAY-1989 11:22:51.01
%DCL-S-RETURNED, control returned to process RAY
```

```
parent> show process

23-MAY-1989 11:22:55.58   RTA2:                  User: RAY
Pid: 00002C8F   Proc. name: RAY                  UIC: [12,5]
Priority:   4   Default file spec: PCL$CCSROOT:[RAY]
Devices allocated: RTA2:
```

Notice that LOGOUT killed the child process, and control was passed back to the parent. Also note that the parent process has been allocated the user's terminal, RTA2:, but the child process has no devices allocated.

Instead of specifying the name of the process to attach to, we can use the /IDENTIFICATION qualifier (commonly abbreviated to /IDENT) and specify the PID (Process Identification Number) instead. First we need to find out the PID values; this can be done by using the SHOW PROCESS command, as follows:

```
child> show process

23-MAY-1989 11:23:47.36                          User: RAY
Pid: 00002C9E   Proc. name: RAY_1                UIC: [12,5]
Priority:   4   Default file spec: PCL$CCSROOT:[RAY]

child> attach ray

%DCL-S-RETURNED, control returned to process RAY

parent> show process

23-MAY-1989 11:24:02.08   RTA2:                  User: RAY
Pid: 00002C8F   Proc. name: RAY                  UIC: [12,5]
Priority:   4   Default file spec: PCL$CCSROOT:[RAY]
Devices allocated: RTA2:
```

So in the above example we could have specified:

```
child> attach/ident=2c8f
%DCL-S-RETURNED, control returned to process RAY
```

to attach to the parent form the child process, and

```
parent> attach/ident=2c9e
%DCL-S-RETURNED, control returned to process RAY_1
```

to attach to the child from the parent process. These commands perform the same function as:

```
child> attach/ident=ray
%DCL-S-RETURNED, control returned to process RAY
```

and

```
parent> attach/ident=ray1
%DCL-S-RETURNED, control returned to process RAY_1
```

respectively.

Chapter

9

Batch and Print Queues

9.1 Introduction

There are two major types of queues on VAX/VMS—print queues and batch queues. A queue is created in software to replicate a queuing system, such as we see in everyday life, e.g. at a bus stop or outside a cinema. On a computer, items that need to be processed have to join the back of the appropriate queue and wait their turn to be processed. Once the computer has finished processing the item at the front of the queue, the next one in turn is dealt with and each item in the queue moves forward a place. This is repeated until the last process is completed and the queue becomes "empty".

To place a file into a queue, the user places an entry into a "queue table" requesting that a certain file be executed, in the case of the batch queue, or printed, in the case of the print queue. In doing this, the user is said to "submit" a "job" to a queue. Unless the user has been granted privileges over those normally allocated to other users, the request will join the queue at the back and gradually work its way to the front as the preceding jobs in the queue are finished.

Although jobs can be placed in both the print and the batch queues and left there to be completed in their own time, there are several essential differences in the operation of the two queues and of course they process two entirely different types of jobs. Because of this we will describe the two types of queue separately, but it is important to realize that many of the main commands and qualifiers, apply equally well to either queue. For example, consider the following commands:

```
SHOW QUEUE queue_name

DELETE/ENTRY=entry_numberqueue_name
```

These can equally well be applied to either job type. The other main commands are SUBMIT (to place a job in the batch queue) and PRINT (to place a file in the queue for printing). Any of the qualifiers apply equally well to either type of queue.

9.2 Batch Queues

9.2.1 Introduction

Normally we use VAX/VMS in interactive mode. That is, we type commands to the operating system from a terminal and VAX/VMS attempts to execute each command (program or procedure) and displays a resulting message on the screen. This mode of interactive operation can have a number of drawbacks:

1. When the computer is heavily loaded, either because it has too many users using it simultaneously or, alternatively, because some users are running large application programs, the "user response time" (the time it takes to execute each command typed) can be quite slow. Consequently, any programs that are run also take longer to complete.
2. During the period of time it takes to run your own large programs, your terminal is unavailable to execute any other commands or programs. The SPAWN/NOWAIT command can be used to avoid this problem.
3. On some computers, limits are imposed as to the size of a program that can be run during the normal working day. This has the benefit of speeding up the machine for users in general, but it also makes it impossible to run large programs, e.g. those that need either a lot of memory or CPU time.

All these potential problems can be overcome by using batch jobs.

A batch job is a command procedure that can execute a program without the user's intervention. This command procedure may run one or more programs or utilities. These programs may be passed data, from the command procedures that run them.

In running a batch job VAX/VMS logs into the user account from which the job was submitted into the queue. A process is then created in much the same way as when we log in interactively and the command procedure is executed. Batch jobs are normally run at a priority level that is one less than for normal interactive users—level 3 as opposed to level 4. While it will make the procedure run slower than under normal circumstances, the fact that it can be entered into the queue to run at a specified time when the system is not heavily loaded may outweigh the lower priority allocation.

The System Manager is responsible for setting up queues, and therefore there may be differences between systems depending on local conditions. Although most computers have the default batch queue, SYS$BATCH, other batch queues may have been added. Usually, each additional queue is assigned for a specific use or application. Queue priorities may be altered to make them comparable with running jobs interactively. Unlike print queues, batch queues can be configured so that several jobs in the same queue can run simultaneously. For example, if the limit was set to three, the first three jobs in the queue would execute, and as soon as one is finished, the fourth job in the queue could start running. Complications may arise if two or more jobs were dependent on each other, i.e. if one job needed to have completed running, before a second job could start (e.g. if the second job processed results produced by the first job). The processing of such jobs is controlled by a program known as the Queue Manager. This process ensures correct interaction between jobs in the same queue that need to exchange data. It also organizes the queue from within the batch environment to the printer.

Batch jobs are used a great deal for processing large tasks, i.e. processes involving large amounts of data, such as mailing lists, invoicing (i.e. gas bills, phone bills, etc.), collating scientific data etc. Running processes over a long period of time at a low priority makes batch jobs ideal for these type of tasks.

9.2.2 Submitting batch files

First of all we need to create a command procedure (command procedures are covered in Chapter 14) that is capable of running without user intervention. To do this we run the editor EVE and type in the program (see Chapters 5 and 6 pertaining to EVE). The example that follows is simple and can be enhanced, using lexical functions, to obtain and manipulate the data. To start we run EVE and specify a filename (in this case WHO.COM):

```
$ edit/tpu who.com
```

We then type in the file:

```
$! Program to find the number of users on the system
$!
$ write sys$output "A list of the users on the system:- "

$ show users
$!
```

and exit the editor (press the ⟨PF4⟩ key then type EXIT).

The file contains just one DCL command, SHOW USERS. We may have preceded the command with SHOW TIME to obtain the date and time on the output, but this information is contained in the header generated by the SHOW

USERS command anyway. With any batch file, it is a good idea to run it interactively at first to check that it works satisfactorily:

```
$ @who.com

A list of the users on the system :-
          VAX/VMS Interactive Users
           19-JUN-1989 09:57:55.99
    Total number of interactive users = 5

 Username      Process Name    PID       Terminal
 $OPER         BR              00001E7D  TXA4:
 $OPER_1       CRAIG           00001E83  LTA1878:
 ALISTAIRW     alistair        00001E9B  LTA1888:
 BEN           BEN             00001E9D  LTA1889:
 RAY           RAY             00001EA0  RTA1:
```

Then we can submit it into the batch queue:

```
$ submit who.com

Job WHO (queue SYS$BATCH, entry 5) started on SYS$BATCH
```

which will submit the file into the default batch queue SYS$BATCH. To submit into another queue we simply use the /QUEUE qualifier (this equally applies to print queues). So to submit the job into the batch queue USERS-$BATCH:

```
$ submit/queue=users$batch who.com

Job WHO (queue USERS$BATCH, entry 22) started on USERS$BATCH
```

If an error occurs while the procedure is being run, execution will terminate and the procedure exits.

9.2.3 Log files

When the job has completed a "log file", which contains a report of the batch jobs, execution is automatically queued to the printer and then deleted. The log file contains a complete record from the time the command procedure started until it finished. This includes logging in to the system, running the command procedure, and logging out. When procedures that create large log files are being run, the data is written out to the log file once a minute. This can be altered by placing the command $ SET OUTPUT_RATE time_interval at the beginning of the procedure. It is possible to display the log file on the screen before the procedure has finished writing it. If, however, you receive a "file locked by another user" error message, then wait a few seconds and try again. This occurs because the command procedure is updating the log file at precisely the same time that you wish to look at it. Alternatively, we can use the EVE editor with the qualifier /READ_ONLY, which will allow us to read, but not to alter the log file.

The following complete log file generated by the procedure "WHO.COM":

```
MOLE will be down TUESDAY 10 JULY until TUESDAY 24 JULY 1989 to
                install software upgrades.

$!    Login command procedure - LOGIN.COM
$!
$     define/nolog/job    LNK$LIBRARY    SYS$LIBRARY:VAXCRTL
$     mail      :==  mail/edit
$!
$     if f$mode() .eqs. "INTERACTIVE" then goto interactive
$        goto end
$end:
$! Check is then is BATCH if so EXIT the LOGIN.COM Prodcedure
$     if f$mode() .eqs. "BATCH" then exit
$!
$! Program to find the number of users on the system
$!
$ write sys$output "A list of the users on the system :- "
A list of the users on the system :-
$ show users
          VAX/VMS Interactive Users
           19-JUN-1989 10:00:24.62
    Total number of interactive users = 3

 Username      Process Name     PID       Terminal
 BRENDA        BRENDA           00001E7F  LTA1876         LTA1876:
 FRANCES       FRANCES          00001E92  LTA1884         LTA1884:
 GREENWOOD     GREENWOOD        00001E8E  LTA1882         LTA1882:
$!
  RAY          job terminated at 19-JUN-1989 10:00:25.28

  Accounting information:
  Buffered I/O count:          73      Peak working set size:    395
  Direct I/O count:            63      Peak page file size:     2426
  Page faults:                713      Mounted volumes:            0
  Charged CPU time: 0 00:00:01.90     Elapsed time:   0 00:00:06.82
```

9.2.4 SUBMIT qualifiers

We shall now look at some of the queue qualifiers that are of most interest when used with batch queues (SUBMIT command), although they also work with the PRINT command.

The /AFTER qualifier

We are able to place a job in the batch queue and suspend its execution until a specified time, or until after a specified time period has elapsed. Consequently when it reaches the front of the queue and is able to run, it will not do so until the time stated by the /AFTER qualifier is reached. This is useful in many instances; for example, by placing WHO.COM in the batch queue with the /AFTER qualifier we are able to see who is using the system at any given time. The following command submits WHO.COM to the batch queue, but withholds its execution until midnight on 15 April 1989 (notice the format used to specify the date and time):

```
$ submit who.com/after=16-apr-1989:00:00:00

Job WHO (queue SYS$BATCH, entry 42) holding until 16-apr-1989 00:00
```

Execution begins when the time specified by the system clock matches that specified by the /AFTER qualifier. This example uses an “absolute time”. We will show examples of alternative ways of specifing the time in the next section.

The /AFTER qualifier can also be used with the PRINT command although its usefulness is somewhat limited.

Since the /AFTER qualifier is used a great deal, it will be useful now to look at the three different methods of specifying the time. These are called absolute, delta, and combination times.

Absolute time

This is a specific time of day (as used in the example above). The date/time must be in the following format, although certain parts may be omitted:

```
DD-MMM-YYYY:HH:MM:SS.CC
```

where:

DD	Date—Must be an integer between 1 and 31.
MMM	Month—first three characters of the name of the month: JAN, FEB, MAR, APR, MAY, JUN, JUL, AUG, SEP, OCT, NOV, DEC.
YYYY	Year—the year as an integer (i.e. 1989).
HH	Hour—must be an integer between 0 and 23.
MM	Minute—must be an integer between 1 and 59.
SS	Second—must be an integer between 1 and 59.
CC	1/100 second—must be an integer between 1 and 99.

We can either omit the date field (DD-MMM-YYYY), or the time field

(HH:MM:SS:CC), but if we specify both fields we must place the colon between them. When omitting fields in the date or time parts we must include the separating hyphens for the date fields, or the separating colons for time fields. For example, 12::30 is 30 seconds past midday, and 23- is midnight on the 23rd of the current month.

Instead of specifing a time in the format shown above we can specify one of the following:

TODAY	Midnight of the current day.
TOMORROW	Midnight tomorrow night.
YESTERDAY	Midnight last night.

For example, to run the program WHO.COM tonight at midnight, we use the command:

```
$ submit who.com/after=today
```

Let us look at some more examples:

7:15	A quarter past 7 this morning.
12-	12th of this month.
09-JAN	8 January at midnight (i.e. 00:00 on 9 January) this year.
22-APR-1989:20	22 April 1989 at 8 p.m. (24-hour clock)
20-::45	The 20th of this month at 45 minutes past midnight.

Delta time

Delta time enables you to specify a time interval that has to elapse before the procedure can run. Once that time period has expired, the program executes. For example, to execute the command procedure WHO.COM 2 hours after submission:

```
$ submit who.com /after="+2"
```

The general format of the date/time specification is:

```
DDDD-HH:MM:SS.CC
```

where:

DDDD	Number of days—must be an integer between 1 and 9999.
HH	Number of hours—must be an integer between 0 and 23.
MM	Number of minutes—must be an integer between 1 and 59.
SS	Number of seconds—must be an integer between 1 and 59.

CC	Number of hundredths of a second—Must be an integer between 1 and 99.

You can omit various parts of the date/time field, but you must adhere to certain rules. If you specify days you must include the hyphen. If you omit time fields you must still include the colons that separate them. Delta times can be truncated on the right.

Let us look at some examples of delta times:

7:30	7 hours 30 minutes from now.
:15	15 minutes from now.
2	2 hours from now.
2-	2 days (48 hours) from now.
2-::20	2 days and 20 seconds from now.

Combination times

We can also use absolute and delta times together. First, we specify the absolute time and then subtract (-) or add (+) a delta time. The format is given below; notice that when we use a plus symbol, we need to enclose the complete string in quotes.

```
"absolute time + delta time"

absolute time - delta time
```

Be careful not to confuse the subtraction symbol with the hyphen field separator! The same rules and formats apply for combination times as for absolute and delta times. You can omit either the absolute or the delta time. If the absolute time is missing, the delta time is offset from the current date and time.

The following are some examples of combination times:

-:15	15 minutes before the current time.
"+45"	45 minutes from the current time.
"+2"	2 hours from the current time.
-3-00	3 days ago. The first "–" is a subtraction sign specifing minus 3 days, the second "–" is a hyphen separating day and time fields.

The /KEEP qualifier

This qualifier prevents the log file from being deleted after printing. For example:

```
$ submit stats.com/keep
```

The /LOG NAME qualifier

The /LOG_NAME qualifier allows you to change the name of the log file from that specified by the default. By default, the log file is given the same name as the batch file that generated it, but with a file extension of .LOG (i.e. WHO.COM would create a log file called WHO.LOG). The file is created in the user's default directory.

The example below runs a command procedure called CALC.COM, which creates a log file called RUN2.LOG (as specified by the /LOG_NAME qualifier) and stores it in a subdirectory called TEST:

```
$ submit calc.com/log_name=user0:[biology.test]run2.log/keep
```

The /KEEP qualifier ensures that the log file is not deleted after printing.

The /RESTART qualifier

If the system were to crash (i.e. a fault develops and the operating system stops running) while a batch job is being executed, the job will not be completed. When the system is rebooted (the operating system is restarted) the next job in the queue will start running. In order to rerun a job from the beginning after a machine crash, specify the /RESTART qualifier as follows:

```
$ submit stats.com /restart
```

9.2.5 The SHOW command

Once we have submitted a job in a queue we can watch its progress with the SHOW QUEUE command:

```
$ show queue sys$batch

Batch queue SYS$BATCH
(System Batch Queue)

  Jobname          Username      Entry          Status
  -------          --------      -----          ------
  RESULT           RAY               7          Executing
```

where SYS$BATCH is the name of the batch queue. The show queue commands for print and batch queues are very similar and the same qualifiers apply. The following example shows the /ALL and /FULL qualifiers, used in conjunction with batch queues SYS$BATCH and SYS$CONTROL, respectively:

```
$ show queue sys$batch/all

Batch queue SYS$BATCH
(System Batch Queue)

  Jobname          Username      Entry             Status
  -------          --------      -----             ------
  RESULT           RAY               7             Executing
  WHO              RAY               8             Executing
```

```
$ show queue sys$control/full

Batch queue SYS$CONTROL
(Control Batch Queue)
/BASE_PRIORITY=4/CPUMAXIMUM=00:30:00/JOB_LIMIT=3/OWNER=[AUSTAFXN,SYSTEM]
/PROTECTION=(S:E,O:D,G:R,W:W) /WSEXTENT=350 /WSQUOTA=250

  Jobname          Username      Entry             Status
  -------          --------      -----             ------
  RESULT           RAY              12             Executing
Submitted 19-JUN-1989 09:59 /KEEP /PRIORITY=100
File: _DUA2:[CCSROOT.RAY]RESULT.COM;1 (executing)
```

9.2.6 The DELETE/ENTRY command

To stop a job running, or to delete it from the queue, we use the DELETE/ENTRY command. This command applies to both print and batch queues.

Before we can delete a job from the queue, we need to know its "entry number". This is a unique number assigned to each job as it enters the queue. To obtain the entry number we use the SHOW ENTRY command, followed by the DELETE/ENTRY command to delete the job from the queue. Therefore to delete an entry from the queue, use the following procedure:

```
$ show entry

 Jobname  Username  Entry  Blocks  Status
 -------  --------  -----  ------  ------
 WHO      RAY          42         Holding until 20-JUN-1989 12:00

    On batch queue SYS$BATCH

$ delete/entry=42 sys$batch
```

9.2.7 Examples of resubmitting a batch job

Introduction

We shall now consider two versions of a procedure that once run, will automatically resubmit itself into the batch queue for subsequent execution.

This procedure will be repeated indefinitely until the procedure is deleted from the batch queue (with the DELETE/ENTRY command). The first example is less complex but not as accurate as the second.

First program—a procedure that resubmits

We can modify our earlier example WHO.COM so that it runs every hour. At first sight, the simplest way to do this is to place a SUBMIT command in the procedure itself, which automatically resubmits the procedure each time it runs. There are, however, two major problems with this method:

1. Each time the procedure runs, it takes a short, but finite, period of time to log in. Then if the next command in the procedure resubmits the file to run in an hour, the program will actually be resubmitted in one hour from that statement, and not one hour from the moment the procedure started to execute. Therefore it takes a little over an hour each time the program is submitted (the additional time depends on how long it takes for the batch file to log in and to execute as far as the submit statement). Placing the submit statement further down the file further exaggerates the problem. If the program is to run each hour for only 24 hours, this may not be a major problem, but over say a period of a week, it may well be.
2. A more serious problem, however is if the procedure did not work correctly first time, but had, for instance, a syntax error that caused the procedure to be resubmitted every second instead of every hour; the procedure then would replicate itself very quickly and soon become out of control. Such a procedure would be very difficult to stop since each procedure (especially in this example—WHO.COM) is small and consequently quick to execute. So before we can delete it, it has finished running and again submitted a new process that is now running and so on, i.e. it creates a "runaway chain reaction".

The following procedure (once carefully checked) would produce a report (contained in the file WHO.LOG) of users on the system approximately once an hour:

```
$! Program to find the number of users on the system
$!
$ submit who.com /after=1
$ write sys$output "A list of the users on the system :- "
$ show users
$!
```

Second program—an enhanced resubmitting procedure

A safer, more accurate way of resubmitting would be to use a data file containing a single record, corresponding to the time at which the procedure is to run next. The command procedure will then open the file, read the time, add one (hour) to it, and use the new time to resubmit the procedure. Finally, the new time is written back into the file. The following procedure, called WHO2.COM, shows this method:

```
$! Produce an hourly list of system users
$ open/read time_file next.dat
$ read time_file time
$ time = time + 1
$ show symbol time
$ if time .eqs. 24 then time = 0
$ close time_file
$ submit who2.com /after='time'
$ show users
$ open/write time_file next.dat
$ write time_file time
$ close time_file
```

The data file thus contains the time the program is to run. We shall start the program at midnight. So HOUR.DAT looks like:

```
$! The Program will run again at :
00
```

Note that the time is stored as data and therefore is not preceded by a dollar sign.

Each time the procedure is run, one is added to this record, until it reaches 24 (midnight) and the count is reset to 00.

The examples above are short, but they are typical of a procedure created to run in a batch queue to provide routine system statistics. The examples can be used as a model for related applications.

9.3 Print Queues

9.3.1 Introduction

Most printing on a VAX computer is done on a main system printer(s), which may be situated in another room or building, as opposed to a microcomputer, or a standalone machine (i.e. one not in a network), where the printer is connected directly to an output port on the back of the individual computer. In this way printers connected to computers such as the VAX, can be shared amongst all the computer users. By saving on initial cost (one printer for all the users to share as opposed to one each) and maintenance costs, this arrangement allows for more expensive (and so higher quality, or higher speed) printers to be purchased. By placing such a printer in a location central to the users and the computer staff, it enables the printer to be supervised more easily, and makes it readily available to the users.

Many timesharing computers have more than one printer. It is usual to have a central fast printer which produces reasonable quality copy—this would be primarily used for listing program code or data files. There may also be a high-quality printer, such as a laser printer or daisy-wheel type, for more demanding requirements such as letters and documents. Depending on the software running on the computer, there may also be a plotter to produce drawings and diagrams. There may be other printers and plotters for more specialist use, or for local printing/plotting needs; these may well be located in users' offices.

Since the theory of printer and plotter queuing is the same, we shall consider only printer queues.

9.3.2 Printer queues

As with microcomputers, each printer has to be connected to a socket on the computer. This need not be physically on the computer cabinet itself, but may be a terminal server connected to that computer. A printer socket, sometimes known as a printer port, is generally the same as a socket connected to a terminal except that it has been configured by the System Manager in a slightly different way. Each printer has to have a queue associated with it. Users enter files into the queue; each file in the queue is known as a job, and the printer prints them one at a time. When a job is entered in a queue, it immediately goes to the back of the queue and waits its turn to be printed. In some instances, the queue may be configured so that all the small print jobs, i.e. files that are less than a certain number of blocks, can jump near to the front of the queue, so preventing a lengthy wait for these users while large files are being printed. Each time a job has finished printing, all the files waiting to be printed move up one position towards the front of the queue. Finally, as each job finishes printing, its entry is removed from the queue.

The processing and management of queue entries is the responsibility of a program called the print symbiont. This program is constantly running on the computer, and deals specifically with managing a particular queue. Another program that runs continuously is the Queue Manager, which deals with any interaction between queues (e.g. a batch job that then needs to be printed). Queue Manager processes and symbiont processes need no interaction from the user, and therefore we will not consider them any further.

Each job output from the queue has a "flag page". This is the first page and contains in large characters the username of the person who printed the file, and the file name. This aids distribution to the user. Also contained on the banner page is the date and other information relating to the file and VAX/VMS.

9.3.3 Printing files

Each print queue on the computer must have a unique queue name. The default VAX/VMS print queue has the name SYS$PRINT. This is usually the queue assigned to the main system printer, which is responsible for the majority of printing work. Any other print/plot queues on the system are also given names, e.g. a plot queue may be called PLOT_QUEUE, and a letter-quality queue for a laser printer SYS$LASER. Since SYS$PRINT is the default, we do not need to specify the queue name when printing. Thus to place an entry in the queue SYS$PRINT we type:

```
$ print prog.for

Job PROG (queue SYS$PRINT, entry 44) pending
     pending status caused by queue paused state
```

which places an entry, requesting that the file PROG.FOR (residing in our current directory) be printed, in the queue SYS$PRINT. VAX/VMS responds with a message informing us that the job has been entered into the queue, but that activation of the queue has been paused. To print files in another directory (assuming we have privilege) we specify the file description:

```
$ print user0:[godzilla.coursework]tokyo.dat
```

or if we were currently in the directory GODZILLA, we can abbreviate the command to:

```
$ print [.coursework]tokyo.dat;2
```

In the above example we have specified that the second version of the file be printed; the default is to print the last version (newest version) of the file.

We can also use the asterisk wildcard character to print specific groups of files, or place several files in the queue to be printed by separating the list of filenames with commas. The next two examples illustrate both of these points.

```
$ print prog*.dat
```

prints all files that have a filename beginning with PROG and with a filename extension of .DAT.

```
$ print prog_2.dat,prog_3.dat
```

places two files, PROG_2.DAT and PROG_3.DAT, into the print queue SYS$PRINT and requests that they are printed.

Do not attempt to print any files that contain special characters or escape sequences. The printer will try and interpret these characters and end up by creating a unintelligible listing—thereby wasting large amounts of paper. Amongst the types of files that contain such characters are files with file extensions of .JNL (journal files created by the EVE editor) and .EXE (program image files).

9.3.4 Useful qualifiers

In this section we introduce a selection of the most useful qualifiers we can employ to tailor our printed output.

The /BURST qualifier

A burst page is identical to the flag page (see page 150) and precedes it when the file is printed. This makes it easier to see where one file ends and another begins. The same rules apply to its use as for /FLAG.

```
$ print/burst buzby.tmp
```

When using /BURST we need not specify the /FLAG qualifier, since a flag page will automatically follow a burst page.

The /CONFIRM qualifier

In order to display a list of selected files before printing them and then choose certain files from that list to print, we use the /CONFIRM qualifier. We can see how this works in the following example:

```
$ print who*.com/confirm

PRINT PCL$CCSROOT:[RAY]WHO.COM;6 ? [N]:
PRINT PCL$CCSROOT:[RAY]WHO2.COM;5 ? [N]: Y
Job WHO2 (queue SYS$PRINT, entry 10) started on SYS$PRINT
```

To print each file we answer each prompt with a Y; if we do not want to print the file we type N, or simply (as "no" is the default) press the ⟨Return⟩ key.

The /COPIES qualifier

If we wish to print more than one copy of a file, we specify the /COPIES qualifier as follows:

```
$ print/copies=2 prog_2.for
```

which queues two copies of the file PROG_2.FOR to the default system printer (i.e. the queue SYS$PRINT).

The /DELETE qualifier

It is important to realize that by placing an entry in a queue we do not place a copy of the file in the queue. What in fact happens is that a record that contains information about the contents of the file we wish to be printed is placed in the queue. This record contains information on the file's type, size, etc., but most importantly it contains the file's specification. When the file reaches the front of the queue, the entry "tell's" the "print spooler", the program that organizes and runs the queues, in which directory the file can be found, as well as the filename itself. It is at this point that the file is copied to the printer. If we place a job (a job entry) into the queue and then delete the file to which that entry refers the file will not be printed, instead the following message below will be printed on the listing:

```
%PSM-E-OPENIN, error opening _DUA2:[CHRIS]OLD_DATA.DAT;1 as input
-RMS-E-FNF, file not found
```

We can use the /DELETE qualifier, to delete automatically the file from our directory after printing. The following example deletes the file OLD_DATA.-DAT after it has been printed on the main system printer (queue SYS-$PRINT):

```
$ print/delete old_data.dat
```

The /FLAG qualifier

By default the print symbiont always adds a flag page. This page, which is output at the start of the file, contains such information as the date and time the file was printed, the version of VAX/VMS running on the computer, the computer's node name, but perhaps most importantly, the username of the person who queued the file to the printer together with the name of the file. These two are output in large characters, to aid distribution to the user. At the top and bottom of the page are lines identifying the computer. It is possible that the flag page has been modified by the System Manager to display other information that may be more relevant to the institution than that given by the default. Figure 9-1 shows a typical flag page.

Any notes that are added to the flag page (see /NOTES qualifier) appear in the line following the file name, in this instance after RUBBISH.DAT.

We can suppress the printing of a flag page by using the /NOFLAG qualifier; while this saves paper, it may be difficult for a user to identify their file amongst the others being printed.

Normally, if we print several files from a single print command (by using wildcards or a list of files separated by commas), only one flag page is printed.

```
IIIIII 77777777777777777777777777777777777777777777777777 IIIIII
IIIIII 7777777 Pcl Computer Services - VAX/VMS 5.1 7777777 IIIIII
IIIIII 77777777777777777777777777777777777777777777777777 IIIIII

                         RRR    AA    Y   Y
                         R   R  A    A    YY
                         RRR    AAAA    YY
                         R   R  A    A    YY

RRRR    U    U  BBBB   BBBB   III    SSSS  H    H      DDDD     AA    TTTTT
R    R  U    U  B    B  B    B   I    S        H    H      D    D A   A     T
RRRR    U    U  BBBB   BBBB    I     SSSS  HHHHH      D    D AAAA     T
R    R  U    U  B    B  B    B   I         S H    H ..  D    D A   A     T
R    R    UUU   BBBB   BBBB   III    SSSS  H    H ..  DDDD  A   A     T

File _DUA0:[CCSTAFF.RAY.WASTEBASKET]RUBBISH.DAT;1 last revised on
the 31-MAY-1988 9:35, is a 7 block sequential file owned by [12,5].
Job RUBBISH (719) queued to SYS$PRINT on 12-JUN-1989 by user RAY.
IIIIII 77777777777777777777777777777777777777777777777777 IIIIII
IIIIII 7777777 Pcl Computer Services - VAX/VMS 5.1 7777777 IIIIII
IIIIII 77777777777777777777777777777777777777777777777777 IIIIII
```

Fig. 9-1 A typical flag page.

This precedes the first file and contains as the filename the name of the first file output.

The relative position in which the /FLAG or /NOFLAG qualifiers are placed on the command line affects the output, as shown in the following example:

```
$ print/flag=all file1.dat,file2.dat,file3.dat
```

causes a flag page to be printed for each file output.

```
$ print/flag=one file1.dat,file2.dat,file3.dat
```

prints a single flag page for the first copy of the first file only—this is the default.

```
$ print file1.dat/flag,file2.dat,file3.dat/flag
```

prints flag pages for files FILE1.DAT and FILE3.DAT, although since a flag page is always printed for the first file output, the first flag qualifier is unnecessary.

The /FORMS qualifier

If we wish to print a file that needs different paper, e.g. A4 size paper as opposed to A5, or perhaps we wish to output addresses on sticky labels as opposed to the normal listing paper, we can specify a different type of form other than the default. By using the /FORMS qualifier, the request remains in the queue until the correct type of form (i.e. the same type as specified with the /FORMS qualifier) is mounted in the printer.

```
$ print address.dat/forms=labels/copies=2
```

prints two identical sets of forms, in this instance labels, on the printer. This job will wait in the queue until the default listing paper is removed, labels inserted, and the operator notifies the print symbiont of the new form type (i.e LABELS). All the jobs in the queue with the form type LABELS will then be output. Usually once all the queue entries needing a "special" type of form are output, the paper type is switched back to the default (usually shown as DEFAULT). Managing queues in this way is useful since it means that a single printer can be used for producing output on various types of stationary.

The /HEADER qualifier

The /HEADER qualifier produces a one-line header line at the top of each page output. For example:

```
$ print/header add.c
```

causes a status line of the form:

```
DUA0:[RUPERT]LOGIN.COM;1     19-JUN-1989 09:58          Page 1
```

to be printed at the top of each page output.

The /NAME qualifier

Instead of printing the file name on the banner (if more than one file is being printed, the file name of the first file will be printed) we can specify another name by using the /NAME qualifier:

```
$ print prog.for/name="Fortran Program"
```

replaces the file name PROG.FOR with the text "Fortran Program" on the flag page.

The /NOTE qualifier

In many instances it may be useful to output a short message on the banner page, so that a user can easily identify their output. This is done by using the /NOTE qualifier:

```
$ print salary.dat/note="Confidential Info."
```

If the message to be output contains tabs or spaces, then it must be contained within quotation marks. It is advisable to keep the message short, or else it will be truncated.

The /NOTIFY qualifier

We can request that we be notified on our terminal after a file queued to a printer has been printed. For example:

```
$ print prog.for/notify

Job WHO (queue SYS$PRINT, entry 16) pending
     pending status caused by queue busy
```

When it has finished printing, we receive the message:

```
Job WHO (queue SYS$PRINT, entry 16) completed
```

The /PAGES qualifier

If you wish to print only a few pages from a file, you can use the /PAGES qualifier. There are several formats this qualifier can take, but in general these are two values enclosed in parentheses, which correspond respectively to the number of the first and the last page to be printed. If, however, only one value is specified, then pages are printed from the start of the file up to that page number (we can omit the parentheses in this instance). The value of the last page can be given as quotation marks if we are uncertain of the number of pages the file contains. For example:

```
$ print book.txt/pages=25
```

prints the first 25 pages of the file BOOK.TXT.

```
$ print book.txt/pages=(25,30)
```

causes the six pages 25–30 to be printed.

```
$ print book.txt /pages= (30,"")
```

prints from page 30 until the end of the file.

The /PASSALL qualifier

Another useful qualifier for the print command is /PASSALL. Some files, such as file listings produced by FORTRAN, various data files, etc., may contain special characters to format the output. These may be useful when displaying the file on the terminal screen, but cause problems when printing. Such special characters (i.e. clear screen) and all print qualifiers affecting formatting (e.g. /HEADER, /PAGES, and /PAGE_SETUP qualifiers) will be suppressed by the print symbiont and not output. When using /PASSALL to print a group of files, its relative position on the command line governs the files it affects. For example, the following command will apply the qualifier to all files, while the second command shown only effects the last file (PASCAL.DAT):

```
$ print/passall cobol.dat,pascal.dat

$ print cobol.dat,pascal.dat/passall
```

The /PRIORITY qualifier

When jobs are placed in the print queue, they are assigned a priority by VAX/VMS, and it is this that governs the files' entry point in the queue. By default, most jobs are assigned the same priority and so join at the back of the queue, although small files may start nearer the front—these are quicker to print and thus bottlenecks are prevented. However, if our account has been granted privilege to raise the value of the files' priority, it is possible to modify the priority and so enter the queue at a higher level, nearer the front of the queue. We do this via the /PRIORITY qualifier:

```
$ print prog.c/priority=200
```

Note that no privilege is needed to lower the priority level of your file. Priority values range from 0 to 255. The default for all jobs entering the queue is specified by a system parameter, called DEFQUEPRI, which is normally set to about 100. Therefore specifying a priority greater than 100 results in your file being printed more quickly.

The /QUEUE qualifier

To place an entry in a print queue other than the default we need to specify the queue's name. For example, to print a file called LETTER.TXT on a laser printer with queue name SYS$LASER, we use the /QUEUE qualifier as follows:

```
$ print/queue=sys$laser letter.txt
```

The /REMOTE qualifier

We are able to queue files to a printer that does not exist on our current node, but it is on a disk attached to another node in a DECnet network. The file will be queued to the default printer attached to the remote node. An example would be:

```
$ print/remote stoat::user0:[mouse]wheel.txt
```

which causes file WHEEL.TXT to be entered into print queue SYS$PRINT on node STOAT.

The /RESTART qualifier

If a file is being printed and subsequently the queue is stopped, this is done via the operator command STOP/QUEUE/RESTART. The job will then automatically start printing again when the queue is restarted via the operator START/QUEUE command. The default is /RESTART so we need not normally specify it as a qualifier.

The /TRAILER qualifier

All jobs are given a flag page by default, but we can also have a trailing page printed by specifing the /TRAILER qualifier. Trailing pages are similar in format to flag pages but they appear as the page following the print job. The rules for using this qualifier are the same as for /FLAG (see p. 150).

9.3.5 Displaying the print queue

To see how our entry is progressing in the queue, we use the SHOW QUEUE command:

```
$ show queue sys$print

  Terminal queue SYS$PRINT, on _TXA2:, mounted form DEFAULT
  (Main System Printer)

   Jobname          Username      Entry  Blocks  Status
   -------          --------      -----  ------  ------
   RAYPRINT         RAY             263      48  Printing

   Terminal queue SYS$PRINT, on _TXA2:, mounted form DEFAULT
```

Notice that we need to specify the queue name, or else the system displays all the queues. The SHOW QUEUE command only displays our entries and not any other entries in the queue. If we wish to display all entries, we add the /ALL qualifier:

```
$ show queue sys$print/all

  Terminal queue SYS$PRINT, paused, on _TXA2:, mounted form DEFAULT

  (Main System Printer)

   Jobname          Username      Entry  Blocks  Status
   -------          --------      -----  ------  ------
   WHO              RAY              44       1  Pending
   LOGIN            VAXVMS_20        45       1  Pending
   RAY              RAY              43      15  Pending
```

To obtain more detailed information on each entry, we add the /FULL qualifier. By omitting the /ALL qualifier we see our jobs only:

```
$ show queue sys$print/full

Terminal queue SYS$PRINT, paused, on _TXA2:, mounted form DEFAULT
(Main System Printer)
/BASE_PRIORITY=4/DEFAULT=(FEED,FLAG,FORM=DEFAULT)/NOENABLE_GENERIC
  Lowercase/OWNER=[AUSTAFXN,SYSTEM]/PROCESSOR=PCL_FLAG/PROTECTION=(S:E,O:D,
G:R,W:RW)

 Jobname          Username      Entry  Blocks  Status
 -------          --------      -----  ------  ------
 WHO              RAY              44       1  Pending (queue paused)

    Submitted 20-JUN-1989 09:53 /FORMO DEFAULT /PRIORITY=100
    File: _DUA2:[CCSROOT.RAY]WHO.COM;6

 RAY              RAY            43       15  Pending (queue paused)
```

```
Submitted 20-JUN-1989 09:52 /FORM=DEFAULT /PRIORITY=100
File: _DUA2:[CCSROOT.RAY]RAY.LIS;1
```

9.3.6 Manipulating the print queue

If we decided that we do not want to print the file after all, we may, by using the /ENTRY qualifier in conjunction with the DELETE command, delete the entry from the queue. First we need to find the job's entry number, which is done by using the SHOW ENTRY command. We then specify this, along with the queue name, as parameters to the DELETE/ENTRY command:

```
$ show entry

  Jobname          Username      Entry  Blocks  Status
  -------          --------      -----  ------  ------
  WHO              RAY              17       1  Pending
    On terminal queue SYS$PRINT

$ delete/entry=17 sys$print

  Job WHO2 (queue SYS$PRINT, entry 17) terminated with error status
  %JBC-F-JOBDELETE, job deleted before execution
```

We only have privilege to delete the entries that we have placed in the queue and not for any of the others.

If the job has already started printing, the STOP command with the /QUEUE qualifier will stop the output and abort the job from the queue. To do this, we specify the commands:

```
$ show entry

  Jobname          Username      Entry  Blocks  Status
  -------          --------      -----  ------  ------
  RESULT           RAY              15       1  Printing
    On terminal queue SYS$PRINT

$ stop/queue/entry=15 sys$print
```

where the entry number of the job has been obtained from the SHOW ENTRY command.

Chapter

10

Program Development

10.1 Introduction

In this chapter we shall follow an example program through the various stages of its development cycle. The first stage—known as the program specification—ascertains what the program should achieve. Then comes the stage of designing an algorithm, or a set of actions that will enable the program to reach those goals. This is followed by translating the program design into a programming language (i.e. the coding stage) and inputting it into the computer. The code is then converted inside the computer into a machine-executable format, which involves compiling, linking, and then running the program. This is equivalent to the computer comparing the code with its own internal specification, and joining together the appropriate parts of the code. This is repeated until there are no more errors detected. The whole program is then executed. There are usually some errors present, either due to coding faults or just due to typing errors, therefore it is expected that one has to go through a stage of "debugging", or error correction, until all the errors have been removed. Finally there is usually a period of "settling in", with the program.

Depending on the complexity of the program, the development can take months or even years. After the program is finally running, continuing maintenance is usually needed, as new faults (called "bugs") come to light. The program may also be upgraded several times during its lifetime to incorporate new features, or to speed up its execution. Some programs never reach a point where work on them is complete, but require constant modifications. This involves the need for updated documentation of any changes and recording the reason for these changes.

In this chapter we shall follow each of the stages of program development on VAX/VMS, from inputting the program to debugging. Then we shall trace the progress of a simple program from its conception through all the stages to its completion.

10.2 Inputting the Program

Programs are input into the computer using an editor, such as EVE, in the same way as we would enter any other text. The default VAX/VMS editor EVE is covered in Chapters 5 and 6. Some computers may have LSE (Language Sensitive Editor) installed. This will help the user by prompting for the correct syntax when inputting the program. LSE recognizes in which programming language the file is being input, by reference to the program's filename extension. It will then set up a series of programming templates for you to use inside the editor. In fact it has been said that by using LSE it is possible to create a syntactically correct program, in a programming language you have never used before!

Whichever editor you choose to use, an extension to the filename is necessary to indicate the programming language the file is written in. Files containing programming instructions in a specific programming language are known as source files. Table 10-1 gives a list of the default file types. A source file containing lines of FORTRAN code may therefore be called PROG1.FOR. It is good practice to give your programs meaningful names, so that in the future you may have an idea as to what that program was designed to do. For example, SUBTRACT2.PAS may indicate a Pascal source program for subtracting numbers. The computer languages listed in Table 10-1 (with the exception of MACRO) use "English-like" expressions—these are known as "high-level languages".

Table 10-1 Some default programming language source files and extensions

Filename Extension	Programming Language of Source file
BAS	VAX BASIC
B32	VAX BLISS-32
C	VAX C
COB	VAX COBOL
COR	VAX CORAL-66
FOR	VAX FORTRAN
MAR	VAX MACRO
PAS	VAX Pascal
PLI	VAX PL/1

10.3 Compiling or Assembling the Program

10.3.1 Introduction

The computer is unable to execute programming code directly. The code needs to be compiled, i.e the source listing is read and then translated into a machine-readable form in accordance with the language rules. This is done by invoking the respective compiler. After compilation, a compiled version of the file is stored in a new file with a file extension of .OBJ, and with the same filename as the source. This object file, also called the object code, contains binary machine code, which the computer is able to interpret.

Unlike the other languages, MACRO is not a high-level language but an assembler. Assembler languages are called "low-level languages" because the instructions refer to the status and content of memory locations. The code is of "low level" (i.e. simple) and its location, in comparison with the high-level languages, is nearer to the computer's "machine interface". Assemblers are usually machine dependent, and are assembled as opposed to compiled. To the user, however, the compile and assemble commands are very similar. When a MACRO source program is assembled, each line of source code produces a line of machine code, whereas the high-level languages for each compiled line, usually produce several lines of machine code. Table 10-2 gives a list of compilers and assemblers. Note that the programming language PL/1 is known as PLI (the number one is swapped for the character "I"). It may also be of general interest to note that when we write the name Pascal, this is not written entirely in uppercase, as are the names of the other programming languages, since this is not an acronym but refers to a person's name.

Table 10-2 Commands for invoking the appropriate programming language

Command	Compiler/Assembler Invoked
BASIC	VAX BASIC
BLISS	VAX BLISS-32
CC	VAX C
COBOL	VAX COBOL
CORAL	VAX CORAL-66
FORTRAN	VAX FORTRAN
MACRO	VAX MACRO (Assembler)
PASCAL	VAX Pascal
PLI	VAX PL/1

10.3.2 Running the FORTRAN and other compilers

To run the FORTRAN compiler, in order to compile the program TEST.FOR, we type the following:

```
$ fortran test
```

We do not need to specify the file extension as the compiler will assume it is of type FOR. The output file (sometimes referred to as an output module) containing the binary machine code is created—this file is named TEST.OBJ. In the same way, a Pascal program is compiled using the Pascal compiler, i.e. TRIAL.PAS will be compiled with the command:

```
$ pascal trial
```

This produces the object file TRIAL.OBJ.

10.3.3 Running the MACRO assembler

The following command is used to assemble a MACRO program called GET_TIME.MAR:

```
$ macro get_time
```

Here, the file type MAR is assumed by the computer.

If there are any programming errors, VAX/VMS will detect and display them while attempting to compile the source code, otherwise a dollar prompt will be displayed, indicating that the process is successfully completed and VAX/VMS is ready for the next command.

10.3.4 Compiler/assembler qualifiers

In this section we shall briefly describe some of the qualifiers that can be used in conjunction with the compile/assemble command.

The /LIST qualifier

If compilation errors are present we may attempt to recompile the program, this time adding the /LIST qualifier to force a listing file to be produced. To produce a listing file of the MACRO program GET_TIME we type in:

```
$ macro get_time /list
```

We shall look at the contents of a listing file in more detail when we describe a typical example of program development later on in this chapter.

The /OPTIMIZE and /NOOPTIMIZE qualifiers

The /OPTIMIZE qualifier is set on by default, so we generally need not specify it. By optimizing the code during compilation, the image produced is more efficient. This is due to the optimizer using additional rules to use not just an acceptable version of the code, but a superior version if possible. Unfortunately, compilations in this case take longer since the compiler needs to find the most effective methods of building the image code, i.e. the code that will eventually run on the computer. In most cases it is better to use the /NOOPTIMIZE qualifier while developing the program, and then OPTIMIZE for the final code. In general /NOOPTIMIZE should be used on code that needs to be debugged. The example below compiles the program PLUS.FOR without optimizing the code:

```
$ fortran/nooptimize plus
```

The DEBUG qualifier

The DEBUG qualifier causes the source program to be compiled with a debugging code contained within it. This extra code enables the user to run the program via the VAX/VMS debugger. It gives the user the opportunity to stop the program's execution at various stages and to examine the contents of variables. (See Section 10.8 on the VAX/VMS debugger below.) Normally we also need to specify the /NOOPTIMIZE qualifier. For example:

```
$ cobol/nooptimize/debug salary
```

This compiles file SALARY.COB ready for debugging.

10.4 Linking the Files

Once a program has been compiled, it then needs to be linked with any of the library files it may use. The object file usually references other programs or routines and these must be combined with the object, to form the executable program. The linker searches the system libraries to locate and include routines and symbols that are referred to by the object modules, and then links them all together. You can link several object files into a single executable file and specify libraries for it to search. The executable file is called an "image" and has the default file extension.EXE.

```
$ link exam
```

This command links the object file EXAM.OBJ with the relevant system library files and places the executable code into the image file EXAM.EXE.

The next example combines two object files (TEST1.OBJ and TEST2.OBJ), which have been written in the C programming language, along with system libraries and the VAX C runtime library, VAXCRTL. The executable image is called TEST1.EXE. First we need to define the logical name LNK$LIBRARY, so C knows which library files to search for unresolved functions when linking.

```
$ define lnk$library sys$library:vaxcrtl

$ link test1,test2
```

When writing programs in C it is useful to have the definition of lnk$library in the LOGIN.COM, so it is automatically defined on login.

SYS$LIBRARY is the VAX/VMS default directory for storing program libraries.

10.5 Running the Programs

To execute (i.e. run) a program image, use the RUN command:

```
$ run testprog
```

As no file extension is specified, .EXE is assumed.

At this stage you may notice that your program does not perform as expected. Once you have located the source of the error, use the editor to correct the source file, then recompile, link, and run the program. This process may be repeated several times before the program is running satisfactorily.

10.6 Summary

We have seen how a program progresses from being entered into the computer, through the various stages to being run. The stages are as follows:

- Source program written in high-level language or in the low-level (assembler) language, e.g. TEST.FOR
- Compile, to produce an object module written in binary machine code, e.g. FORTRAN TEST.FOR—produces TEST.OBJ

- Link to combine object modules and produce an executable image, e.g. LINK TEST.OBJ—produces TEST.EXE
- Run to run the executable image, e.g. RUN TEST.EXE

In the above examples the file extensions have been shown to indicate which file the command acts upon. These are defaults and therefore they can be omitted.

10.7 Development of a Simple Program

10.7.1 Introduction

We shall now follow a simple program through the various stages of its development. As the example we shall use a program written in C, although the method is identical for any other high-level language or assembler.

10.7.2 Aim(s) of the program

First we need to identify the task that the program is to achieve. This may be to provide a service to other users, automate certain system facilities, or any other uses. At this point we need to consider any additional features or enhancements to the aims of the basic program. An appreciation of the program's maintenance and any possible future upgrades should also be sought. By spending a little more time considering the program design, much effort can be saved in later stages of the development cycle. It is not untypical for one to spend 80 percent of the time on program design, 10 percent on coding, and 10 percent on running the program. It may also be relevant to consider which programming language to write the code in. Some languages lend themselves to specific tasks better than others.

We shall write a simple program to accept two integers input from the keyboard, add them together, and display the total along with the calculation. The program then asks if the user wants to add another two values. If the user answers "yes" the program will repeat and ask for another two values to be input; if the user answers "no" the program will finish. A program this small will probably not need any future enhancement or maintenance.

The programming language we have chosen is C, although languages such as Pascal and FORTRAN would be equally viable. COBOL may be unnecessarily "lengthy" for a simple program such as this, and MACRO possibly too complex. It should be added that COBOL is extremely good at business-type applications, and MACRO at low-level machine coding, such as writing disk interfaces, etc. As stated earlier, each programming language has its strengths and weaknesses, but the development cycle for each program is basically the same.

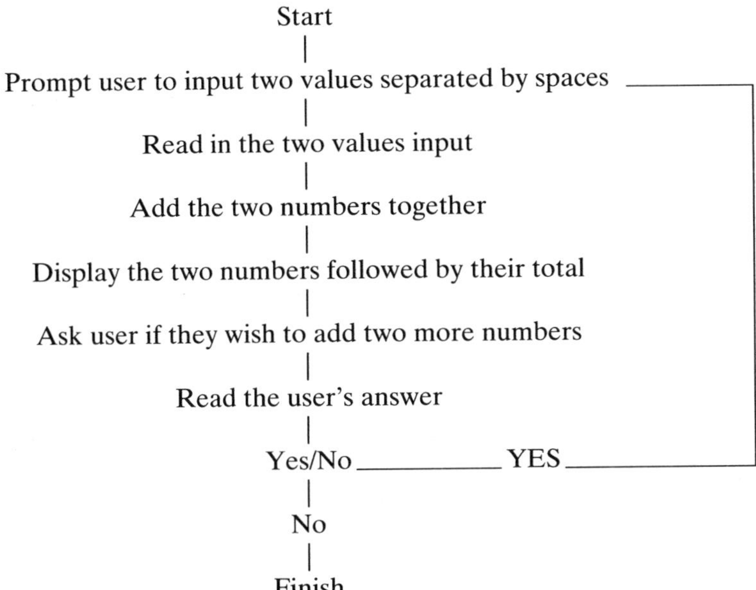

Fig. 10-1 Algorithm for the interactive addition of two numbers.

10.7.3 Planning the program

Many methodologies can be used to plan the program—flowcharts, schemas, top-down structure, etc. We shall use a simplified structure diagram as shown in Figure 10-1.

The next stage is to write the program in the chosen language using the structure diagram as a guide. An example of the program written in C is shown in the next section.

10.7.4 Inputting the program

As our program is written in C and adds two numbers we shall call it ADD.C. After ensuring that the terminal is set up correctly, using the command SET TERMINAL/INQUIRE to do this, we run the EVE editor to create the file ADD.C, and input the C program. Note the deliberate misspelling on input (as "inpot").

```
$ edit/tpu add.c
```

Then we type in the following C program:

```
/* C Program to add two numbers, print calculation and result.
   Program will repeat as often as required                  */

#include <stdio.h>  /* Include C STandarD Input/Output library */

main()

{
float a = 0.0;               /* First  value to add - A */
float b = 0.0;               /* Second value to add - B */
char answer[] = "YES";       /* Repeat program variable */

printf ("C Program to add two floating point numbers\n\n");

while (answer[0] == 'Y' || answer[0] == 'y')
{
 printf ("Please inpot two values to add : "); /* Ask for input*/
 scanf  ("%f%f",&a,&b);                         /* Read input   */
 printf (""%f + %f = %f\n\n",a,b,a+b);           /* Display total*/
 printf ("Do you wish to do any more calculations ? "); /*More?*/
 scanf  ("%s",answer);
}
printf ("\n\n--- Program Complete ---\n\n");    /* End of Prog. */
}}
```

We now have a file containing the source code which is ready for compilation.

10.7.5 Compiling the program

To compile using the C compiler (the file extension can be omitted as the default for the C compiler is.C) we type the following:

```
$ cc add

}}
%CC-E-SYNTAXERROR, Found "}" when expecting
          one of { arithmetic-operator "int" "auto" "char" "enum"
"long" "void" "const" "float" "short" "union" "_align" "double"
etc.
          Listing line number 165.
          At line number 24 in PCL$CCSROOT:[RAY]ADD.C;10.
     }}
%CC-F-FATALSYNTAX, Fatal syntax error.
          Listing line number 165.
          At line number 24 in PCL$CCSROOT:[RAY]ADD.C;10.
     }}
%CC-I-NOBJECT, No object file produced.
          Listing line number 165.
          At line number 24 in PCL$CCSROOT:[RAY]ADD.C;10.
```

There are errors in the program, so we shall recompile the program but this time use the /LIST qualifier to produce a file containing a list of the code together with the relevant error messages.

```
$ cc add/list
```

produces a listing file called ADD.LIS. If we type this file, we find it contains the following:

```
$ type add.lis

ADD  23-MAY-1989 11:02:01    VAX C     V2.4-026             Page 1
V1.0      23-MAY-1989 11:01:10    PCL$CCSROOT:[RAY]ADD.C;10 (1)

  1       /* C Program to add two numbers, print calculation and
  2       Program will repeat as often as required             */
  3
  4       #include <stdio.h>        /* Include STandarD Input/Output
146
147       main()
148
149       {
150   1   float a = 0.0;             /* First  value to add - A */
151   1   float b = 0.0;             /* Second value to add - B */
152   1   char answer[] = "YES";     /* Repeat program variable */
153   1
154   1   printf ("C Program to add two floating point numbers\n\n");
155   1
156   1   while (answer[0] == 'Y' || answer[0] == 'y')
157   1   {
158   2   printf ("Please inpot two values to add : "); /* Ask for
159   2   scanf  ("%f%f",&a,&b);                       /* Read in
160   2   printf ("%f + %f = %f\n\n",a,b,a+0 b);        /* Display
161   2   printf ("Do you wish to do any more calculations ? "); /*
162   2   scanf  ("%s",answer);
163   2   }
164   1   printf ("\n\n--- Program Complete ---\n\n");    /* Program
165   1      }}
%CC-E-SYNTAXERROR,   Found   "}"   when   expecting
one  of   {arithmetic-operator "int" "auto" "char" "enum" "long"
"void" "const" "float" "short" "union" "_align" "double"  etc.

%CC-F-FATALSYNTAX, Fatal syntax error.
%CC-I-NOBJECT, No object file produced.
```

Now we need to correct the error. To do this we run the editor and change the last line in the source file. Therefore }} is now altered to }. We then exit from the editor and recompile, again using the /LIST qualifier in case we have any further errors:

```
$ cc add /list

$
```

This time we have no errors and the source code has successfully compiled, to create an object module called ADD.OBJ.

10.7.6 Linking the program

C differs from most of the other languages at this point, since you have specifically to include the runtime library—SYS$LIBRARY:VAXCRTL (see also Section 10.4). We do this by defining the logical name LNK$LIBRARY in order to incorporate some of the runtime object modules in the image when linking. Therefore, before we can link, we must issue the following command (or have the following line in our LOGIN.COM file):

```
$ define lnk$library sys$library:vaxcrtl
```

We can then link using the VMS linker. This linker is used by all the languages and the assembler.

```
$ link add
```

This links ADD.OBJ with the system and the VAX C RunTime LIBrary, to produce the executable image—ADD.EXE.

10.7.7 Running the program

To execute image ADD.EXE on VAX/VMS, type the following:

```
$ run add

C Program to add two floating point numbers


Please inpot two values to add :
3 11
3.000000 + 11.000000 = 14.000000


Do you wish to do any more calculations ?
n

--- Program Complete ---
```

This time the program seems to perform as predicted, although there is a typing error in the input message to the user. We therefore need to run the editor and correct the line. We use EVE to edit the line:

```
printf ("Please inpot two values to add : "); /* Ask for input*/
```

so it becomes:

```
printf ("Please input two values to add : "); /* Ask for input*/
```

We then need to repeat the previous three stages again. We now know that there are no programming errors in the program, so we need not produce a listing file. Therefore to recompile, link, and run the code again, we type:

```
$ cc add

$ link add

$ run add

C Program to add two floating point numbers


Please input two values to add :
2 5
2.000000 + 5.000000 = 7.000000


Do you wish to do any more calculations ?
y
Please input two values to add :
23.7 54.2
23.700001 + 54.200001 = 77.900002


Do you wish to do any more calculations ?
no

--- Program Complete ---
```

The program development is now complete.

It would now be useful to PURGE all previous incorrect versions of the program; all the object files can also be deleted, along with any listing (.LIS) files. We now run the DIRECTORY/SIZE/DATE command to see the files that have been created and retained after purgeing the earlier versions during the development of this program, with their respective sizes and dates/times of creation.

```
$ purge add.*

$ directory/size/date add.*

Directory PCL$CCSROOT:[RAY]

ADD.C;11                 2  23-MAY-1989 11:02:49.91
ADD.EXE;3               88  23-MAY-1989 11:03:25.78
ADD.LIS;4                4  23-MAY-1989 11:03:06.65
ADD.OBJ;7                2  23-MAY-1989 11:03:06.65

Total of 4 files, 96 blocks.
```

Notice the variation in the size of the files.

You might find, however, that while the program executes correctly there are logical errors present that the compiler is unable to detect. For this we use the VAX/VMS debugger. An overview of a simple debugging session is given in the next section.

10.8 The VAX/VMS Debugger

The VAX debugger enables you to debug programs interactively. The debugger runs the program image and enables the user to check the contents of various parameters while the program is running. It does this by stopping execution of the code at locations specified by the user and allows the user to inspect the value assigned to a given variable. By stepping through the program one instruction at a time or by setting stops at suitable positions, one can trace the change in value as it progresses through the various operations.

The debugger allows you to do the following:

- Start, stop, and continue program execution.
- Trace the program's flow of execution through the code.
- Examine selected locations, variables, and events.
- Monitor and change the contents of variables.

The debugger can be used with all the VAX/VMS-supported compilers and assemblers. To use the debugger, the source code must be compiled and linked using the /DEBUG qualifier. It is also advisable to use the /NOOPTIMIZE qualifier when compiling, as some compilers by default use /OPTIMIZE which may affect the values of some of the program's variables.

To enable debugging of PLUS.FOR, we compile, link, and run:

```
$ fortran/debug/nooptimize plus

$ link/debug plus

$ run plus
```

For a Pascal program called SUBTRACT.PAS that also produces a listing file the corresponding sequence is:

```
$ pascal/debug/nooptimize/list subtract

$ link/debug subtract
$ run subtract
```

When compiling ENABLE=DEBUG may be stated instead of DEBUG. To turn off the debugger when running a program compiled and linked with the debugger option, type:

```
$ run/nodebug subtract
```

if the image name is SUBTRACT.EXE.

Within the debugger you can use the default editor, EVE, although you may choose an alternative editor by using the SET EDITOR command.

Let us see how we can use the debugger to examine the execution of ADD.C. First we need to ensure the terminal is set to its correct type:

```
$ set terminal/inquire
```

We can then compile and link the program using the /DEBUG qualifier:

```
$ cc/debug/nooptimize add

$ link/debug add

$ run add
```

We then receive an introductory message followed by the debugger prompt. At this stage press the ⟨PF3⟩ key to enter screen mode.

```
DEBUG⟩

DEBUG⟩ ⟨PF3⟩
```

The debugger now enters screen mode as shown in Figure 10-2. The top window shows the source listing of the program, along with imposed line numbers down the left-hand side. The arrow shows the next line to be indicated.

The middle window contains the current state of the program and any output from the program. For example, the statements prompting for input will appear in this window.

```
—SRC: module ADD$MAIN —scroll—source ——————————————————————
    8:         {
→  9: float a = 0.0;            /* First  value to add — A */
  10: float b = 0.0;            /* Second value to add — B */
  11: char answer[] = "YES";    /* Repeat program variable */
  12:
  13: printf ("C Program to add two floating point numbers\n")
  14:
  15:while (answer[0] == 'Y' || answer[0] == 'y')
  16:{
  17: printf ("Please input two values to add : "); /* Ask for
—OUT—output ————————————————————————————————————————————————
stepped to ADD$MAIN\%LINE 6
stepped to ADD$MAIN\%LINE 7
stepped to ADD$MAIN\%LINE 8
stepped to ADD$MAIN\%LINE 9
— PROMPT —error—program-promt ——————————————————————————————
DBG>Step
DBG>Step
DBG>
```

Fig. 10-2 The VAX/VMS debugger screen.

The bottom window is used to type commands into the debugger. A few of the main commands are:

STEP — or KEYPAD⟨0⟩—to execute the current instruction and move on to the next line of code in the source listing.

EXAMINE — or KEYPAD⟨1⟩—to view the contents of a variable. This instruction takes two forms: EXAMINE (for integer, floating-point numbers, etc.), and EXAMINE/ASCII for text strings. For example, to examine the contents of the floating-point variable "a" we type:

```
DBG> examine a
```

The value appears in the middle window.

DEPOSIT — To modify the contents of a variable. For example:

```
DBG> deposit a = 1.2
```

This makes the floating-point variable equal to 1.2, or for a text string:

```
DBG> deposit answer = 'yes'
```

HELP to provide help on the debugger. For example:

```
DBG〉 help
```

There are many other debugger commands, some of which are similar to EVE, DEFINE KEY, SPAWN, etc. Type HELP to get information on these commands. Pressing the ⟨PF2⟩ key displays a keypad diagram.

Chapter

11

Communicating with Other Users

11.1 Introduction

Communication with other users of the VAX/VMS system is logically divided into two main processes. These processes evolved from consideration of the major requirements encountered by users and it is modeled to some extent on everyday experiences.

In the first process, MAIL simulates the receipt of post with the facility to store the "letters", either in a basic filing system provided by VAX/VMS, or in a customized set of folders created by the user into which the incoming mail is moved. Unwanted mail is assigned to a WASTEBASKET folder.

Numerous qualifiers can be used to enhance the operation of MAIL both in terms of organization and retrieval via pattern and word search. The operation of MAIL is described in the next section.

The second process, PHONE, corresponds to another everyday experience, whereby one user rings another and if the call is accepted a two-way communication is initiated. The dialog is terminated when one of the two parties "hangs up". The PHONE process is described in Section 11.3.

11.2 MAIL

11.2.1 Introduction to MAIL

In this section the different stages involved in sending, receiving, and the efficient storage of messages are introduced. We then proceed to describe the various qualifiers that can be used, and introduce the pattern searching and printing facilities. Finally, we show how to establish or modify the MAIL environment to suit our own individual requirements.

We start by showing how to "invoke" the MAIL facility and then how to send messages to a single user, or to a number of users. This can be extended to users on a different system that is connected to the sender's system through Digital's networking architecture DECnet. The messages are either composed directly, via the MAIL process, or by using an editor such as EVE.

Messages are usually stored in three folders, which are provided by the system:

NEWMAIL	holds unread messages.
MAIL	holds read and retained messages.
WASTEBASKET	for messages that have been marked for deletion but not yet deleted.

In addition, customized folders can be created by users for their own special requirements.

VMS MAIL is invoked by the MAIL command:

```
$ mail

MAIL⟩
```

the prompt MAIL⟩ indicates that the system is ready to accept a command.

As with other VMS utilities, on-line help is available through the HELP command. For example:

```
$ mail

MAIL⟩ help

HELP
```

Allows you to obtain information about the MAIL utility.

To obtain information about all of the MAIL commands, enter the following command:

```
MAIL⟩ help *
```

To obtain information about individual commands or topics, enter HELP followed by the command or topic name.

```
HELP [topic]

Additional information available:
```

```
/EDIT     /PERSONAL_NAME     /SELF     /SUBJECT ANSWER    ATTACH
BACK      COMPRESS COPY      CURRENT   DEFINE   DELETE    DIRECTORY
EDIT      ERASE    EXIT      EXTRACT   FILE     FIRST     Folders
FORWARD   GETTING_STARTED    HELP      KEYPAD   LAST      MAIL
MARK      MOVE     NEXT      PRINT     PURGE    QUIT      READ
REMOVE    REPLY    SEARCH    SELECT    SEND     SET-SHOW SPAWN
V5_CHANGES

Topic?
```

Some of the more common MAIL commands that are available are discussed below.

11.2.2 Sending MAIL

The MAIL command—SEND

This command is used to send a MAIL message to one or more users. An example on its use is given at the end of this section.

MAIL first prompts you for the name of the user who is to receive the message. If you wish to send the message to more than one user, then enter each username separated by a comma. MAIL then prompts you first for the subject of the MAIL, and then for the content of your MAIL message. You should enter the message that you want to send and then press ⟨Ctrl⟩Z to indicate the end of input.

After you have typed a line and pressed the ⟨Return⟩ it is not possible to modify that line of text, but you can decide not to send the complete message by typing ⟨Ctrl⟩C.

Example

```
$ mail

MAIL> send

To: susan

Subj: lunch

Enter your message below. Press CTRL/Z when complete, or
CTRL/C to quit:

  How about lunch on Thursday?       Would 12:30 be ok?

          see you,

                Mike.
  <Ctrl>Z
```

Sending a carbon copy

There is an option of being prompted to supply a list of usernames to whom carbon copies (CC) of the mail message should be sent; this option is system dependent but you can modify it for yourself (see Section 11.2.7).

If the CC option is on, then you will be prompted to supply a list of usernames as illustrated in the following example. By pressing the ⟨Return⟩ key in response to this prompt no carbon copies are sent.

```
$ mail

MAIL⟩ send

To: peter, susan, terry

CC: alex

Subj: Agenda for next meeting

Enter your message below. Press CTRL/Z when complete, or
CTRL/C to quit:

Please let me have items for next weeks meeting by Friday.

⟨Ctrl⟩Z
```

Sending MAIL across DECnet

A message can be sent to a user with an account on another DECnet node by prefixing the username(s) with the node name. For example, to send a message to user KATIE on node OTTER:

```
$ mail

MAIL⟩ send

To: otter::katie

Subj: Agenda

Enter your message below. Press CTRL/Z when complete, or
CTRL/C to quit:

  Can you send me the agenda for the meeting on 16th?

⟨Ctrl⟩Z
```

Editing messages

The /EDIT qualifier to SEND invokes a text editor (such as EVE) for you to compose the text of your mail message. The message is sent when you exit the editor. It is usual to create messages this way as it allows you to modify the message should it be necessary.

You can set the /EDIT qualifier to MAIL by including the following definition in your LOGIN.COM file:

```
$ MAIL :== MAIL/EDIT
```

Sending files

You can include a file specification with the SEND command. If you specify a file with the SEND, the text in that file is sent to the specified user(s).

Example

```
$ mail
MAIL> send agenda.txt
To: peter, susan, terry
Subj: Agenda for next meeting
```

You should note that if you have used the /EDIT qualifier, then you enter the editor with the file that you wish to send. The message will be sent when you exit from the editor.

Note that sending mail is particularly useful for transferring text files from one user to another. The recipient of the file then uses the mail EXTRACT command to extract the file from the mail folder into a file. Suppose, for example, that user SUSAN wishes to send a Pascal source program in a file HELLO.PAS in her default directory to a user MIKEN. User SUSAN would send the file as follows:

```
$ mail
MAIL> send hello.pas
To: miken
CC:
Subj: A useful little program;
```

```
program hello(input, output)
begin
     writeln('Hello world')
end
MAIL> exit
```

User MIKEN then logs into VMS and enters MAIL:

```
$ mail
say GREETING.PAS, by using the EXTRACT command:

MAIL> extract greeting.pas

%MAIL-I-CREATED, PCL$CCSROOT:[MIKEN.EVEFOR.EX]GREETING.PAS;1
created

MAIL> exit
```

User MIKEN then decides to view the file by using the TYPE command:

```
$ type greeting.pas

From:      MOLE::SUSAN       "MikeN" 28-NOV-1988 12:13:22.72
To: MIKEN
CC:
Subj: A useful little program

program hello(input, output);
begin
     writeln('Hello world')
end.

$
```

As you can see, the mail message is extracted complete with header (giving sender, receiver, CC, and subject). This can be removed by using a text editor such as EVE or we could have specified that the message be extracted without this header by using the /NOHEADER qualifier to EXTRACT:

```
MAIL> extract greeting.pas/noheader
```

We should emphasize that only text files (e.g. program source files) can be sent through mail. Binary files (such as those with file type.OBJ or. EXE) cannot be sent.

Distribution lists

Often you may wish to send the same MAIL message to a group of users. This is most readily accomplished by setting up a distribution list.

A distribution list consists of a file created by a text editor such as EVE which has a name (ideally reflecting the purpose of the list) and the file extension .DIS. This file should contain a single username on each line. Any line starting with an exclamation mark is treated as a comment. For example, a file called LUNCHTIME_DRINKING.DIS could contain the following text:

```
! This line is a comment
RAY
CHRIS
MIKE
BOB
```

and could be used as follows:

```
$ mail

MAIL> send

To: @lunchtime_drinking

Subj: lunch

Enter your message below. Press CTRL/Z when complete, or
CTRL/C to quit:

  How about a meeting at 13:00 in the Ship on Friday

<Ctrl>Z
```

This MAIL would be sent to the users specified in the file LUNCHTIME_DRINKING.DIS, i.e. users RAY, CHRIS, MIKE, and BOB.

11.2.3 Folders

Before looking at how we can read messages sent to us by other users, it is useful to look at how mail is organized into folders since this is central to the use of VMS MAIL.

What is a Folder?

All mail is organized into folders. When you use MAIL, three folders exist by default:

- The NEWMAIL folder contains all messages that have not yet been read. It is thus the NEWMAIL folder that receives all new mail messages.

- The MAIL folder contains all messages that have been read. When you have read a message it is deleted by the MAIL process from the NEWMAIL folder and added to your MAIL folder.
- The WASTEBASKET folder contains messages that have been read and then deleted.

11.2.4 Reading messages

You can read unread messages from the NEWMAIL folder if you press ⟨Return⟩ or type READ immediately after you enter the MAIL utility. If there are no unread messages, then MAIL will use the MAIL folder and display each message starting with the oldest and working towards the newest. You can move between messages by using the following commands:

BACK — Moves you to the message immediately before the current message.

NEXT — Moves you to the next message after the current message.

SEARCH string — Moves you to the first message containing the characters in the specified string. For example:

```
MAIL⟩ search agenda
```

will search all messages in the current folder for the string "agenda". To continue searching from the current message for the same string use SEARCH without specifying a string:

```
MAIL⟩ search
```

Printing messages

PRINT queues a copy of the current message for printing. The files created by MAIL are not entered into the print queue until you exit from MAIL and create a single print job. The PRINT command from within MAIL can take qualifiers, e.g. to select the print queue used. Details of these qualifiers can be found by accessing the HELP facility within MAIL.

Example

```
$ mail

MAIL⟩ 25
```

```
25        28-NOV-1988 12:13:22.72                    MAIL
From:     MOLE::SUSAN
To:  MIKEN
CC:
Subj:     A useful little program

program hello(input, output);
begin
    writeln('Hello world')
end.

MAIL> print/copies=2

MAIL> exit

Job MAIL (queue SYS$PRINT, entry 12) started on SYS$PRINT

$
```

This example shows how to print two copies of the message number 25.

Obtaining a directory of messages

The MAIL DIRECTORY command:

```
MAIL> directory
```

displays a list of the messages in the current mail file, including message number, sender's name, date, and subject. You can also include the following qualifiers:

/BEFORE=date	Displays a listing of all the mail messages received before the specified date, where "date" is of the format DD-MMM-YYYY.
/CC_SUBSTRING=text	Selects messages that contain "text" in the CC field of the message. The CC (carbon copy) field is used to send copies of a mail message to one or more users.
/EDIT	Invokes the editor using the output of the DIRECTORY command as input to the editor. Enables you to find messages easily by scrolling through the folders or searching text.

/FROM_SUBSTRING=text	Selects messages that contain "text" in the FROM field of the message.
/FOLDER	Displays a listing of all the folders contained in the current mail file. For example:

```
MAIL> directory/folder

Listing of folders in DISK1:[MIKEN.-
MAIL]MAIL.MAI;1
     Press CTRL/C to cancel listing
ADVISORY                    AGENDA
MAIL                        MICROS
MINUTES                     NETWORK
PROJECTS                    TASKS
```

/FULL	Displays the number of records in the message and the external id (identification) number. Also displays attributes such as whether you have replied to the message, whether the message is marked, and whether the message is new.
/[NO]MARKED	Selects messages that have been marked (indicated by an asterisk). The /NOMARKED qualifier selects messages that are not marked.
/NEW	Displays a listing of any new (unread) MAIL messages.
/[NO]REPLIED	/REPLIED qualifier selects messages that have been replied to; /NOREPLIED qualifier selects messages that have not been replied to.
/SINCE=date	Displays a listing of all the MAIL messages received on or after the specified date.
/START=start-point	Indicates the first message number you want to display. For example, to display all the messages beginning with number three, enter the command line DIRECTORY_/START=3.
/SUBJECT__SUBSTRING=text	Selects messages that contain "text" in the SUBJECT field of the message.
/TO__SUBSTRING=text	Selects messages that contain "text" in the TO field of the message.

11.2.5 Deleting MAIL

The DELETE command is used to delete the current message:

```
MAIL> delete
```

or a list of messages specified by their message numbers.

```
MAIL> delete 1,3,8-11,15
```

deletes messages 1, 3, 8–11, and 15. Note that a hyphen may be used to give a range of message numbers. As an alternative to the hyphen, a colon may be used.

When you delete a message, it is automatically moved into the WASTEBASKET folder. Deleted messages collect in the WASTEBASKET folder until you empty it. To empty the WASTEBASKET folder, enter either EXIT or PURGE. It is important that you regularly delete obsolete MAIL since a large number of MAIL messages can use up a considerable amount of your disk storage quota.

To recover a message that has been accidentally deleted (while it is still in the WASTEBASKET folder), SELECT the WASTEBASKET folder, READ the desired message, and MOVE it to another folder as shown in the following example:

```
MAIL> search program

#25         28-NOV-1988 12:13:22.72                               MAIL
From:      MOLE::SUSAN
To:  MIKEN
CC:
Subj: A useful little program

program hello(input, output);
begin
   writeln('Hello world')
end.

MAIL> delete

MAIL> set folder wastebasket

%MAIL-I-SELECTED, 1 message selected

MAIL> directory

                                                        WASTEBASKET
#From                    Date          Subject

1 MOLE::MIKEN             28-NOV-1988  A useful little program
```

We can now make message #1 the current message by:

```
MAIL> 1

#1          28-NOV-1988 12:13:22.72                    MAIL
From:      MOLE::SUSAN
To:  MIKEN
CC:
Subj: A useful little program

program hello(input, output);
begin
    writeln('Hello world')
end.
```

and move the message to the MAIL folder:

```
MAIL> move mail
```

We then set our folder back to the MAIL folder and can check for the existence of the message:

```
MAIL> set folder mail

%MAIL-I-SELECTED, 27 messages selected

MAIL> 25

#25         28-NOV-1988 12:13:22.72                    MAIL

From:      MOLE::SUSAN
To:  MIKEN
CC:
Subj:      A useful little program

program hello(input, output);
begin
    writeln('Hello world')
end.

MAIL> exit
```

11.2.6 Using folders

In addition to the default folders NEWMAIL, MAIL, and WASTEBASKET, you can create your own MAIL folders for organizing your electronic messages much as you might create and maintain paper folders for paper mail.

Folders can be created by moving (see page 187) a MAIL message to a folder that does not exist at this time. You will then be asked if you wish to create a folder with this name.

A mail folder is removed when all the messages in it have been deleted.

The MAIL command—MOVE

This command moves the current message to the specified folder.

The FILE command performs the same function as MOVE, and these commands can be used interchangeably.

```
MAIL> move schedules
```

moves the current message to the folder SCHEDULES.

Example

```
$ mail

MAIL> 1


#1         23-NOV-1988 10:15:21.71                        MAIL

From:      MOLE::JOHN
To:  MIKEN
CC:
Subj:      Squash

Dear Mike,

Can you play on Monday 28th Nov. at 18:30?

           Best wishes - John.

MAIL> move sports

MAIL> set folder sports
%MAIL-I-SELECTED, 2 message selected

 MAIL> directory
                                                        SPORTS
# From                   Date          Subject

1 MOLE::SUSAN            13-NOV-1988  Football match
2 MOLE::JOHN             23-NOV-1988  Squash

MAIL> exit
```

You can also specify a filename to which the current message is to be moved. If the specified file does not exist, it is then created for you. If the filename is omitted, the message is moved to the specified folder in the current file.

If you do not supply a folder name, you will be prompted for one. If a folder name is given that does not exist, then you will be asked if that folder is to be created. This procedure can thus be used to create a new folder.

```
MAIL⟩ move
_Folder: schedules

_File: ⟨Return⟩

Folder SCHEDULES does not exist.
Do you want to create it (Y/N, default is N)?  Y

%MAIL-I-NEWFOLDER, folder SCHEDULES created
```

If you enter the MOVE command, supply a folder name and then decide that you do not want to move the message, press ⟨Ctrl⟩Z. ⟨Ctrl⟩Z aborts the operation but keeps you within MAIL.

MOVE/ALL

This command moves all the messages in the current folder to the specified folder. For example:

```
$ mail

MAIL⟩ set folder sports

%MAIL-I-SELECTED, 2 messages selected

MAIL⟩ move/all oldseason

MAIL⟩ exit

$
```

moves all messages from the SPORTS folder to the OLDSEASON folder.

The MAIL command—SELECT

This command selects the current folder.

Example

```
$ mail

MAIL> directory

                                                   NEWMAIL
#From              Date         Subject

1 MOLE::MIKEN      10-OCT-1988  Software Advisory Red Lion Sq.
2 MOLE::MIKEN      10-OCT-1988  Software Advisory for Mbone Rd
3 MOLE::MIKEN      10-OCT-1988  Software Advisory for Wells St.

MAIL> select advisory

%MAIL-I-SELECTED, 1 message selected

MAIL> directory

                                                   ADVISORY
# From              Date         Subject

1 MOLE::MALCOLM     16-SEP-1988  NEW ADVISORY ARRANGEMENTS

MAIL> select newmail

%MAIL-I-SELECTED, 3 message selected

MAIL> move/all

_Folder: advisory

_File: <Return>

MAIL> select advisory

%MAIL-I-SELECTED, 4 messages selected

MAIL> directory

                                                   ADVISORY
# From              Date         Subject

1 MOLE::MALCOLM     16-SEP-1988  NEW ADVISORY ARRANGEMENTS
2 MOLE::SUSAN       10-OCT-1988  Software Advisory Red Lion Sq.
3 MOLE::PETER       10-OCT-1988  Software Advisory for Mbone Rd
4 MOLE::TERRY       10-OCT-1988  Software Advisory for Wells St.

MAIL> exit
```

The MAIL command—DIRECTORY

You can enter the DIRECTORY/FOLDER command in order to see a display of the names of folders existing in the current mail file. You can optionally include a folder name to give a list of messages in that folder. For example:

```
MAIL> directory meetings
```

lists all messages in the MEETINGS folder.

11.2.7 Your MAIL environment

Your MAIL environment may be shown by typing:

```
MAIL> show all

Your mail file directory is DISK1:[MIKE.MAIL].
Your current mail file is DISK1:[MIKE.MAIL]MAIL.MAI;1.
No folder is currently selected.
The wastebasket folder name is WASTEBASKET.
Mail file DISK1:[MIKE.MAIL]MAIL.MAI;1
contains 31317 deleted message bytes.

You have 0 new messages.

You have not set a forwarding address.
Your personal name is "MIKE".
Your editor is TPU.
CC prompting is enabled.
Automatic copies to yourself are disabled.
Automatic deleted message purge is enabled.
Your default print queue is SYS$PRINT.
You have not specified a default print form.
```

Here we can see that the information provided consists of the following:

1. The name of the MAIL file directory.
2. The current MAIL file and folder.
3. The name of the WASTEBASKET folder.
4. The amount of deleted message space.
5. The number of any new (unread) messages.
6. The forwarding address, if set (see the SET FORWARD command).
7. The personal name, if set (see the SET PERSONAL_NAME command).
8. Whether a CC: (carbon copy) prompt is generated when sending mail.
9. Whether or not copies are received of MAIL messages sent or answered (see the SET COPY_SELF command).

10. Whether or not MAIL empties the WASTEBASKET folder when the EXIT or SET FILE (see the SET AUTO_PURGE command) command is used.
11. The default print queue.
12. The default print form for printing MAIL messages.

You can modify your MAIL environment by using the SET command. Except where indicated, changes performed with the SET command remain in effect from one session of MAIL to another.

The following are some of the more commonly used characteristics:

AUTO_PURGE

You should set AUTO_PURGE so that messages that you have deleted and are placed in the WASTEBASKET folder are removed every time that you exit from MAIL. The SHOW command is used to verify the action.

```
MAIL> set auto_purge

MAIL> show auto_purge

Automatic deleted message purge is enabled
```

CC_PROMPT

Setting CC_PROMPT enables the carbon copy (CC:) prompt when sending a message:

```
MAIL> set cc_prompt
```

You should SET NOCC_PROMPT to turn off prompting for carbon copies.

EDITOR

Allows you to specify the editor you wish to use within MAIL:

```
MAIL> set editor tpu
```

where TPU stands for Text Processing Utility and is the utility in which the editor EVE is defined.

FILE

Specifies the file that is to be used as your current MAIL file. Each time you enter MAIL your default MAIL file is MAIL.MAI. Changing the value of FILE is not preserved from one session of MAIL to another.

```
MAIL> set file minutes
```

FOLDER

Changes the current folder within the MAIL file. You can also include qualifiers to select only messages that satisfy one or more specified conditions, e.g.:

```
MAIL> select folder agenda/from_substring=susan
      /since=10-oct-1988
```

selects all messages from the folder AGENDA that are dated after 10-OCT-1988 and include the substring SUSAN in the FROM entry.

MAIL_DIRECTORY

Most users find it convenient to keep all MAIL files in a subdirectory. The following example shows you how this can be achieved:

```
MAIL> show mail_directory

DISK1:[MIKE]

MAIL> set mail_directory [.mail]

%MAIL-I-CREATED, DISK1:[MIKE.MAIL] created

MAIL> show mail directory

DISK1:[MIKE.MAIL]

MAIL> exit

$ directory [mike.mail]

Directory DISK1:[MIKEN.MAIL]

MAIL$00040091930D975C.MAI;1       MAIL$0004009193FAB1FE.MAI;1
MAIL$000400919C8D5579.MAI;1       MAIL$000400919E234193.MAI;1
MAIL$00040091A2EC81A9.MAI;1       MAIL$00040091A468A4A8.MAI;1
MAIL.MAI;1

Total of 7 files.
```

PERSONAL_NAME

Allows a user to attach a personal name to the end of the "From:" text of mail messages that are sent. This can in fact be any text you like. For example:

```
MAIL> set personal_name "The Joker"
```

QUEUE

Sets the default print queue. For example:

```
MAIL> show queue

Your default queue is SYS$PRINT.

MAIL> set queue laser

MAIL> show queue

Your default print queue is LASER

MAIL> select/subject=coursework

%MAIL-I-SELECTED, 4 messages selected

MAIL> 1


#1          16-OCT-1988 12:31:53.07                    MAIL
From:       MOLE::SUSAN         "The Joker"
To:  MIKE
CC:
Subj:       The Latest Coursework

Are you making much headway with this?

MAIL> print

MAIL> exit

Job MAIL (queue LASER, entry 156) started on LASER
```

In this example the default printer queue is initially shown to be SYS$PRINT. The SET command then modifies this to be LASER which is verified by the SHOW QUEUE command. The messages in the current folder that contain COURSEWORK in the subject field are selected and by typing "1" the first of these is made the current message. The PRINT command sends the current message to the queue LASER.

11.3 The PHONE Utility

11.3.1 Introduction

Unlike the MAIL utility on VMS, users wishing to communicate via PHONE must be using the system concurrently, i.e both users—the "sender" and the "receiver"—must be logged onto the system at the same time. MAIL can be considered analogous to the postal system, where you need not be at home when the post arrives, and the PHONE utility to the telephone system, where of course you need to be at home to answer a ringing telephone.

11.3.2 Using the PHONE utility

To contact someone via PHONE you must first ensure that your terminal is set up correctly, i.e. it is set for the appropriate terminal type: the SET TERMINAL/INQUIRE command selects the correct type. Secondly, ensure that the person you wish to contact is currently using the same computer system, or another reachable system in the DECnet network. There are various methods for checking this, as shown below. To check for a user on the same system as you, type in:

```
$ show users
```

or if you know the username is RAY:

```
$ show users ray

            VAX/VMS Interactive Users
             19-JUN-1989 10:23:12.91
       Total number of interactive users = 18
 Username      Process Name        PID       Terminal
 RAY           RAY                 00001EB2  RTA1:
```

If user RAY is using the system you can phone him with the command:

```
$ phone ray
```

Alternatively, after invoking the PHONE utility, you can check for a specific user. To invoke the PHONE utility, simply type:

```
$ phone
```

In response the screen will be redrawn with a horizontal line across its center, to form upper and lower window of communication. Along the top a small input window also appears which contains your username and the title "phone". It is

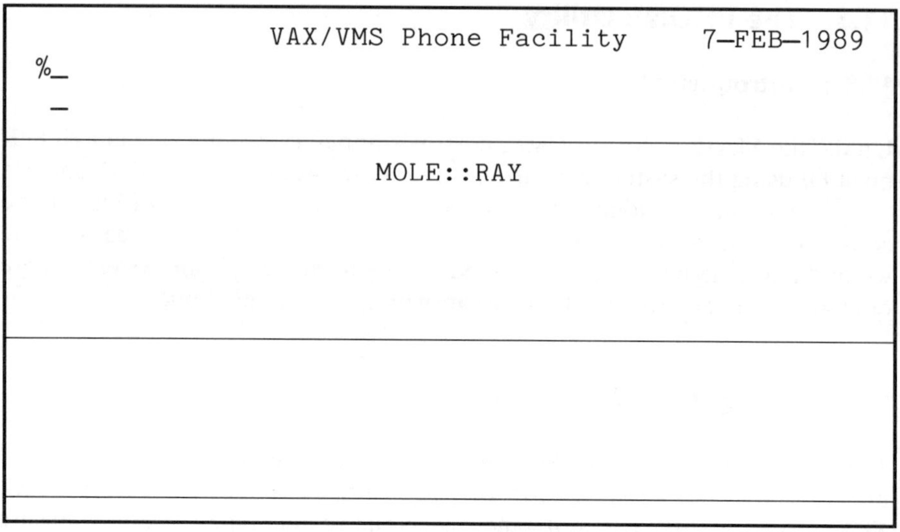

```
                    VAX/VMS Phone Facility     7—FEB—1989
 %_
  _
-------------------------------------------------------------
                          MOLE::RAY



-------------------------------------------------------------



-------------------------------------------------------------
```

Fig. 11-1 Screen display on start of phone call.

in this top window that commands to PHONE are typed. Text sent in conversation appears in the larger two windows, i.e. text typed by you in the top window, and text received by you in the bottom window. The cursor is at the top left-hand corner (see Figure 11-1). Note that once the PHONE utility is invoked, the prompt is the percentage sign shown in the command window.

To check if a specific user is currently using the computer, type the following command in the command window:

```
% directory
```

This causes phone to perform the SHOW USERS command. If a user you wish to contact is on the system, and has username RAY, then type:

```
% dial ray
```

To contact a user on another computer in the DECnet network, precede the username and the directory command in the above examples by the computer's node name, followed by two colons. For example, if user RAY is on a computer called MOLE:

```
% dial mole::ray
```

The message

```
Ringing RAY - press any key to cancel the call and continue
```

should appear repeatedly in the command box at the top of the screen.

If you wish to stop the phone ringing and cancel the call, type any key. The receiver might have disabled the PHONE utility at his or her terminal by using the SET TERMINAL/NOBROADCAST command, in which case you will be informed with the message:

```
That person's phone is unplugged (\NOBROADCAST).
```

If the user you are wishing to contact does not have the PHONE disabled, then the following message will be received on the screen:

```
$

MOLE::RAY is phoning you on MOLE::      (10:07:21)

$

MOLE::RAY is phoning you on MOLE::      (10:07:31)
```

Messages appear repeatedly at 10-second intervals each time the sender receives the "Ringing..." message. Each message shows the node the user is phoning from and the time.

To answer the following call, first run the PHONE utility and then respond with the command ANSWER:

```
$

MOLE::MIKE is phoning you on MOLE::      (10:07:21)

$

MOLE::MIKE is phoning you on MOLE::      (10:07:31)

$ phone
```

Figure 11-2 shows the conversation.

Alternatively, PHONE can be answered directly from VMS by typing:

```
$ phone answer
```

Once the call has been answered, the other user's name appears in the bottom window of the screen. From this point on, the screens of both users are identical, with whatever is typed appearing in the top section of the screen (on both the user's and the caller's terminal) and the caller's text in the bottom

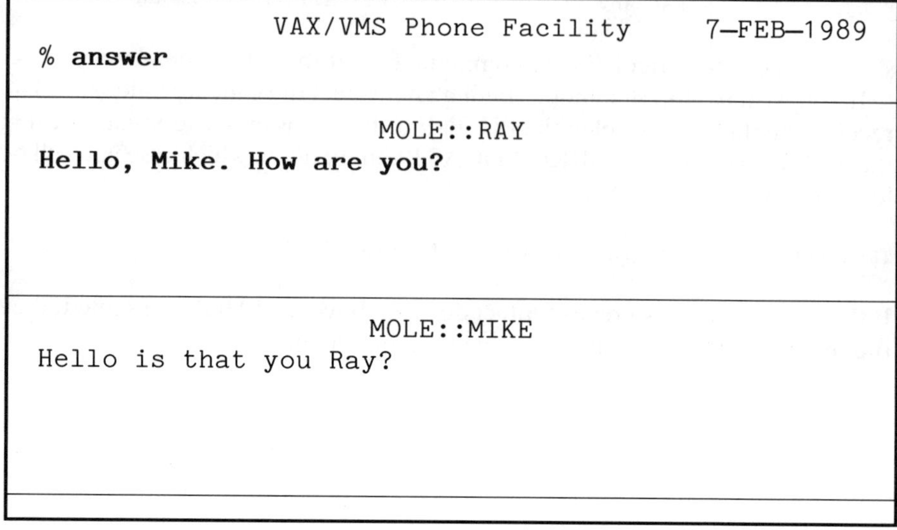

Fig. 11-2 Screen display of two-way phone call.

window. Note that both users can type simultaneously at their respective terminals.

11.3.3 Phone text formatting

Although PHONE does not provide a full editor, some text formatting and editing is available by using the keys shown in Table 11-1.

Table 11-1 PHONE line-text editing commands.

Key	Function
⟨Delete⟩	Deletes character to the left of the cursor
⟨Line feed⟩	Deletes word to the left of the cursor
⟨Return⟩	New line
⟨Tab⟩	Moves to the next tab position
⟨Ctrl⟩G	Rings bell at all terminals involved in conversation
⟨Ctrl⟩L	Clears text from your window
⟨Ctrl⟩S	Stops characters appearing on the screen (freezes the screen)
⟨Ctrl⟩Q	Restarts screen scrolling after a ⟨Ctrl⟩S
⟨Ctrl⟩U	Deletes the current line
⟨Ctrl⟩W	Redraws the entire screen.

If at any time during the "conversation" you need to type commands directly to the PHONE utility, press the percentage key. This will return the cursor to the command window. Pressing the ⟨%⟩ key twice allows you to type a percentage into your message window.

Multiway conversations can be achieved by returning to the command window and using the DIAL command to contact other users as shown below.

To contact another user, type:

```
⟨%⟩
```

to return to the command window, and then

```
% dial stoat::jim
```

to phone username JIM on DECnet computer STOAT. Figure 11-3 shows this sequence of commands and the ensuing conversation.

To leave PHONE, press ⟨%⟩ to move to the command window and then type:

```
% hangup

% exit
```

Typing ⟨Ctrl⟩Z at any time during the conversation is equivalent to using the HANGUP command and disconnects the current call. Typing ⟨Ctrl⟩Z at

```
                    VAX/VMS Phone Facility     7—FEB—1989
 % dial stoat::jim
--------------------------------------------------------------
                          MOLE::RAY
 Hello, Mike. Have you met Jim?
--------------------------------------------------------------
                          MOLE::MIKE
 Hello Everyone.
--------------------------------------------------------------
                          STOAT::JIM
 No, I haven't met Mike before! How are you Mike?
--------------------------------------------------------------
```

Fig. 11-3 Screen display for multi-way phone calls.

command mode (the percentage prompt) will terminate and exit from the session.

11.3.4 Useful phone commands

While running the PHONE utility, it is possible to invoke several useful features. We have already discussed the DIRECTORY, DIAL and HANGUP commands; now we shall describe some of the others. To perform these commands, you must be in command mode.

The PHONE command—FACSIMILE

In the command mode, the contents of files in your directory can be listed over PHONE by using the FACSIMILE command, which displays the file's contents in the window. The contents of file MYPROG.TXT can be displayed as shown in Figure 11-4.

The PHONE command—HELP

Phone has its own HELP facility. Figure 11-5 shows how to invoke HELP and obtain a list of PHONE commands. Alternatively, HELP on a particular topic can be invoked directly. For example:

```
% help hangup
```

provides help on the HANGUP command.

The PHONE command—HOLD

It is also possible to put a conversation "on hold", dial another user, and then return to the original conversation. The person put on hold will be notified with a message. To do, this type:

```
% hold
```

The PHONE command—REJECT

If you are busy when someone tries to phone you, you can reject the call. The caller is informed that the call has been rejected. The following commands run

```
                    VAX/VMS Phone Facility     7-FEB-1989
% facsimile myprog.txt
-------------------------------------------------------------
                          MOLE::RAY
This is the first line of my file. The file is called
myprog.txt, because it is about my program.
It's a very boring program about sheep....
-------------------------------------------------------------
                         MOLE::CHRIS
Can I have a look at your famous program Ray?
```

Fig. 11-4 Use of FACSIMILE command in conjunction with phone call.

```
                    VAX/VMS Phone Facility           7-FEB-1989
% help
Press any key to cancel the help information and continue.
- - - - - - - - - - - - - - - - - - - - - - - - - - - - - - - -
HELP
The HELP command allows you to obtain information about the
PHONE facility.
To obtain information about an individual command or topic,
type HELP followed bby the command or topic name:

   HELP topic

HELP also accepts all of the other standard VMS help argument
formats.

The information you request is displayed at your terminal
until you type any character at your keyboard.

Additional information available:

ANSWER   Characters DIAL DIRECTORY EXIT        FACSIMILE HANGUP
HELP     HOLD       MAIL REJECT    Switch_hook UNHOLD
```

Fig. 11-5 Example of PHONE–HELP facility.

PHONE and reject an incoming call:

```
$ phone

% reject
```

The PHONE command—MAIL

Messages can be left for those users who are not currently logged in to the computer. In order to do this, PHONE uses the MAIL utility to send a short message to the user's mailbox. The example shown below is mailing username MIKE with the message in double quotes. As with some of the other commands, the username may be preceded by a node name if on a network.

```
% mail miken "Do you fancy going for a drink after work?"
```

When PHONE is running, typing PHONE at the command line performs the same function as typing DIAL—The two commands are interchangeable.

Chapter

12

Using VAX/VMS Libraries

12.1 Introduction

There are two main libraries on VAX/VMS—the help library and the VMS Common Run-Time library. These are both similar in that they contain a set of features that the users can access. The help library contains a set of help topics, each one providing information on a feature of VAX/VMS. The Run-Time library contains a series of routines, each one performing a specific function. Additional features can be added to, or deleted from each library by the System Manager.

We have shown how to access the help library in Chapter 3 (Section 3.4). In this chapter we will show how to add additional information into the library.

12.2 The Help Library

12.2.1 Accessing help

To read articles from the help library, type HELP followed by the name of the subject you require information on. For example:

```
$ help show queue

SHOW

 QUEUE
```

```
Displays information about queues and jobs that are currently
in queues.

o Display characteristic names and numbers that are available
  on queues (see /CHARACTERISTIC).

o Display form names and numbers that are available on queues
  (see /FORM).

Format:
            SHOW QUEUE  [queue-name]

Additional information available:

Parameters Command_Qualifiers
/ALL_ENTRIES /BATCH  /BRIEF   /BY_JOB_STATUS /DEVICE
/FILES       /FULL   /GENERIC /OUTPUT        /SUMMARY
/CHARACTERISTIC      /FORM

SHOW QUEUE Subtopic?
```

At this prompt you type in the name of the subtopic or press ⟨Return⟩ twice to exit, and return to the DCL prompt.

12.3 Adding and Deleting Library Information

12.3.1 Introduction

The help library is organized as a hierarchy. Main topics are placed at the top level (level 1), with information associated with these topics being stored at lower levels. For instance, if SHOW was a subject at the top level, SHOW's parameters (QUEUE, SYSTEM, USERS, etc.) would be the second level with qualifiers relating to each of these parameters (/FULL, /ALL, etc.) being on a third level (see Figure 12-1).

If we wish to add information into the library, we must place the text in a file and then insert it into the relevant library.

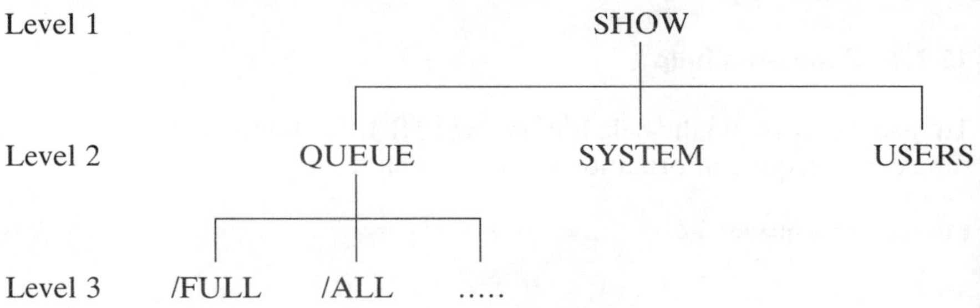

Fig. 12-1 The hierarchy of library information (SHOW).

12.3.2 Inserting information into the help library

To insert information in a help file, we first need to place the text in a file. We can do this using the EVE editor, as follows:

```
$ edit/tpu pclprinters.hlp
```

we then type in the contents of the file:

```
1 PCL_printers

This text is to help you use the printers at the Polytechnic
of Central London.

2 Room3.1

To use the printer located in room 3.1, type the following:

PRINT/QUEUE=ROOM31 test.dat

where:

'test.dat' is the name of the file to be printed.

2 Room3.6

To use the printer located in room 3.6, type the following:

PRINT/QUEUE=ROOM36 test.dat

where:

'filename.ext' is the name of the file to be printed.
```

The text starts with the number "1", this is known as "key-1" and states that the first section of the text is to be a major topic of help (this is equivalent to level 1 on Figure 12-1). The topic name "PCL_printers" follows this. The next section starts with the number "2", this is "key-2" and so depicts a subtopic relating to key-1. The last section, also "key-2", is another subtopic of key-1, and is placed on the same level as any other key-2 topics. We thus obtain the structure shown in Figure 12-2.

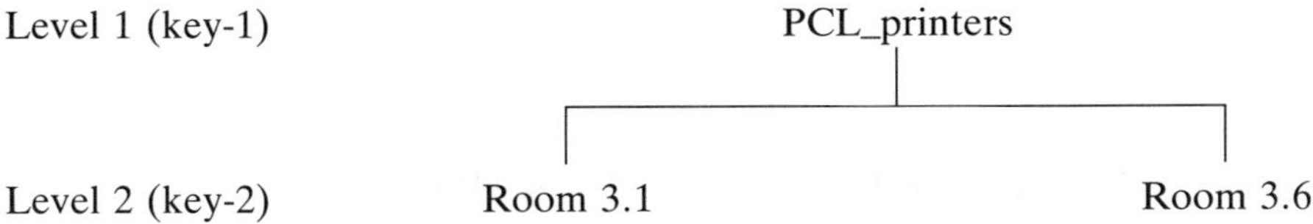

Fig. 12-2 The hierarchy of printers in PCL.

To insert this into the main help library, SYS$HELP:HELPLIB.HLB, type:

```
$ library/help/insert sys$help:helplib.hlb pclprinters.hlp
```

where:

LIBRARY	runs the VAX/VMS Librarian Utility;
/HELP	updates a help library;
/INSERT	inserts a new module into an existing library;
SYS$HELP:HELPLIB.HLB	is the name of the library we wish to modify;
PCLPRINTERS.HLP	is the name of the file we wish to insert into the library.

The default file extension for help libraries is .HLB and for help files .HLP.

The previous command inserts the text into the library only if the module does not already exist. To insert text into a library overwriting (and so updating) an existing module if it exists, use the /REPLACE qualifier:

```
$ library/help/replace sys$help:helplib.hlb pclprinters.hlp
```

To display the text we run the HELP facility:

```
$ help pcl_printers

This text is to help you use the printers at the Polytechnic
of Central London.

Room3.1   Room3.6

Topic: room3.1

Room3.1

To use the printer located in room 3.1, type the following:

  PRINT/QUEUE=ROOM31 filename.ext

where:

 'filename.ext' is the name of the file to be printed.

Topic: <Ctrl>Z
```

12.3.3 Deleting information from the help library

To delete a module from the library we use the /DELETE qualifier:

```
$ library/help/delete=pcl_printers sys$help:helplib.hlb
```

which deletes the module PCL_PRINTERS from the main help library.

12.3.4 Creating a help library

It is unlikely that your account has been given sufficient privilege to modify the main help library. It is possible, however, for you to create your own libraries, containing information that is helpful to you. To create a library of your own use the /CREATE qualifier:

```
$ library/help/create myhelp pclprinters
```

This command creates a help library called MYHELP.HLB, which contains the file PCLPRINTERS.HLP. The library can then be modified as and when the need arises.

To access this library, you first need to redefine the logical name HLP$LIBRARY, so that it contains the file specification for your personal help library. HLP$LIBRARY is used by the HELP command when searching for help libraries:

```
$ define hlp$library dua0:[ray]myhelp.hlb

$ show logical hlp$library

"HLP$LIBRARY" = "DUA0:[RAY]MYHELP.HLB"(LNM$PROCESS_TABLE)

"HLP$LIBRARY" = "SYS$HELP:CCS.HLB" (LNM$GROUP_000012)
```

By displaying the logical name, we can see there are two help libraries assigned to HLP$LIBRARY. The first, which has been stored in the user's "process table", is for the library we have just created; the second, stored in the "group table", is an additional library added previously for use of the group that user RAY is a member of.

When we run HELP, both these additional libraries appear in the output, for our use:

```
$ help

  Information available:

  8086_68000_C    :=      =       @       ACCOUNTING ADVICE
  .
  .
  .
  UNIX_Utilities  UNLOCK  V50_NewFeatures   WAIT     Wells_St
```

```
  WRITE

  Additional help libraries available (type @name for topics):

  MYHELP  CCS

Topic? @myhelp

  Information available:

  Pcl_printers

  Additional help libraries available (type @name for topics):

  MYHELP  CCS

@MYHELP Topic? pcl_ printers

Pcl_printers


This information describes how to use the printing facilities at
the Polytechnic of Central London.


  Additional information available:

  Room3.1    Room3.6

@MYHELP Pcl_printers Subtopic? room3.1

PCL_PRINTERS

  Room3.1


    To use the printer in room 3.1 type:

          PRINT/QUEUE=ROOOM31 filename.ext

    where filename.ext is the name of the file to be printed.

@MYHELP Pcl_printers Subtopic?    <Ctrl>Z

$
```

Notice that apart for having to specify a leading "at" sign ("@") when we specify the directory name, the library from our point of view becomes integrated with the main help library. Other users, will not be able to access the library that we have created and it will not appear on the list of topics output when they execute the HELP command.

12.4 Other Libraries

In this chapter, we have considered only help libraries, but it is possible to have other types of libraries. Table 12-1 shows some possible types. These libraries are modified in much the same way as the Help library. Table 12-1 shows the parameters needed to modify the various possible library files.

12.4.1 The object library

Object libraries can be built to contain many useful modules. Modules can be written and then inserted into the library for later use. These can then be searched when linking new programs to incorporate the necessary library routines into the code. This saves the time and effort of rewriting the same routine several times.

To create an object library containing two modules, we use the LIBRARY command with the /CREATE qualifier (the default library type is object, so we need not use the /OBJECT qualifier):

```
$ library/create mylib add,subtract
```

which creates a new object library called MYLIB.OLB comprising files ADD.OBJ and SUBTRACT.OBJ.

If at a later stage we wish to add further modules to this file, we use the /ADD qualifier to the /OBJECT qualifier, to the /INSERT qualifier, to the LIBRARY command.

```
$ library/add/object/insert mylib string_test
```

This adds the module in file STRING_TEST.OBJ to the object library MYLIB.OLB, which we created above.

Table 12-1 Library types.

Library Type	Qualifier	Library Extension	File Extension
HELP	/help	.hlb	.hlp
MACRO	/macro	.mlb	.mar
OBJECT	/object	.olb	.obj
TEXT	/text	.tlb	.txt
SHARE	/share	.olb	.exe

To specify an object library for the VAX/VMS linker to search when linking programs, use the /LIBRARY qualifier with the LINK command. For example, the following commands compile the file SORT.C to create an object file SORT.OBJ, which is then linked with any necessary modules contained in the object library USEFUL.OLB to produce an image file SORT.EXE:

```
$ cc sort

$ link sort/library+useful
```

12.5 The VAX/VMS Common Run-Time Library

The VAX/VMS Common Run-Time library, also known as the Run-Time library, contains a set of routines that can be called from any VAX programming language, as well as the MACRO assembler and interpreted languages (see Table 12-2). Use of these routines enables us to perform a wide range of operations without having to write any additional programs.

All the Run-Time library routines are shared among all the users, hence there is no need for duplication and therefore they take up less space in the computer's memory.

Before we continue, let us define what we mean by the term "routine". In this instance, a routine is a set of instructions (similar to a computer program) that performs some task. There are two types of routines, those that return a result (or value) of a given type, these are called "functions", and others called "procedures".

The Run-Time library routines are grouped into various sets, each set having its own unique prefix. Each routine in the set has its routine name preceded by the group prefix. For example, for the mathematics routines each routine name begins with MTH$. Table 12-3 shows the different groups.

Each group contains a large number of routines. We shall look at a few of the more immediately useful routines from each group to obtain an idea of the scope of each section.

Table 12-2 Languages that can call Run-Time library routines.

VAX Ada	VAX DATATRIEVE (interpreter)
VAX BASIC	VAX DSM (interpreter)
VAX BLISS-32	VAX FORTRAN
VAX C	VAX MACRO (assembler)
VAX COBOL	VAX Pascal
VAX COBOL-74	VAX PL/1
VAX CORAL	VAX RPG
VAX DIBOL	VAX SCAN

Table 12-3 VAX/VMS Run-Time library groups.

Prefix	The Run-Time library routine groups
DTK$	DECtalk routines
LIB$	Routines which: Get records from devices Manipulate character strings Convert I/O data types Perform resource allocation Get system information Handle signal exceptions Detect hardware exceptions Process cross-reference data
MTH$	Mathematic routines.—These are capable of performing algebraic, arithmetic and trigonometric operations
OTS$	General purpose routines, such as data type conversion for compilers and some mathematical routines
PPL$	Parallel processing routines—useful for VAXs with more than one CPU
SMG$	Screen management routines
STR$	String manipulation routines

DTK$ DECtalk routines

DTK$ANSWER_PHONE	Wait for and answer a ringing phone.
DTK$DIAL_PHONE	Dial the phone.
DTK$HANGUP_PHONE	Hang up the phone.

(There are a total of 21 routines in the DECtalk section.)

LIB$ library routines

LIB$ATTACH	Attach terminal to a process.
LIB$CREATE_DIR	Create a directory.

LIB$DATE_TIME	Return date and time as string.
LIB$DAY_OF_WEEK	Return the day of the week as an integer.
LIB$DELETE_FILE	Delete file(s).
LIB$DELETE_LOGICAL	Delete a logical name assignment.
LIB$DISABLE_CTRL	Disable interception of ⟨Ctrl⟩ characters.
LIB$DO_COMMAND	Execute a DCL command.
LIB$ENABLE_CTRL	Enable interception of ⟨Ctrl⟩ characters.
LIB$FIND_FILE	Locate a file.
LIB$GET_DVI	Get device and volume information.
LIB$GETJPI	Get job and process information.
LIB$GETQUI	Get queue information.
LIB$GETSYI	Get system information.
LIB$LEN	Calculate the length of a character string.
LIB$LOCC	Find a character.
LIB$PAUSE	Pause execution of a program.
LIB$PUT_OUTPUT	Output a line to SYS$OUTPUT.
LIB$SET_LOGICAL	Set logical name.
LIB$SHOW_VM	Display virtual memory characteristics.
LIB$SPAWN	Spawn a subprocess.
LIB$STOP	Stop process execution and signal state.
LIB$TRA_ASC_EBC	Translate ASCII to EBCDIC
LIB$TRA_EBC_ASC	Translate EBCDIC to ASCII
LIB$WAIT	Wait for a specified time period to elapse.

(There are a total of 155 routines in the library section.)

MTH$ mathematics library routines

MTH$xACOS	Give arc cosine of angle in radians*.
MTH$xASIN	Give arc sine in radians*.
MTH$xATAN	Give arc tangent in degrees*.
MTH$CLOG	Give complex natural logarithm**.
MTH$COSH	Give hyperbolic cosine*.
MTH$xEXP	Give exponential*.
MTH$HTANH	Computes hyperbolic tangent***.
MTH$RANDOM	Generate random number (uniform distribution).
MTH$SQRT	Give the square root.
OTS$CNVOUT	Convert D, G, and H floating data types to character string.
OTS$CVT_L_TO	Convert (unsigned) integer to octal text.
OTS$CVT_L_TU	Convert (unsigned) integer to decimal text.
OTS$CVT_L_TZ	Convert (unsigned) integer to hexadecimal text.
OTS$DIVCx	Do complex division.
OTS$MULCx	Do complex multiplication.

* Applies to F, D, and G floating-point data types.
** Applies to F floating complex value.
*** Applies to H floating-point value.
F, D, G and H indicate the levels of precision in floating-point numbers in programming languages.

(There are a total of 42 routines in the maths section.)

PPL$ parallel processing library routines

PPL$AWAIT_EVENT	Wait for an event.
PPL$CREATE_EVENT	Create an event.

PPL$CREATE_SPIN_LOCK	Create a spin lock.
PPL$CREATE_SHARED_MEMORY	Create shared memory.
PPL$RELEASE_SPIN_LOCK	Release a spin lock.
PPL$SPAWN	Start parallel execution.
PPL$STOP	Stop a processes in parallel execution.

(There are a total of 29 routines in the parallel processing section.)

SMG$ screen management library routines

SMG$ADD_KEY_DEF	Create a key definition.
SMG$CREATE_SUBPROCESS	Create a subprocess.
SMG$CREATE_VIRTUAL_DISPLAY	Create a virtual display.
SMG$CREATE_VIRTUAL_KEYBOARD	Create a virtual keyboard.
SMG$CURSOR_COLUMN	Return column cursor position.
SMG$CURSOR_ROW	Return row cursor position.
SMG$DEFINE_KEY	Define a function key (DEFINE/KEY).
SMG$DELETE_KEY_DEF	Delete key definition.
SMG$DELETE_LINE	Delete line.
SMG$DELETE_SUBPROCESS	Delete a subprocess.
SMG$DRAW_CHAR	Output specified character.
SMG$DRAW_LINE	Output a line.
SMG$DRAW_RECTANGLE	Output a rectangle.
SMG$ERASE_CHARS	Delete characters.
SMG$ERASE_COLUMN	Delete a column from the screen.
SMG$ERASE_DISPLAY	Delete virtual display.
SMG$ERASE_LINE	Delete a line from the screen.
SMG$FLUSH_BUFFER	Clear the buffer.
SMG$GET_TERM_DATA	Obtain terminal data.
SMG$HOME_CURSOR	Moves cursor to top left of screen.
SMG$LIST_KEY_DEF	List key definitions.
SMG$RING_BELL	Ring bell on terminal.

(There are a total of 117 routines in the screen management section.)

STR$ String manipulation library routines

STR$ADD	Add together two decimal strings.

STR$APPEND	Append a string.
STR$COMPARE	Compare two strings.
STR$DUPL_CHAR	Copy a character N times.
STR$MATCH_WILD	Match a wildcard specification.
STR$TRIM	Remove trailing blanks and tabs.
STR$UPCASE	Convert all characters to uppercase.

(There are a total of 32 routines in the string manipulation section.)

12.6 Using the Run-Time Library

A program that uses a Run-Time routine needs to have this incorporated into the program. The LINK command does this automatically for us by searching two system libraries—IMAGELIB.OLB and STARLET.OLB.

The system default shareable image library, IMAGELIB.OLB, contains the most commonly used routines. This file is searched by default when linking to resolve any undefined symbols. Any routines, in the form of shareable images, are then linked with the program to form a executable image.

The system default object module library, STARLET.OLB, is then searched to resolve any routines that are not in IMAGELIB.OLB. The object module of the routine is then copied into the program's executable image.

If the routine is found in the shareable image library, the routine does not need to be copied into the program's executable image. This has the following advantages:

1. Several programs can use the same copy of the shareable image, making each program smaller and thus saving memory and disk space.
2. Several programs can use the routine simultaneously, again saving memory.
3. There is no need to relink program when a new version of the Run-Time library has been installed.

12.6.1 An example of a Run-Time library call

To use a subroutine from some high-level language program we need to use the CALL statement. This applies to languages such as COBOL, FORTRAN, PL/I and BASIC. Pascal and C, however, can call Run-Time library routines as they would call other routines and functions internal to the program.

Before a specific routine is used, we have to ensure, first, that the correct information is passed to it, and secondly, that we have somewhere to store the data it returns. To call a function, we therefore first need to know the type and number of variables it requires (if any), and the type of result we would expect to receive, as a result of the call (if any). Most of these details can be found in various manuals supplied by Digital to help you use the Run-Time library fully. A complete list of routines can be found in the *Introduction to the VMS Run-Time Library* manual along with a complete description of the CALL command. This manual is published by Digital, and forms part of their documentation set.

For the example here, we shall use a FORTRAN program to call a Run-Time library routine that gets the date and the time.

First we locate the routine we need to use. In the Digital Run-Time library manual it states: "LIB$DATE_TIME – Return Date and Time as a string." Alternatively we can look up the function in the on-line Help library.

```
$ help rtl—routines lib$ lib$date—time

RTL_ROUTINES

  LIB$

    LIB$DATE_TIME

        The Date and Time Returned as a String routine returns the VMS
        system date and time in the semantics of a user-provided string

          Format:

            LIB$DATE_TIME  date-time-string

          Argument

        date-time-string

        access: write only
        mechanism: by descriptor

        Destination string into which LIB$DATE_TIME writes the system date
        and time.  The  date-time-string  argument  is  the  address  of a
        descriptor pointing to the destination string.
```

Thus we have found the routine and know it returns a character string as a result of being called. So we can start to write the program, using the FORTRAN programming language:

```
    program time
    character*23 day_of_week
    call lib$date_time(day_of_week)
    write (6,100) day_of_week
100 format ('The date and time is ',a23)
    stop
    end
```

The first line of the program is the program's name. The second line "character*23 day_of_week" creates a character array called "day_of_week" consisting of 23 elements, which is large enough to store a character string returned as result of a call to the date and time routine. The next line "call lib$date_time-(day_of_week)" calls the Run-Time library routine. Note that it does not pass variables to the routine. As a result of the call a character string is passed back to the calling program and stored in the array "day_of_week". We then display the output along with a message.

To compile, link and run the program, called GETTIME.FOR:

```
$ for gettime

$ link gettime

$ run gettime

The date and time is 4-JUN-1989 18:10:27.83
```

Remember that on linking, the Run-Time library is automatically searched for routines.

This program could then be further developed. For example, by splitting the array and changing the date, which is currently a character field, into integers, we can use the program to calculate the number of days until say Christmas.

We have given a simple arbitrary example. However, Run-Time routines can be very useful for extracting data that is otherwise difficult to get, such as system and process information. Also, if the VAX you are using has more than one CPU, the PPL$ series of routines are useful to write programs that can run across more than one CPU, with all the advantages of parallel processing.

There are many uses of Run-Time routines, we have only given a brief overview of their type and uses as a means of illustrating how one can utilize and access them from within a program.

Chapter

13

Symbols and Logical Names

13.1 Introduction

In this chapter we shall describe the use of symbols and logical names. Although there are significant differences between them, there are also enough similarities for us to consider them together.

Symbols enable the user to manipulate numbers and character strings. A number or a string is assigned to a symbol. The symbol can then be used to access that variable. A symbol has a limited lifespan, depending on the type of definition. It can exist only for the time it takes the program containing the symbol definition to execute, or for the duration of your current login session.

Logical names assign a character string to a equivalence string. This enables the use of shorter strings, and so shorter and more easily typed commands, which can be equated to quite lengthy commands. Logical names also provide device independence for files. Parts of a command that refer to a particular disk area can be assigned to a logical name. If the files are then moved to a different area, the new area specification can be equated to the original logical name. From then on, each time the logical name is specified in VAX/VMS commands, the new area will be searched from the files. This technique can be very useful for setting up disk areas that are accessed by a group of users.

First we shall describe the use of symbols. In the second part of the chapter we shall consider the use of logical names.

13.2 Symbols

Symbols are used to store data, although unlike files, which also store data, their existence is only temporary. It is possible to assign symbols automatically when you log in, giving the appearance of permanent storage, by placing their definitions in a LOGIN.COM file. There are two types of symbol definition in VAX/VMS—"local" and "global". Note that local symbols with the same name take precedence over global symbols.

13.2.1 Local symbols

After a local symbol has been defined, it is available for use at that level of DCL, at the interactive level of level 0, and at all levels below that. For example, if we define a symbol when we first log in to the system, when we have subsequently the VAX/VMS prompt, this will be at level 0. That symbol can then be accessed by any programs or command procedures. Command procedures are files containing those DCL commands that we run (see Chapter 14). If, however, we define a symbol inside a command procedure, then that symbol has been defined at level 1, and that symbol will not be available for use at higher levels, in this instance level 0. If a command procedure that defined a symbol runs a second command procedure, then that symbol would remain defined for the second, and any subsequent command procedures, whether run by the original command procedure or any child procedures. The highest level is the command level (level 0) and the lowest level 32.

Since local symbols defined in command procedures are only in existence while the procedure runs, it enables the user to redefine (reuse) symbols that are defined at higher levels without altering the contents of the original symbol definition.

To define a local symbol we type its name, a single equals sign, then the equivalent string or number. For example:

```
$ prog1 = "run dua1:[compstaff.ray.c_progs]world.exe"
```

This sets up a symbol name PROG1 that can be used, instead of the command RUN DUA1:[COMPSTAFF.RAY.C-PROGS]WORLD.EXE, to execute the image file WORLD.EXE. For example, if the program WORLD displayed a "Hello, World" text string, then we would get the response:

```
$ prog1

  Hello, World
```

which is much shorter than:

```
$ run dua1:[compstaff.ray.c_progs]world.exe

 Hello, World
```

Alternatively, when defining a symbol, we can include a colon in front of the equals sign and avoid the need for quotation marks around the equivalence string, as follows:

```
$ prog1 := run dua1:[compstaff.ray.c_progs]world.exe
```

This produces similar results to using quotation marks, except the string is converted to uppercase and multiple spaces between words are replaced by a single space.

13.2.2 Global symbols

Unlike local symbols, global symbols can be accessed regardless of the level of operation of DCL. These may be defined and are available for use at any level.

To define a global variable we add a second equals sign to the command line. To redefine the local symbol of the previous example as a global symbol, we type:

```
$ prog1 == "run dua1:[compstaff.ray.c_progs]world.exe"
```

or

```
$ prog1 :== run dua1:[compstaff.ray.c_progs]world.exe
```

The rules about quotation marks also apply to global symbols.

13.2.3 Using symbols

We have already explained the differences between local and global symbols. In the following examples the processes can equally well be applied to either type of symbol (any exceptions will be stated).

In the following example we shall check for the existence of a symbol called "today", then define that symbol and ensure it is set up correctly. We shall then use that symbol, and finally delete it.

To see if a symbol exists, and if it does what is the equivalence string it contains, we type:

```
$ show symbol today

%DCL-W-UNDSYM, undefined symbol - check validity and spelling
```

This command invokes the SHOW command, to display the content (equivalent string) of the symbol named "today". In this instance VAX/VMS produces a warning message which states that no such symbol exists, or that we spelt the symbol name incorrectly. In any case we now know that "today" has not been defined as a symbol.

We now define a global symbol for "today". This is done by the command:

```
$ today :== directory/size/protection/since=today
```

The "today" symbol has been made equivalent to the DCL directory command, together with several additional qualifiers, these cause the directory to display for each file its size and protection for each file created today.

If we now display the symbol "today", we can make sure it has been defined correctly:

```
$ show symbol today

TODAY == "DIRECTORY/SIZE/PROTECTION/SINCE=TODAY"
```

It may be of interest to note that although we choose to define the symbol using the comma and no quotation marks syntax, the response from VAX/VMS shows no colon and the equivalent string surrounded by quotation marks.

To use the symbol, we simply type the symbol name. The equivalent string is then executed. For example:

```
$ today

Directory DUA1:[COMPSTAFF.RAY]

SETHOST.LOG;9                1  (RWED,RWED,RWE,)
SETHOST.LOG;8               15  (RWED,RWED,RWE,)
SETHOST.LOG;7                8  (RWED,RWED,RWE,)
SYM.LOG;2                    0  (RWED,RWED,RWE,)
SYM.LOG;1                   17  (RWED,RWED,RWE,)

Total of 5 files, 41 blocks.
```

This displays all the files created since midnight. We can still specify the command directly and achieve the same result, as shown in the following example:

```
$ directory/size/protection/since=today

Directory DUA1:[COMPSTAFF.RAY]

SETHOST.LOG;9                1  (RWED,RWED,RWE,)
SETHOST.LOG;8               15  (RWED,RWED,RWE,)
SETHOST.LOG;7                8  (RWED,RWED,RWE,)
```

```
SYM.LOG;2                  0   (RWED,RWED,RWE,)
SYM.LOG;1                 17   (RWED,RWED,RWE,)

Total of 5 files, 41 blocks.
```

To delete a global symbol we need to specify its type. To delete the symbol "today", which was defined as a global symbol, we therefore type:

```
$ delete/symbol/global today
```

In contrast, when deleting local symbols, we need not specify the type. If "today" had originally been declared as a local symbol (i.e. if we had used one equal sign in the assignment command instead of two), then we would use the following command to delete it:

```
$ delete/symbol today
```

13.2.4 Abbreviating symbol names

It is possible to reduce the amount of typing necessary to specify a symbol name. This is done by placing an asterisk in the symbol name during the definition of the symbol. The symbol name can subsequently be shorted to the characters preceding the asterisk. Characters following the asterisk can also be typed when referring to the symbol, without producing any errors. As an example, we shall define a symbol assigned to an equivalent string which produces a directory listing displaying the creation date and size of all text files, i.e. files that have the extension .TXT, in a user's area. The command will include a search of all the subdirectories. To define a local symbol such that abbreviation is possible, we use the command:

```
$ memo*randum := dir dua1:[christopher.text]*.txt/date/size
```

So instead of typing:

```
$ memorandum

Directory DUA1:[CHRISTOPHER.TEXT]

DCL_NOTES.TXT;1            2  20-AUG-1987 10:29:52.92
BARBARA.TXT;6              2   1-DEC-1988 11:38:44.15
BARBARA.TXT;5              2   1-DEC-1988 11:33:09.28

Total of 3 files, 6 blocks.
```

we can abbreviate the symbol name, as follows:

```
$ memo

Directory DUA1:[CHRISTOPHER.TEXT]

DCL_NOTES.TXT;1              2  20-AUG-1987 10:29:52.92
BARBARA.TXT;6                2   1-DEC-1988 11:38:44.15
BARBARA.TXT;5                2   1-DEC-1988 11:33:09.28

Total of 3 files, 6 blocks.
```

If we lengthen the command syntax, the command still works:

```
$ memor

Directory DUA1:[CHRISTOPHER.TEXT]

DCL_NOTES.TXT;1              2  20-AUG-1987 10:29:52.92
BARBARA.TXT;6                2   1-DEC-1988 11:38:44.15
BARBARA.TXT;5                2   1-DEC-1988 11:33:09.28

Total of 3 files, 6 blocks.
```

However, attempting to shorten the command further generates an error message from VAX/VMS, as shown in the following instance:

```
$ mem

%DCL-W-IVVERB, unrecognized command verb - check validity and spelling
\MEM\
```

13.2.5 Predefined symbols

As you log in to the system, the logging process automatically activates a system file that sets up your working environment. This file is maintained by the System Manager, and it usually includes the definition of various symbols and logical names. To see which symbols this process has defined for you, type the following command:

```
$ show symbol *

  $RESTART == "FALSE"
  $SEVERITY == "1"
  $STATUS == "%X00030001"
  ACCOUNTM*ENU == "@PCL$OPS:ACCOUNTMENU"
  ACCU == "@PCL$CCS:RUN_ACCUTYPE"
  ADA == "ada/nooptimize"
  ARCH*IVE == "$ SYS$ARCHIVE:[MASTER]ARCHIVE"
```

```
.
.
.
TRANSF*ER == "@MGR:JANET_DOWN.COM"
TSA == "@PCL$PUBROOT:[TSA]TSA.COM"
US*ERS == "show users"
VT100 == "@U$PROC:VT100.COM"
WC == "$u$prog:wc"
WHAT == "$PCL$OPSP:WHAT"
WHO == "$u$prog:who"
```

We have shown only a few of the first and of the last symbols defined by the system—There are over 180 in total! Any symbols defined by you earlier in the session would also appear on the list.

13.2.6 Symbols and numbers

So far in this chapter we have dealt exclusively with storing strings in variables. We can, however, also store numerical values, and even combine them to perform simple calculations. Care must be taken to specify values that lie in the range −2 147 483 648 to 2 147 483 647. Numbers outside this range do not cause error messages to be displayed but result in incorrect values being produced. Before we see how to assign values to symbols, we must become familiar with the various types of values that we can specify.

Types of numerical values

Values can be categorized into one of three radices (a radix is a counting set). The three radices are:

- *Decimal* counting in sets of 10. Decimal numbers contain the values 0–9.
- *Hexadecimal* counting in sets of 16. Hexadecimal numbers contain the values 0–9 and A–F.
- *Octal* counting in sets of 8. Octal numbers contain the values 0–7, *not* the values 8 and 9.

Table 13-1 compares the different radices up to the decimal value of 20. We can assign values in any of the radixes to a symbol. Negative and positive values can equally well be specified.

Assigning values to symbols

To assign a decimal value to a symbol, we shall use local symbols though the process is the same for global symbols. We simply specify the symbol name, an

Table 13-1 Equivalence of decimal, octal and hexadecimal numerical values.

Octal	Decimal	Hexadecimal
1	1	1
2	2	2
3	3	3
4	4	4
5	5	5
6	6	6
7	7	7
10	8	8
11	9	9
12	10	A
13	11	B
14	12	C
15	13	D
16	14	E
17	15	F
20	16	10
21	17	11
22	18	12
23	19	13
24	20	14

equals sign—or two for global symbols—and the value to be held in that symbol. For example, to assign the decimal value 4 to the symbol number1:

```
$ number1 = 4
```

We then use the SHOW command to display the contents of symbol "number1":

```
$ show symbol number1

  NUMBER1 = 4    Hex = 00000004  Octal = 00000000004
```

Notice that the value is shown not only in decimal, but also in hexadecimal and octal.

By using the SHOW SYMBOL command to display the contents of the symbol in the various radices, VAX/VMS provides a simple facility for converting between the various counting sets.

Preceding the value with a minus sign enables us to specify negative numbers.

We can also specify values in hexadecimal and octal radixes. To store hexadecimal values we type a "%X" before the value, and "%O" (the character "O", not zero) for octal values. The following example shows local hexadecimal and octal symbols being defined:

```
$ hexnumber = %X1F

$ octnumber = %O16
```

Displaying these symbols gives the following:

```
$ show symbol hexnumber

  HEXNUMBER = 31    Hex = 0000001F  Octal = 00000000037

$ show symbol octnumber

  OCTNUMBER = 14    Hex = 0000000E  Octal = 00000000016
```

Using symbols to add values

Symbols can be used to perform rudimentary calculations. Values can be added, subtracted, multiplied, and divided. We shall demonstrate this with a simple example that adds two numbers. First we need to define the two symbols and their values. This is done by the command:

```
$ number_a == 4

$ number_b == 3
```

We have defined global symbols this time, but the method applies equally well to local symbols. Next, we add the two values together and store the result in a third symbol named "total". To do this, we specify the calculation as follows:

```
$ total = number_a + number_b
```

To display the result of the calculation we use the SHOW command:

```
$ show symbol total

  TOTAL = 7   Hex = 00000007  Octal = 00000000007
```

We can also state values to be added directly to existing symbols. For example, if we had wanted to multiply the value of "number_a" by 12, then add it to "number_b" and finally assign the result to "total", we can specify the command:

```
$ total = 12 * number_a + number_b
```

```
$ show symbol total

  TOTAL = 51    Hex = 00000033  Octal = 00000000063
```

13.2.7 Using symbols to add character strings

Not only can we use symbols to add numbers, but we can also use them to join together character strings. We first assign the strings to symbols and then "add" them together. The following example adds two strings to create a third:

```
$ word1 = "Hello, "

$ word2 = "World"

$ phrase = word1 + word2

$ show symbol phrase

  PHRASE = "Hello, World"
```

This is equivalent to the command:

```
$ phrase = "Hello, " + "World"
```

Additional text can be inserted when concatenating (joining together) the strings by specifying any additional text between quotation marks. In the following example, which adds three strings together, we first assign string values to the symbols and then add the contents of the symbols together. Notice particularly the format of the command line that concatenates the strings.

```
$ string1 = "What"

$ string2 = "load"

$ string3 = "Rubbish !!"

$ opinion = string1 + " a " + string2 + " of " + string3

$ show symbol opinion

  OPINION = "What a load of Rubbish !!"
```

13.2.8 Using symbols to store character strings

By enclosing a symbol name in apostrophes and placing it in a command line, the symbol is automatically substituted for the equivalence string before the command is executed. For example, to define a symbol called "home" whose equivalent string is the specification of the user's default directory, we would use the following command to set up the (global) symbol:

```
$ home == "dua1:[student.rebecca]"
```

By placing "home" between apostrophes and preceding it with the directory command, we can generate a listing of that directory:

```
$ directory 'home'

Directory DUA1:[STUDENT.REBECCA]

EXERCISE_1.PAS;2        CALCULATE.PAS;1     EXERCISE_1.EXE;1
EXERCISE_1.OBJ;1        TEXT.DIR;1

Total of 5 files.
```

If we add *.DIR to the command we can list all the main subdirectories:

```
$ directory 'home'*.dir

Directory DUA1:[STUDENT.REBECCA]

TEXT.DIR;1

Total of 1 files.
```

This produces the same result as typing the command line:

```
$ directory dua1:[student.rebecca]*.dir


Directory DUA1:[STUDENT.REBECCA]

TEXT.DIR;1

Total of 1 files.
```

13.2.9 Summary of character and numerical symbol types

We have viewed character symbols and numerical symbols separately because that is the way they are generally used. In fact, the two types are not permanently set and are interchangeable. The type that a symbol takes, either character or numerical, depends on the context in which it is used. In Section 13.2.6 on symbols and numbers we saw how we can assign numbers to symbols by omitting the quotation marks. If, however, we include the quotation marks and thus define the numerical value as a "character string", we can still use them as numbers. Consider the following example:

```
$ integer1 = "12"
```

which defines a local symbol to contain a character string comprising of a 1 and a 2. But we are still able to use the "integer1" as a numeric value. We can multiply "integer1" by a number (10 in this example) and store the result in the symbol "sum" as follows:

```
$ sum = integer1 * 10
```

then the character string is converted to a numerical value and we obtain the following result:

```
$ show symbol sum

  SUM = 120    Hex = 00000078   Octal = 00000000170
```

13.2.10 Using symbols to run programs and command procedures

A symbol can be defined to run a program. When the symbol name is entered on the terminal keyboard, the program will be executed. To do this we need to set up a symbol that has as its equivalence name the file specification of the program that is to run. It is important to note that the equivalence string must have a leading dollar sign inserted.

For example, by defining the following symbol:

```
$ check == "$dua1:[compstaff.programs]checkdisk"
```

we can run CHECKDISK.EXE by typing the symbol name, as follows:

```
$ check
```

Similarly, we can run command procedures if we replace the $ by an @:

```
$ test == "@dua0:[engineering.fred]testdat"


$ test
```

which would execute the command procedure TESTDATA.DAT in the directory area specified.

13.2.11 Symbols and lexical functions

Various system information may be available by using lexical functions. The status of print and batch queues, system and user processes, as well as general system information can all be accessed by lexical functions. Other types of lexical function enable manipulation of text strings. A third type enables the user to extract information about files and directories. Their usefulness in these areas makes lexical functions invaluable in writing command procedures. When used in command procedures, they can be used in place of symbols. In the following examples we assign the result of the lexical function to a symbol, using the equals sign; after the assignment, the two must be equivalent and so can be substituted for each other in various expressions.

Lexical functions are identified by a name that always begins with the characters F$. Immediately following the function name is a list of arguments in parentheses.

Many lexical functions are available to the user. All are listed in the VAX/VMS Help facility, along with a short description of their use. In this section we provide an overview and look at a few of the more commonly used commands. First we shall consider how to use lexical functions to obtain system information. In the second and third parts, we deal with string manipulation and with file and directory information.

System lexical functions

System lexical functions provide information on the operating environment. This may be information relating to the computer as a whole, or information associated with a particular user or process. The first function described, F$GETSYI, is a general function, which returns system information of various types depending on the associated arguments. We give two examples here. The other functions mentioned are of a more specific nature.

F$GETSYI

When a new version of the operating system is released by Digital, the minor version number of the software is incremented. For instance if the existing version is 5.2, then the next version would be 5.3. Between the releases of VAX/VMS, other enhancements may be applied to the existing version of the operating system to fix any bugs that were not apparent when the most recent update of the software was released. Any major alterations to the operating system result in a increment of the major version number (i.e. from 4.7 to 5.0).

The lexical function F$GETSYI obtains system information. By specifying "version" as an argument to the function, we can obtain the version number of the operating system that is currently running. This is done by first defining a symbol and equating it to the lexical function, then using the SHOW command to display the result:

```
$ sysversion = f$getsyi("version")

$ show symbol sysversion

  SYSVERSION = "V5.0-2 "
```

In this instance the computer is running major version 5, release 0 of the VAX/VMS operating system. The system has had two (bug) fixes applied to it, as denoted by "-2".

Each computer has a software serial number that identifies it from all the others, similar to a license plate on a car. This enables Digital to license the VAX/VMS software running on this machine, such as the programming languages and the operating system. It also enables hardware engineers uniquely to identify the computer for modification and other purposes.

This number is also obtained by assigning a symbol and using the F$GETSYI lexical function and specifying "SID" (short for system identification) as the argument:

```
$ sysid = f$getsyi("sid")

$ show symbol sysid

  SYSID = 133272462   Hex = 0A000002  Octal = 01200000002
```

F$TIME

By using the F$TIME lexical function, we can find out the time as set by the system clock. F$TIME takes no arguments, but we still need to include the brackets. To find the time, type:

```
$ clock = f$time()

$ show symbol clock

  CLOCK = "18-FEB-1989 11:05:32.10"
```

F$GETJPI

This function takes two arguments, the first being the process number, obtainable by the SHOW PROCESS command, and the second a description of the information to be extracted. We can run a test by asking F$GETJPI to give a user's username. This can then be checked against the SHOW USERS command. This is best shown by the following elementary example:

```
$ show process

19-JUN-1989 10:34:56.75    RTA1:                    User: RAY
Pid: 00001EB5    Proc. name: RAY                    UIC: [12,5]
Priority:    4   Default file spec: PCL$CCSROOT:[RAY]
Devices allocated: RTA1:

$ who = f$getjpi("00001EB5","username")

$ show symbol who

 WHO = "RAY "

$ show user ray

          VAX/VMS Interactive Users
           19-JUN-1989 10:35:44.59
    Total number of interactive users = 19
 Username      Process Name       PID     Terminal
 RAY           RAY              00001EB5  RTA1:
```

F$PROCESS

The lexical function F$PROCESS can be used to find the process name of the user's current process. This is done as follows:

```
$ iam = f$process()

$ show symbol iam

  IAM = "RAY"
```

Character manipulation lexical functions

Lexical functions can be used to calculate the length of a character string, trim strings, extract characters, split the string into sections, and for various other functions. We shall demonstrate their action on applying various lexical functions to a series strings.

F$LENGTH

To find the length of the string, we apply the F$LENGTH lexical function. First we define a symbol to hold the result and call the function, passing as the argument the text string. Then we display the contents of the symbol. This is performed as follows:

```
$ size = f$length("I've got a lovely bunch of coconuts.")

$ show symbol size

  SIZE = 36   Hex = 00000024   Octal = 00000000044
```

Spaces and the full stop are counted as characters.

F$EXTRACT

The function F$EXTRACT selects a portion of a string and stores it in a symbol. It takes three arguments: the position of the start of the characters to be extracted (the first character in the string being position 0); the number of the characters to be extracted; and the name of the string. We can demonstrate F$EXTRACT with the following example, which separates a person's name into three separate fields:

```
$ name = "Mary Jane Smythe"

$ first = f$extract(0,4,name)

$ middle = f$extract(5,4,name)

$ last = f$extract(10,6,name)

$ show symbol first

  FIRST = "MARY"

$ show symbol middle

  MIDDLE = "JANE"

$ show symbol last

  LAST = "SMYTHE"
```

Lexical functions for use with files and directories

F$SEARCH

If we need to check for the existence of a file, we can use the F$SEARCH lexical function. In the following example we shall use F$SEARCH with a single argument, which is the file specification of the file to be found:

```
$ need = f$search("dua1:[student.fred]login.com")

$ show symbol need

  NEED = "DUA1:[STUDENT.FRED]LOGIN.COM;2"
```

If the file cannot be found and the search fails, then when using SHOW to display the symbol, we get:

```
$ show symbol need

  NEED = ""
```

13.2.12 Symbols as values for other symbols

We have already seen in Section 13.2.6 that we can substitute a symbol for a value in expressions. By specifying the symbol name as an argument and omitting the quotation marks, we can pass a symbol as an argument to a lexical function. To demonstrate this we shall rewrite the F$LENGTH example given above but to produce, in its new form, the same result. First, we assign the string to a symbol (as before), then we use the lexical function to calculate the length of the character string assigned to that symbol, and finally display the result.

```
$ string = "I've got a lovely bunch of coconuts."

$ size = f$length(string)

$ show symbol size

  SIZE = 36   Hex = 00000024   Octal = 00000000044
```

All lexical functions can be used in this way.

As shown in the previous example, we can substitute a symbol for a lexical function in expressions. We can also use more than one lexical function in an expression. To demonstrate this, we shall combine the F$LENGTH and F$EXTRACT lexical functions to strip away the first four words, i.e. the first 18 characters and the full stop (denoted by the −1 in the example), and leave us with the string "bunch of coconuts". This is done as follows:

```
$ string = "I've got a lovely bunch of coconuts."

$ newstring = f$extract(18,f$length(string)-1,string)

$ show symbol newstring
```

```
NEWSTRING = "BUNCH OF COCONUTS"
```

We shall discuss the use of symbols to store the logical values, true or false, in Chapter 14 on command procedures.

13.3 Logical Names

Logical names share many similarities with symbols. When declared, a logical name is assigned an equivalence string, called a definition. The definition is interchangeable with the logical name in commands.

By assigning directory specifications to logical names, programs and command procedures can become device independent. That is, if your current default directory is moved to another disk or directory, you only need to change the assignment of one logical name in order to correct all your programs that reference your disk area. Shorter and/or more descriptive logical names can be specified to shorten and clarify commands.

Logical names are stored in four tables: process, job, group, and system. Each logical name defined is in one or more of these tables, depending on its initial definition. The tables are searched in a particular order to locate the required logical name.

There are two methods we can use to create logical names—assign and define. Define is the most commonly used, and as the syntax is different we shall refer only to the define command.

13.3.1 Using logical names

The basic process of creating, using, and deleting logical names is quite simple. In this section we give a quick guide to the major commands.

An example of a logical name definition would be:

```
$ define class dua1:[engineering.students]
```

We can then use "class" to reference the directory DUA1:[ENGINEERING.-STUDENTS]. For example:

```
$ dir class
```

is equivalent to specifying,

```
$ dir dua1:[engineering.students]
```

The SHOW LOGICAL command displays the definition of a logical name:

```
$ show logical class

CLASS = "DUA1:[ENGINEERING.STUDENTS]"  (LNM$PROCESS_TABLE)
```

To delete a logical name, use the DEASSIGN command. The following command removes the logical name "class" from the logical name table:

```
$ deassign class
```

Before we continue to review the logical name commands in detail, we need to obtain an understanding of the tables in which the definitions are stored.

13.3.2 The logical name tables

Logical names and their definitions are stored in tables. The four logical name tables are specified in the order of which they are searched:

- Process table.
- Job table (assigned to your process).
- Group table.
- System table.

Each table itself has a system name: LNM$PROCESS_TABLE, LNM$JOB_xxx, LNM$GROUP_xxx, and LNM$SYSTEM_TABLE. The tables also have their own logical names: LNM$PROCESS, LNM$JOB, LNM$GROUP, and LNM$SYSTEM, respectively. It is simpler to refer to the table you wish to use by specifying its logical name. Two of the system-assigned names—LNM$JOB_xxx and LMN$GROUP_xxx—require further explanation. In the case of the job table, "xxx" is a value (actually an address) known as the job information block which varies from process to process. With the group table, "xxx" is the group part of the user's UIC.

We shall now examine each of these tables in detail. An example of a typical definition for system-defined logical names follows, together with their description in the tables.

The process table—LNM$PROCESS TABLE

This is the default table for logical names when using the DEFINE LOGICAL command. Names in this table are available for your process and subprocesses. When you log in there are various default logical names created by the system. The following are the default logical names created in the process table:

SYS$COMMAND The terminal or file from where DCL commands are

	read. Although commands to VAX/VMS are usually input from the terminal we can input them from a file. Example: _TXA7:
SYS$DISK	Default disk. The disk that contains your directory. Example: DUA1:
SYS$ERROR	The terminal or file to which VAX/VMS sends error messages. Example: _TXA7:
SYS$NET	Defined during task-to-task DECnet operations.
SYS$OUTPUT	The terminal or file to which DCL writes output. Example: _TXA7:
TT	Default device name for terminals. Example: _TXA7:

The job table—LNM$JOB_xxx

All logical names available to your process and to any subprocesses you may have are contained in the job table. Various logical names are placed here by the system when you log in, as are those associated with any magnetic tapes or disks you may mount.

The following job table logical names are defined by the system:

SYS$LOGIN	The default directory specification when you log in. Example: DUA1:[ROBERT]
SYS$LOGIN_DEVICE	The default device when you log in. The is usually the terminal you log in on. Example: DUA1:
SYS$REM_ID	For use with DECnet. The identification of the process on the original computer from which the process was run. Example: ROBERT
SYS$REM_NODE	On DECnet networks the name of the computer from where the job originated. Example: MOLE
SYS$SCRATCH	Default file specification to which temporary files are written. Example: DUA1:[ROBERT]

The group table—LNM$GROUP_xxx

The group table contains logical names that are available to all users with the same group UIC (this is the first half of the user's UIC). To create or delete a logical name in the group table the user's account must have GRPNAM, GRPPRV, or SYSPRV privileges.

The system table—LNM$SYSTEM TABLE

There is the only one system table on the system. It is available to all users. To create and delete entries, a user must have SYSNAM or SYSPRV or a UIC group number less than 10.

There are many default system logical names, which may be employed by all users. Some of them, such as SYS$SYSTEM, SYS$MANAGER and SYS-$HELP are used often, others less frequently. The following is a complete list with an accompanying explanation of the major names:

DBG$INPUT	Initially set to be the same as SYS$INPUT, DBG$INPUT is the default input device for the VAX/VMS debugger. Example: SYS$INPUT:
DBG$OUTPUT	Initially set to be the same as SYS$OUTPUT, DBG$OUTPUT is the default output device for the VAX/VMS debugger. Example: SYS$OUTPUT:
SYS$COMMON	Directory specification for the files that are shared between more than one directory in SYS$SYSROOT. Instead of having two copies in different directories of the same system file, VAX/VMS stores a single copy in the SYS$COMMON directory, with "links" to that directory from the other directories which should contain versions of that file. Example: DUA0:[SYS0.SYSCOMMON.]
SYS$ERRORLOG	Directory specification to which error log files are written. Error logs are data files kept by the system, to keep track of any developing hardware (and system software) faults. Example: SYS$SYSROOT:[SYSERR]
SYS$EXAMPLES	Directory specification of system examples. Example: SYS$SYSROOT:[SYSHLP.EXAMPLES]
SYS$HELP	Directory specification for VAX/VMS Help library. Example: SYS$SYSROOT:[SYSHLP]

SYS$INSTRUCTION	Directory specification for Computer-Based Instruction programs. Example: SYS$SYSROOT:[SYSCBI]
SYS$LIBRARY	Directory specification for programming libraries. Example: SYS$SYSROOT:[SYSLIB]
SYS$LOADABLE_IMAGES	Directory specification for VAX/VMS loadable images. These are programs that are parts of the operating system (such as device drivers) which are loaded into the computer's memory when the computer is booted (started) and remain "resident" (permanently) in memory. Example: SYS$SYSROOT:[SYS$LDR]
SYS$MAINTENANCE	Directory specification of work area used by Digital's engineers. Example: SYS$SYSROOT:[SYSMAINT]
SYS$MANAGER	Directory specification of system files. Essentially all the operating system programs (such as the computer's startup and shutdown programs) which are tailored (by the System Manager) specifically for this computer are stored here. Operating system programs that apply to all VAX/VMS computers are stored in SYS$SYSTEM. Example: SYS$SYSROOT:[SYSMGR]
SYS$MESSAGE	Directory specification of system error message files. Example: SYS$SYSROOT:[SYSMSG]
SYS$NODE	DECnet node name for the host node. Example: MOLE::
SYS$SHARE	Directory specification of shareable images. A shareable image is a file that when loaded into the computer's memory can be used simultaneously by more than one user. Many of the VAX/VMS programming languages such as C, Pascal, FORTRAN, etc., operate in this mode as it greatly reduces the amount of memory needed. Example: SYS$SYSROOT:[SYSLIB]
SYS$SPECIFIC	Directory specification for files specific to this computer in a DECnet network. Example: DUA0:[SYS0.]

SYS$STARTUP	Directory specification for VAX/VMS operating system files during machine boot (startup). Example: SYS$SYSROOT:[SYS$STARTUP]
SYS$SYSDEVICE	Device name of disk containing system files, the areas SYS$SYSTEM, SYS$MANAGER etc. Example: DUA0:
SYS$SYSROOT	Directory specification for the system directories. SYS$SYSROOT is the parent directory of SYS$SYSTEM and SYS$MANAGER. Example: DUA0:[SYS0.]
SYS$SYSTEM	Directory specification for VAX/VMS operating system files, programs, and procedures. Example: SYS$SYSROOT:[SYSEXE]
SYS$TEST	Directory specification for User Environment Test Package (UETP) procedures. After a new piece of Digital software has been installed, (or existing software upgraded) the System Manager has the option to run a UETP on the product to test whether the installation/upgrade was successful. Example: SYS$SYSROOT:[SYSTEST]
SYS$UPDATE	Directory specification for programs that automate the installation of new software. Example: SYS$SYSROOT:[SYSUPD]

Let us now look at each of logical name commands in detail, stating the various options as we proceed.

13.3.3 Defining logical names

Before we use a logical name it must be defined. To do this we run the DEFINE command, specifying the logical name as its first argument and the logical name's definition as the second:

```
$ define mydir dua1:[engineering.bob]
```

This places MYDIR in the process logical name table. We can then use MYDIR to reference the directory DUA1:[ENGINEERING.BOB]. For example:

```
$ dir mydir
```

is equivalent to specifying:

```
$ dir dua1:[engineering.bob]
```

To place a logical name in your process table, specify /PROCESS as a qualifier to the DEFINE command, as follows:

```
$ define/process myhelp dua0:[chris.help]
```

If you have sufficient privileges, you can create logical names in the group or system logical name tables. To do this, specify the table name as a qualifier. For example:

```
$ define/group work dua2:[sales.workfiles]
```

creates a logical name WORK that can be used by all users with the same group UIC. To define a system wide logical name, we use the command:

```
$ define/system ada dua0:[programs.ada]
```

We can also "conceal" a logical name translation. This causes the logical name for a device, rather than the device name, to be shown when executing DCL commands. To do this type:

```
$ define/translation=(concealed) apps dua3:
```

If we are currently using DUA3: and we execute the SHOW DEFAULT command, we receive the following reply:

```
$ show default

  apps:[application.fortran]
```

instead of

```
dua3:[application.fortran]
```

This method enables us to give devices names that relate to their contents and are therefore more meaningful.

If you need to define a logical name that is only going to be used during the execution of a single program and then is no longer required, specify the /USER MODE qualifier. This creates a logical name in the process table, which is automatically deleted following the next VAX/VMS command. For example:

```
$ define/user_mode data_area dua2:[rebecca.data]

$ show symbol data_area

   "DATA_AREA" = "DUA2:[REBECCA.DATA]"  (LNM$PROCESS_TABLE)

$ show symbol data_area

   %SHOW-S-NOTRAN, no translation for logical name DATA_AREA
```

13.3.4 The SHOW LOGICAL command

The SHOW LOGICAL command displays the definition of a logical name. SHOW causes a search of the four logical names tables in the order process, job, group and system, and definition is displayed once it has been located. For example:

```
$ show logical class

   "CLASS" = "USER0:[FRENCH]" (LNM$PROCESS_TABLE)
```

Notice that the table name in which the definition was found is also displayed.

If the logical name is in more than one table, then all the occurrences will be displayed:

```
$ show logical tpu$section

"TPU$SECTION" = "U$PROG:PCL.TPU$SECTION" (LNM$PROCESS_TABLE)
"TPU$SECTION" = "U$PROG:PCL.TPU$SECTION" (LNM$SYSTEM_TABLE)
```

To search individual tables for a logical name we specify the table name as a qualifier to the SHOW command. The following example searches the system table for the definition of SYS$COMMON:

```
$ show logical/system sys$common

"SYS$COMMON" = "DUA0:[SYS0.SYSCOMMON.]" (LNM$SYSTEM_TABLE)
```

Logical name definitions may themselves consist of logical names. When using the SHOW command to display such a logical name, the search of the tables continues until all logical name definitions have been solved. We can illustrate this with the following example, in which the number on the left hand side represents the level of translation, the first level being 0, and the second level 1:

```
$ show logical sys$users

   "SYS$USERS" = "USER0:[SYSTEM$AREA]" (LNM$PROCESS_TABLE)
1  "SYSTEM$AREA" = "[OPERATORS.SCRATCH]" (LNM$PROCESS_TABLE)
```

Note in this example that SYSTEM$AREA is a logical name.

If you wish to list all the logical names defined for your use, use the command SHOW LOGICAL to display the contents of all four tables.

```
$ show logical

(LNM$PROCESS_TABLE)

  "SYS$COMMAND" = "_RTA1:"
  "SYS$DISK" = "PCL$CCSROOT:"
  "SYS$ERROR" = "_RTA1:"
  "SYS$INPUT" = "_RTA1:"
  "SYS$OUTPUT" [super] = "_RTA1:"
  "SYS$OUTPUT" [exec] = "_RTA1:"
  "TPU$SECTION" = "U$PROG:PCL_VT100_TERM.TPU$SECTION"

(LNM$JOB_80849670)

  "LNK$LIBRARY" = "SYS$LIBRARY:VAXCRTL"
  "SYS$LOGIN" = "PCL$CCSROOT:[RAY]"
  "SYS$LOGIN_DEVICE" = "PCL$CCSROOT:"
  ""SYS$REM_ID" = "RAY"
  "SYS$REM_NODE" = "MOLE::"
  "SYS$SCRATCH" = "PCL$CCSROOT:[RAY]"

(LNM$GROUP_000012)

  "CCS" = "PCL$CCSROOT:[CCSTAFF]"

(LNM$SYSTEM_TABLE)

  "ACP$BADBLOCK_MBX" = "MBA3:"
  "APP1" = "DUA1:[APP1.]"
  .
  .
  .
  "SYS$MANAGER" = "SYS$SYSROOT:[SYSMGR]"
  "SYS$MESSAGE" = "SYS$SYSROOT:[SYSMSG]"
  "SYS$MICROVAX" = "0"
  "SYS$NODE" = "MOLE::"
  "SYS$SHARE" = "SYS$SYSROOT:[SYSLIB]"
```

```
"SYS$SPECIFIC" = "DUA0:[SYS0.]"
"SYS$STARTUP" = "SYS$SYSROOT:[SYS$STARTUP]"
     = "SYS$MANAGER"
"SYS$SYSLOGIN" = "PCL$MANAGER:SYSLOGIN.COM"
"SYS$SYSDEVICE" = "DUA0:"
"SYS$SYSDISK" = "SYS$SYSROOT:"
"SYS$SYSROOT" = "DUA0:[SYS0.]"
     = "SYS$COMMON:"
"SYS$SYSTEM" = "SYS$SYSROOT:[SYSEXE]"
.
.
.
"USER0" = "DUA2:"
"USER1" = "DUA3:"
"WSC" = "PCL$PUBROOT:[WSC]"
```

We have displayed only a sample above; there are in fact about 200 logical names defined on the system (of which 20 are local to the process, none are in the group table, and 175 are in the system table).

The command SHOW TRANSLATION searches through the four logical name tables and displays the first definition of a logical name, along with the table in which it was found. For example:

```
$ show translation tpusecini

TPU$SECTION" = "U$PROG:PCL_VT100.TPU$SECTION" (LNM$PROCESS_TABLE)
```

The SHOW TRANSLATION command does not continue searching the tables once it has found the definition. This means that any logical names that are used in a logical name's definition do not get translated. We can demonstrate this with the following example, which uses the first logical name defined in the definition of the second:

```
$ define work_area [operator.scratch]

$ define tools work_area

$ show translation tools

TOOLS = "WORK_AREA"  (LNM$PROCESS_TABLE)
```

We can now use the SHOW command to translate the logical name fully:

```
$ show logical tools

    "TOOLS" = "WORK_AREA" (LNM$PROCESS_TABLE)
  1  "WORK_AREA" = "[OPERATORS.SCRATCH]" (LNM$PROCESS_TABLE)
```

This is important as lexical functions and some VAX/VMS commands when used with logical names do not fully expand the definition. To check how some commands may be viewing your use of logical names, use the SHOW TRANSLATION command.

A feature of the SHOW TRANSLATION command is that it is memory resident. This means that if you are running a program or command procedure and press ⟨Ctrl⟩Y to halt its execution, you can then use the SHOW TRANSLATION command to display the current definitions of the logical names employed in the program, before continuing the program execution by typing CONTINUE. Using SHOW LOGICAL while a program is temporarily interrupted causes the program to exit.

13.3.5 Using logical names

Before we continue, let us examine how some of the system logical names are used. First notice that in the definitions of the logical names of the system table (pp. 233–238), the definitions of SYS$LIBRARY and SYS$SHARE are identical. That is:

```
SYS$LIBRARY = "SYS$SYSROOT:[SYSLIB]"

SYS$SHARE = "SYS$SYSROOT:[SYSLIB]"
```

This demonstrates that two logical names can have the same definition.

Also from pp. 233–238 notice that many of the logical names use the SYS$SYSROOT logical name in their definition. This makes it simple to move all the system files to another area or disk. By simply changing the definition for SYS$SYSROOT, to reflect that new area, and copying the system files to the new area, all logical names, programs, and procedures that use the SYS$SYSROOT logical name still work. This facility offers a great deal of flexibility.

As an example, we shall consider a few of SYS0's subdirectories:

```
SYS$SYSROOT = DUA0:[SYS0.]

SYS$SYSTEM  = SYS$SYSROOT:[SYSEXE]  = DUA0:[SYS0.SYSEXE]

SYS$MANAGER = SYS$SYSROOT:[SYSMGR]  = DUA0:[SYS0.SYSMGR]

SYS$SYSHLP  = SYS$SYSROOT:[SYSHLP]  = DUA0:[SYS0.SYSHLP]

SYS$UPDATE  = SYS$SYSROOT:[UPDATE]  = DUA0:[SYS0.UPDATE]
```

To move to another disk we copy all the files and modify the definition of SYS$SYSROOT, so we now have DUA1 instead of DUA0:

```
SYS$SYSROOT = DUA1:[SYS0.]
```

```
SYS$SYSTEM  = SYS$SYSROOT:[SYSEXE]  = DUA1:[SYS0.SYSEXE]

SYS$MANAGER = SYS$SYSROOT:[SYSMGR]  = DUA1:[SYS0.SYSMGR]

SYS$SYSHLP  = SYS$SYSROOT:[SYSHLP]  = DUA1:[SYS0.SYSHLP]

SYS$UPDATE  = SYS$SYSROOT:[UPDATE]  = DUA1:[SYS0.UPDATE]
```

Notice that some directory definitions, such as SYS$SYSROOT, end with ".]"; this is so we can use it as a "device name" in the file specification for its subdirectories. For instance, compare the logical translation for SYS$SYSTEM with a user's directory:

```
SYS$SYSROOT:[SYSEXE]

DUA1:[RICHARD]
```

This shows that if we define a logical name ending in ".]" instead of "]", we can then use that logical name (i.e. SYS$SYSROOT) as we would a device name (i.e. DUA1) in directory specifications.

The next section considers an example of the existence of two or more logical names appearing in different logical name tables.

13.3.6 Translating logical names

The system will translate any logical names specified on a command line into its definition before the command is executed. This can be viewed as substituting the definition for the logical name in the command line. The order in which the logical name tables are searched to locate a logical name is specified by two further tables—the logical name directory tables. The default order is job, process, group, and system tables. We need to consider this, as the first definition found will be the one used. We can show an example of this by putting a logical name into two separate tables. Notice that the second definition is never used by this process. The following example uses a logical name TEST$TEMP, which is defined in both process and group tables:

```
$ define/group temp$test dua0:[test.group]

$ define temp$test dua1:[process]

$ show logical temp$test

  "TEMP$TEST" = "DUA1:[PROCESS]" (LNM$PROCESS_TABLE)
  "TEMP$TEST" = "DUA0:[TEST.GROUP]" (LNM$GROUP_000012)
```

```
$ dir temp$test

Directory DUA1:[PROCESS]

DIR.LIS;1       LISTING.COM;1     PROGDEV.LOG;1    SORT.TXT;1
SYM.LOG;1

Total of 5 files.
```

Using the SHOW TRANSLATION command helps to clarify which definition will be used:

```
$ show translation temp$test

  TEMP$TEST = "DUA1:[PROCESS]" (LNM$PROCESS_TABLE)
```

If we subsequently deleted the process table definition, then the first definition for the logical name would be in the group table and that would be translated. For example:

```
$ deassign temp$test

$ show logical temp$test

"TEMP$TEST" = "DUA0:[TEST.GROUP]" (LNM$GROUP_000012)

$ dir temp$test

Directory DUA0:[TEST.GROUP]

AAP2.LOG;1        ADD.C;11          ADD.COM;3       ADD1.C;5

Total of 4 files.
```

13.3.7 Using logical names in logical name definitions

When we use a logical name as part of a longer file specification, the logical name must appear on the leftmost side of the specification, and must be separated from the remainder of the file specification by a colon. An everyday example of this is the SYS$HELP (also SYS$SYSTEM and SYS$MANAGER) logical names. We shall use SYS$HELP in the example that follows.

SYS$HELP is a logical name in the system table which has as its definition the directory specification for the VAX/VMS Help files. As part of this, the directory specification is a logical name SYS$SYSROOT. If we expand the logical name definition, we get:

```
SYS$HELP = SYS$SYSROOT:[SYSHLP]
```

where

```
SYS$SYSROOT = DUA0:[SYS0.]
```

therefore

```
SYS$HELP = DUA0:[SYS0.SYSHLP]
```

If we wish to list the files in this area, we can use the DIRECTORY command as follows:

```
$ directory dua0:[sys0.syshlp]
```

We can use the logical name SYS$SYSROOT in the directory specification as follows:

```
$ directory sys$sysroot:[syshlp]*.hlp

Directory SYS$SYSROOT:[SYSHLP]

EVE.HLP;1    EVE_TVI.HLP;1    HELPLIB.HLP;1     ORACLE.HLP;2

Total of 4 files.

Directory SYS$COMMON:[SYSHLP]

RDBERROR_HELP.HLP;1 RDBHELP.HLP;1 RDMLHELP.HLP;1

Total of 4 files.

Grand total of 2 directories, 7 files.
```

Notice the use of the colon between the logical name and the directory name. Notice also that the directory name needs to be in square brackets. The directory specification can be referred to by its logical name SYS$HELP:

```
$ dir sys$help:*.hlp
Directory SYS$SYSROOT:[SYSHLP]

EVE.HLP;1    EVE_TVI.HLP;1    HELPLIB.HLP;1     ORACLE.HLP;2

Total of 4 files.

Directory SYS$COMMON:[SYSHLP]

RDBERROR_HELP.HLP;1 RDBHELP.HLP;1 RDMLHELP.HLP;1

Total of 4 files.

Grand total of 2 directories, 7 files.
```

13.3.8 The DEASSIGN command

A logical name can be deleted by using the DEASSIGN command. The following command deletes the logical name TEST from the process logical name table:

```
$ deassign test
```

Logical names in other tables may also be deleted by specifying the table name as a qualifier to the DEASSIGN command. You will need to have sufficient privileges to delete names from the system and group tables. To delete a logical name called PIG$SCRATCH from the system table:

```
$ deassign/system pig$scratch
```

All logical names in the process and job tables are deleted automatically when you log out of the computer.

13.3.9 Search lists

A search list is a logical name that has a list of equivalent names. When a logical name is used, the first equivalence name in the search list is translated and that area is searched. If a match is not found, then the second equivalence string in the list is translated and that area searched. The process is continued until a match is found. Let us look at an example:

```
$ define datafiles [chris.old_data],[chris.new_data]
```

defines the logical name DATAFILES to have two equivalence names. We can show this by using the SHOW LOGICAL command:

```
$ show logical datafiles

 "DATAFILES" = "[CHRIS.OLD_DATA]" (LNM$PROCESS_TABLE)
   = "[CHRIS.NEW_DATA]"
```

When we use the logical name first, the directory [CHRIS.OLD_DATA] is checked, if the file is not found, then [CHRIS.NEW_DATA] is searched. For instance, if we use the command:

```
$ dir datafiles:work.dat

Directory USER0:[CHRIS.OLD_DATA]

WORK.DAT;23

Total of 1 file, 1 block.
```

then given the previous DEFINE statement, this would first cause a search of the directory [CHRIS.OLD_DATA] for the file WORK.DAT, and then the directory [CHRIS.NEW_DATA]. Once the file is located, the search terminates. In the example above the file was in directory [CHRIS.OLD_DATA].

If, however, we had specified all files with the file extension .DAT by using the wildcard asterisk, then the search would not end when the first occurrence was detected but would continue until all the directories specified in the search list had been examined. As an example (again using the previous define):

```
$ dir datafiles:*.dat

Directory USER0:[CHRIS.OLD_DATA]

SEARCH.DAT;1

Total of 1 file, 1 block.

Directory USER0:[CHRIS.NEW_DATA]

FILE1.DAT;1          FILE2.DAT;2

Total of 2 files.
```

Notice that the names of the directories are displayed in the order of the search list in which the files were found. If no files are found, an error message to this effect will be displayed.

Let us look at another example. If we wish to search for a file called REPORT.LOG and print it out on the main printer, we could define a search list to look for it in certain areas and then print it out. We would need to define a logical name and an equivalence search list:

```
$ define test user0:[test1],user1:[test2]
```

To check this we use the SHOW LOGICAL command:

```
$ show logical test

 "TEST" = "USER0:[TEST1]" (LNM$PROCESS_TABLE)
  = "USER1:[TEST2]"
```

Then to search for the file, and if it is found to print it

```
$ print test:report.log

Job REPORT (queue SYS$PRINT, entry 18) started on SYS$PRINT
```

this initiates a search and subsequent printing of the first file found that matches the following file specifications:

```
user0:[test1]report.log
```

or

```
user1:[test2]report.log
```

13.4 Customizing the VAX/VMS Environment—the LOGIN.COM File

It is useful to use symbols and logical names to customize your environment to your particular needs when you log in. This is done by placing selected symbol and logical name definitions in a file called LOGIN.COM. As the name may suggest, LOGIN.COM is a command file that runs automatically when the user logs in to the computer. An example LOGIN.COM file is given in Appendix C, and the topic is discussed further in Chapter 14.

In this section we shall concern ourselves with symbols and logical names that we may like to include in LOGIN.COM or in any other command file we may create to customize the VAX/VMS environment for our needs.

13.4.1 Useful symbols

Here we give examples of some useful symbol definitions.

Useful directory symbols

```
$ dsd :== directory/size/date

$ dop :== directory/owner/protection
```

In the example above we have set up two symbols and defined the equivalent strings, which are quite lengthy but nevertheless commonly used commands. This greatly reduces the amount of typing needed to execute the command. When defining symbols such as this, ensure that not only is the symbol unique (for instance we cannot set up a symbol called "dir" as it would be confused with the VMS DIRECTORY command), but also make sure that the name of the symbol is easy to remember.

```
$ nodir   :== directory/size/date/exclude=*.dir
```

Setting up this symbol and typing NODIR will produce a directory listing of all files in the current directory, but excluding any subdirectories.

Symbols to call lexical functions

```
$ u_i_c     =     f$getjpi("","UIC")
```

By defining symbols to be equivalent to lexical functions calls, we provide a quick and easy method of obtaining system information. The example above provides a call to F$GETJPI (get job process information) to obtain the UIC of the current process.

Symbols to run command files or programs

```
$ setenv   :==   @user0:[ray.test]set_environment.com
```

We can assign the name of a command file to a symbol. By placing symbol and logical name definitions in this file, we can run this file to provide a new environment.

In the example above we have created a file that sets up a particular environment, e.g. for program testing. By placing a @ in front of the definition string, we can execute the file by simply typing the symbol name (SETENV).

```
$ logout := @staff$accounts:logout.com
```

If the symbol above is defined by a group of users, it can be used to run a common procedure to be run on LOGOUT. The directory the procedure LOGOUT.COM is kept in must be accessible by the staff who need to use it and is specified by the logical name STAFF$ACCOUNTS.

```
$ salary :== run prog$development:tax_calculator
```

The symbol defined above runs a program call TAX_CALCULATOR.EXE whose directory has been defined previously by the logical name PROG$DEVELOPMENT.

Symbol to run a mail editor

```
$ mail :== mail/edit
```

By default, typing MAIL to use the MAIL utility does not cause the EVE screen editor to be loaded. Typing MAIL/EDIT does. By defining the symbol above the editor is automatically loaded when using MAIL's SEND command.

After the symbol has been defined, in order not to load the editor, we need to run mail with the /NOEDIT qualifier.

Symbols to rename commands

```
$ his*tory :== recall/all
```

If we wish we can use symbols to provide equivalent names for some of the VMS commands. The example above allows the user to type HISTORY (which can be abbreviated to HIS) instead of RECALL/ALL to recall the last 20 commands onto the screen.

Some users can use symbols in this way to customize their environment on VAX/VMS to be similar to another operating system (such as Unix, or MS-DOS) that they may be more familiar with.

Further examples of symbols to provide a Unix-type environment within VMS are:

```
$ ls :== directory

$ who :== show users

$ more :== type/page

$ cd :== set default
```

13.4.2 Useful logical names

Logical names are useful to define certain directories containing files of a particular sort or files that are required for a particular purpose. For example, we could define:

```
$ define project dua0:[staff.chris.programs]
```

then we could use the command:

```
$ @project:add

$ run project:subtract
```

to run the command procedure ADD.COM and the image file SUB-TRACT.EXE, respectively.

Or to set our current directory to DUA0:[STAFF.CHRIS.PROGRAMS], we could specify:

```
$ set default project
```

As long as this logical name was redefined each time we logged in (presumably by placing its definition in LOGIN.COM) we could make use of it in any command procedures we wrote.

Defining logical names in this way provides a method of making the programs we write device independent. If, for example, we had to move all our programs to another disk, say DUA3, or another directory area, all we would need to do is change the logical name assignment and all the programs that make use of that assignment would continue to work.

Chapter

14

Writing Command Procedures

14.1 Introduction

A command procedure is a program that has been written in the DCL (Digital Command Language). So far we have only used DCL as a method of directly inputting command lines to VAX/VMS and having these commands interpreted and performed interactively by DCL. We show in this chapter how to group DCL commands together in a file and run them in the same way as we would a program in a high level programming language such as FORTRAN or C.

Command procedures need not contain only DCL commands, but can include statements to provide flow control equivalent to the FOR, WHILE, and IF statements available in most high-level programming languages. Other statements can read in data from files, or access data contained directly in the command procedure itself.

Although command procedures can be devised that are capable of performing many of the tasks of programs written in a high-level programming language, command procedures are not compiled or assembled, but are run directly. This makes them less efficient and also slower to execute compared with a program written in a programming language to perform the same function. However, for applications where one has to interact directly with VAX/VMS, they are preferred.

A typical application is to use the computer's batch queue; here we need to create a command procedure and then "submit" this to the batch queue. When placing the procedure in the queue, we may specify as a qualifier a time when we wish the procedure to start execution. By making use of this facility, we can execute a series of DCL commands at any time of the day or night. This is also useful if we need to execute a procedure at the same time every day. For more information on batch jobs see Chapter 9.

This chapter starts by looking at a very simple command procedure, followed by a brief section on format, and then continues by looking at the more advanced examples. The last two sections look at two special procedures—LOGIN.COM and LOGOUT.COM—giving examples of each.

14.2 A Simple Command Procedure

First we shall consider the commands we would need to type to VMS to produce a directory listing, and then how we could automate this function by placing the commands in a command procedure.

In order to keep track of the files in a directory at any one time we issue the DCL command DIRECTORY. By specifying the /SIZE and /DATE qualifiers we can extract more information, such as the number of blocks the files occupies of our disk space, and the date and the time the file was created. To do this we type:

```
$ directory/size/date

Directory PCL$CCSROOT:[RAY.HOME]

ADD.C;11                 2  23-MAY-1989 11:02:49.91
CHAP13.LOG;1             0   2-JUN-1989 12:17:56.28
F.C;1                    1  17-DEC-1986 17:01:15.65
LISTING.COM;1            1   2-JUN-1989 12:17:12.00
OLDUSER.C;32            22  10-FEB-1988 17:17:32.92
OPS_OLDUSER.C;2         21  10-FEB-1988 15:56:20.66
TEST1.LOG;1              5   1-JUN-1989 15:54:40.92
WORLD.C;1                1  17-FEB-1989 09:09:13.50

Total of 8 files, 53 blocks.
```

If we then wish to output the listing to a file, instead of the screen, we need to type the ASSIGN command immediately before and the DEASSIGN command immediately after the DIRECTORY command (ASSIGN and DEASSIGN are covered in Chapter 4). In addition, the SHOW TIME command is combined with the directory information request to display the time and date at which the directory listing was taken. So we have the following:

```
$ assign directory.lis sys$output

$ show time

$ directory/size/date

$ deassign sys$output
```

We can then output the contents of DIRECTORY.LIS on the printer by using the print command as usual (by adding the /DELETE qualifier we delete the file from our directory after printing):

```
$ print directory.lis/delete
```

If we wish to keep a regular check on a directory, we need to perform the above series of statements regularly. Obviously, we can save time and effort by automating this set of instructions, by creating a command procedure file that contains these commands. To do this, we run the editor EVE, specifying a file name with an extension of .COM:

```
$ edit/tpu listing.com
```

We then type in the commands exactly as we would enter them to the system, with the exception that each command line needs to begin with a dollar sign, i.e. the VAX/VMS prompt needs to be entered as well. The file is typed as shown in Figure 14-1. Then we exit from the editor. The first line is a comment to tell us what the program does. Comments in command procedure begin with $! instead of a single dollar sign. Everything on a line following the exclamation mark is not executed when the program runs. To run the procedure we press the @ followed by the program name:

```
$ @listing

Job DIRECTORY (queue SYS$PRINT, entry 216) started on SYS$PRINT
```

```
$! Program to produce a Directory listing in a file
$  assign directory.lis sys$output
$  show time
$  directory/size/date
$  deassign sys$output
$  print directory.lis/delete
[End of file]

Buffer: LISTING.COM                 Insert      Forward

Command: exit
```

Fig. 14-1 Screen display showing the procedure LISTING.COM.

Since we have chosen the default file name extension .COM, we do not need to specify the file extension.

Notice that when running this procedure, the commands are not displayed on the screen as they are executed. This is because by default VERIFY was switched off. If you wish to see the procedure being executed—useful when debugging—type the following command before running the command procedure:

```
$ set verify

$ @listing

! Program to produce a Directory listing in a file
$ assign directory.lis sys$output
$ print directory.lis/delete
Job DIRECTORY (queue SYS$PRINT, entry 217) started on SYS$PRINT
```

To switch verification off again, type:

```
$ set noverify
```

If you always wish to see the procedure being executed, you can include the VERIFY command at the top of the procedure.

Now that we have seen how to create command procedures, before we progress to develop their useful features let us proceed to look at the rules governing their syntax.

14.3 Executing Command Procedures

Command procedures may be run either interactively from DCL, or from another command procedure; they can also be placed into a batch queue, to execute at a specified time, as well as run on remote nodes in a DECnet network. In this section we shall look at each of these in turn.

14.3.1 Running command procedures

To run a command procedure, type @ followed by the filename:

```
$ @test
```

There is no need to specify .COM when we run any command procedure with extension .COM as this is the default file extension. To execute a command procedure in a directory other than the current one, we need to add the directory path or the complete specification. For example:

```
$ @user0:[staff.rebecca.commands]test
```

This refers to a file called TEST.COM in a subdirectory REBECCA (where REBECCA is itself a subdirectory of STAFF).

It is usual to assign symbols, or logical names, to a command procedure's file description so that they can be executed easily from any directory. To define a local logical name for the command procedure, use the DEFINE command as shown in the following example:

```
$ define test user0:[staff.rebecca.commands]test
```

We can then run the command procedure TEST.COM from any directory by simply typing:

```
$ @test
```

Alternatively, we could assign a global symbol to a command procedure. An example is shown below. The second command will execute the procedure:

```
$ test == "@user0:[staff.rebecca.commands]test"

$ test
```

By creating symbols and logical names for commonly used command procedures in a LOGIN.COM file, we can save ourselves the trouble of redefining them each time we log in.

14.3.2 Command procedures to run command procedures

It is possible to run a second command procedure from inside a command procedure by placing the RUN command inside the first procedure:

```
$ @procedure1
.
.
.
Procedure 1
.
.
.
$ @user0:[cleaners]tidy_up
.
.
.
Procedure 1
```

would execute TIDY_UP.COM in the directory USER0:[CLEANERS]. As with running the commands from DCL command level, we can create logical names and symbols that refer to the full directory specification of the files. In the case of the symbols shown below, we may choose to make these local to the procedure, thus:

```
$ set verify

$ test = "@pcl$ccsroot:[ray.home]listing"

$ test

$ show symbol test

 TEST = @pcl$ccsroot:[ray.home]listing
```

Since the symbol is defined as local, when the procedure has been completed, the symbol TEST will no longer be defined on return to the DCL command level. Using the SHOW SYMBOL command will give us:

```
$ show symbol test
%DCL-W-UNDSYM, undefined symbol - check validity and spelling
```

This facility of using local procedures is useful if we wish to redefine an existing symbol for use in a command procedure. As soon as the procedure finishes execution, the original value will be recovered. Note, however, that if we wish to retain the redefined symbol, then we would use a global definition.

14.3.3 Running command procedures over DECnet

This section describes how to execute a command procedure on another (remote) computer in a DECnet network.

To run a command procedure on a remote node in a DECnet network we use the TYPE command. This is not the same TYPE command we use to display the contents of files on the screen. If you wish to run a command procedure in the default DECnet account, enter TYPE followed by the node name of the remote computer, two colons ("::"), then TASK=COMMAND_PROCEDURE (where COMMAND_PROCEDURE is the name of the procedure to be executed). For example:

```
$ type stoat::"task=node_users.com"
```

would execute the NODE_USERS.COM file at a remote computer called STOAT and, after execution of the command, return to the current computer.

In the default DECnet account there are usually general procedures that require no additional privileges for their execution.

To execute a command procedure in another user's account, you need the username and the associated password. The username and password are placed in quotation marks between the node name and the double colons. Thus if the username is LESLIE and the password DOGFOOD, the command would be:

```
$ type stoat"leslie dogfood"::"task=node_users.com"
```

Notice that the password appears on the screen!!

14.4 Command Procedure Levels

Before continuing, we shall briefly review the protocol of DCL command levels. Commands entered after the DCL dollar prompt (DCL command level) are being executed at level 0. If, however, we run a command procedure, or use the CALL statement to run a subroutine, then this will be at command level 1. If this command procedure, or subroutine, then runs a second procedure, or subroutine, then this will be at level 2, and so on up to a possible 32 levels. As each command procedure, or subroutine, terminates, the execution will continue at the calling command procedure, or subroutine level, that is at the next lower level. The STOP command will return directly to level 0.

When using local symbols, we need to keep track of the command level at which a procedure is being currently executed. The highest level is the DCL command level, i.e. level 0, and the lowest command level 31.

14.5 Default Input/Output Logical Names

When we log in to VAX/VMS, the operating system automatically defines for us the logical names associated with input/output. These are shown below with typical values:

```
sys$input = txa2:
sys$output = txa2:
sys$command = txa2:
sys$error = txa2:
sys$login = dua0:[sales.shark]
sys$scratch = dua0:[sales.shark]
```

As we can see, each of these are defined by default to have an equivalence string of TXA2: (i.e. the user's terminal), or the user's default directory.

TXA2: represents the terminal. Therefore by default all input and output is directed to the terminal. We can, however, change each of these defaults by reassigning them to some other device. For example, to accept input from a file called INPUT.DAT instead of from a terminal (i.e. the keyboard), we can reassign SYS$INPUT as follows:

```
$ assign sys$input input.dat
```

To redirect output to a file called OUTPUT.DAT, we can similarly reassign SYS$OUTPUT:

```
$ assign sys$output output.dat
```

Such a redirection of input and output can be very useful to input and output data to/from command procedures, especially if they are being run in a batch queue.

To reassign the logical names back to the defaults, we use the DEASSIGN command:

```
$ deassign sys$input

$ deassign sys$output
```

14.6 Major Command Procedure Statements

We have already seen that we need to precede each command in the procedure with a dollar sign, but there are other forms of syntax that must also be obeyed. Here we list the main syntax rules, and give short examples of their use.

14.6.1 Commands

All commands, comments, or labels must start with a dollar sign:

```
$ show users
```

14.6.2 Data

Lines containing data do *not* start with a dollar, i.e. they are placed on their own lines.

```
fred
barbara
sara
```

14.6.3 Continuation

If you need to use commands that are over 80 characters in length, then you can break the command into a number of shorter lines using a combination of the minus sign (−) and underscore ("_") symbols. When typing the program into the computer via the editor, if you wish to continue the command on another line, type a minus sign at the end, press ⟨return⟩ and start the new line with an underscore before the dollar sign. For example:

```
$ inquire/nopunctuation variable_number_one -
_$ "Please input your first value now"
```

14.6.4 Comments

Comments are very important in making a procedure easily understandable for yourself and for anyone else who may need to use it. Lines containing comments start with a dollar immediately followed by a exclamation sign, i.e. $!. All the information that follows the exclamation sign is ignored by the command interpreter, until either the next dollar or the next exclamation sign is reached. In the first example that follows, the whole line is a comment. In the second, only the section following the exclamation mark is a comment while the third type shows how to use the ! as an exclamation mark and not a comment marker, by enclosing the exclamation sign in between quotation marks.

```
$! The whole of this line is a comment.

$ show users ! This part is the comment.

$ write sys$output "What comment !"
```

We can use a dollar sign followed by an exclamation sign, without anything on the line, in order to make it easier to read by breaking the procedure into segments. If you leave blank lines in a command procedure, the DCL will complain and produce an error message.

```
.
.
.
$! End of Section 1

$!

$! Start of Section 2
.
.
.
```

14.6.5 Labels

Labels are used to mark the beginning of a section of code to which reference can be made. The code is executed conditionally on the result of a test, usually a

GOTO statement or a GOSUB or CALL statement being valid. Labels may be up to 255 characters in length. They must not contain blank spaces, and they must finish with a colon. It is usually helpful, when viewing a command procedure, if all the labels are placed next to the dollar sign, without an intervening space. This makes the structure of the procedure more obvious (the interpreter will not complain if you do not do this). An example of a label would be:

```
$finished:
```

and an example of a reference to it would be:

```
$ goto finished
```

14.6.6 The INQUIRE command

The INQUIRE command is used for prompting the user for some input when a procedure is being run interactively (obviously we can not input data directly to a procedure if the procedure is running in a batch queue). The command can output a character string, which can be used to ask the user for an input. It reads in the reply from the user and stores it in a symbol. The following example asks the user to input a directory specification and then assigns the input to a local symbol MYDIR:

```
$ inquire mydir "Please input name of directory"
```

This results in the following message on the terminal:

```
Please input name of directory:
```

Notice that the DCL interrupter has added a colon to the end of the line. To suppress this, add the /NOPUNCTUATION qualifier, as follows:

```
$ inquire/nopunctuation mydir "Please input name of directory"
```

which then displays:

```
Please input name of directory
```

If we wish to store the user's input, which is interpreted by DCL as a character string, in a global symbol, instead of a local symbol, we add /GLOBAL as a command qualifier, as shown below:

```
$ inquire/global mydir "Please input name of directory"
```

As a final point, all the user's input is converted to uppercase characters, with tabs and multiple spaces converted to a single space. To prevent this, place the user's input in quotation marks. You can ask the user to do this, as part of the prompt. For example:

```
$ inquire name "Input your full name in quotation marks"
```

The user would then input their name surrounded by quotation marks:

```
"Donald Richard"
```

14.6.7 Error handling—SET ON and SET NOON commands

The ON command has two forms: ON and NOON (not on). Both are used for error handling.

When an error occurs, VMS provides an indication of its severity by placing a value in the symbol $SEVERITY. These values range between 0 and 4:

0 Warning
1 Success
2 Error
3 Information
4 Fatal

When an error occurs with the ON command set, the severity of the error is taken into account. According to the severity of the error level the following actions are taken.

1. The error is displayed on the screen.
2. Any action (usually in the form of a GOTO) specified by the ON command is carried out.
3. The control is not returned to the next higher command level, instead the fact that an error has occurred is noted and any subsequent errors (which occur before an ON or SET or NOON statement) cause the current procedure to be terminated, with control being returned to the next highest DCL level.

If the error is not of a particularly high level, the command procedure will display the error message and then continue execution.

For example, if an error occurs, the command:

```
$ on error then goto error_handling
```

will cause the program flow to jump to an error-handling routine.

The following command can be used to deal with any warning messages:

```
$ on warning then goto dodgy
```

were DODGY is the label of a routine that processes any errors.

The SET NOON command and SET ON commands disable and enable error checking. Any errors occurring after a SET NOON command and preceding any SET ON command cause an error message to be displayed, but without any further action being taken. For instance:

```
$ set noon      ! Turns error trapping off
.
.
.
$ set on        ! Set error trapping on

$ on error then goto trap_errors
.
.
.
$trap_errors:

$ write sys$output "An ERROR has occurred"
```

14.6.8 ⟨Ctrl⟩Y handling—CONTROL=Y and NOCONTROL=Y commands

Normally, by pressing ⟨Ctrl⟩Y or ⟨Ctrl⟩C, a user can terminate and exit from a running command procedure. There are occasions when this ability is a drawback. We can prevent the user exiting by disabling ⟨Ctrl⟩Y. We include the following commands in the command procedure, to switch the action of ⟨Ctrl⟩Y off and on respectively:

```
$ set nocontrol=y    ! STOP user exiting by pressing <Ctrl>Y
.
.
.
$ set control=y      ! ALLOW user to exit by pressing <Ctrl>Y
```

Alternatively we can specify certain actions to occur:

```
$ on control_y then goto break_out
.
.
.
$break_out:

$ write sys$output "User tried to terminate procedure !!"
```

This causes program flow to continue at the label BREAK_OUT if a user tries to exit from the procedure with ⟨Ctrl⟩Y. This method is preferred because it enables the user to exit in an orderly manner from the procedure.

14.6.9 The READ command

The READ command is similar to the INQUIRE command in as much as it can be used for reading in data while the procedure is being run. Unlike INQUIRE, however, you can specify from which source, i.e. terminal or file, the response is to be read from. Also, READ accepts character strings exactly as they are input and does not convert characters to uppercase, or suppress tabs. By default, the read statement will prompt with DATA: although we can change this by using the /PROMPT= qualifier.

The command syntax is READ, followed by the name of the input source. We can specify the logical names SYS$COMMAND and SYS$INPUT, which default respectively to the terminal or to the name of a file from which data is to be read. The last parameter is the name of the symbol in which the data is to be stored. Let us consider the following example:

```
$ read sys$input name
```

This reads a character string for SYS$INPUT (by default the terminal) and places it in the symbol name.

The user will be prompted by DATA:, although by specifying READ/PROMPT=NAME: instead of READ we can change this prompt to NAME:

```
$ read sys$command answer
```

This will read in a character string from SYS$COMMAND, by default the terminal, and store it in the symbol ANSWER. When run, the command will produce the prompt:

```
DATA:
```

To alter this we use the /PROMPT= qualifier to give the prompt, ANSWER:

```
$ read/prompt="Name: "  sys$command answer
```

prompts with:

```
Name:
```

To read from a file we must first open the file (using the OPEN command described below), and then access the logical name specified in the OPEN command. For example, if we specified the logical name DATAFILE, then to read data from the file and assign it to a symbol DATA_IN we would use the command:

```
$ read datafile data_in
```

If this statement was part of a loop and we wish to keep reading data from the file until we reach the end of the file, we use the /END_OF_FILE=label qualifier. Here "label" is the name of a label to "jump" to when all the data in the file has been read. For example, if the statement above was in a loop that read data from a file, to check for the end of the file we would use:

```
$ open/read datafile results.dat

$ read/end_of_file=data_finished datafile data_in
.
.
.
$data_finished:
.
.
.
```

14.6.10 The OPEN command

To open a file for reading, writing, or appending to, we use the OPEN command. To open a file for reading we use the command along with the /READ qualifier as follows:

```
$ open/read datafile results.dat
```

This opens the file called RESULTS.DAT in the current directory and assigns to it the logical name DATAFILE. It is this logical name that we use from this point onwards to access the file.

To open a file for appending to, we specify the /APPEND qualifier:

```
$ open/append addfile result.dat
```

This will cause data written to the file, such as shown below, to be added onto the end of the data currently stored in the file RESULTS.DAT:

```
$ write addfile  "23 34 34 24 23 34 24 63"
```

To open a file for writing, we use the OPEN command with the /WRITE qualifier:

```
$ open/write newfile "newdata.dat"
```

If the file NEWDATA.DAT does not exist, a file of that name will be created. If NEWDATA.DAT exists, a new version of that file will be created.

By using the /ERROR=label qualifier with the OPEN command, it is possible to check if the open statement was executed successfully. The /ERROR=label qualifier will cause the flow of execution in the procedure to jump to a label. This is useful for suppressing VAX/VMS error messages to the user and either running an error correcting routine inside the command procedure, or displaying a message informing the user of the error and any corrective action that may be taken.

```
$ open/append/error=no_file append_file update.dat
.
.
.
$ exit

$no_file:

$ write sys$output "Cannot append to file UPDATE.DAT"

$ write sys$output "Please correct and run procedure again"

$ exit
```

The /ERROR=label qualifier only works on OPEN, READ, and WRITE commands.

14.6.11 The CLOSE command

The CLOSE command closes a file after we have finished reading, writing or appending to it. The file may subsequently be reopened for other operations. The form of the command is CLOSE followed by the logical name we have assigned as a pointer to the file. For example, the procedure may be:

```
$ open/read in_file dodgy.dat

$ read in_file data_line

$ close dodgy.dat
```

which will read the first line of a file called DODGY.DAT.

14.6.12 The GOTO command

This command causes the flow of the program to go from one section of the code to another. Usually the section of code executed depends on the result of a test.

The simplest form of the GOTO command, is, for example:

```
$ goto finished
.
.
.
$finished:
```

which would cause the procedure to "jump" to the label FINISHED:. It would then start executing the code following the label. Usually GOTOs are conditional on the outcome of a test, which are introduced in the IF statement as described below.

14.6.13 The IF statement

The IF statement evaluates a test to give a boolean logical "true" or "false" answer. In its simplest form, the command comprises of the word IF followed by a test, i.e. is A equal to B? This is followed by the word THEN and a statement that is executed only if the test is true, i.e. in this case if A and B have the same value. If, however, the test is evaluated to be false, i.e A and B have different values, the next command is "skipped" and execution continues at the subsequent command. Let us consider the following section of a command procedure:

```
$ inquire word_1 "Input a word, please"

$ word_2 = "test"

$ if word_1 .eqs. word_2 then goto same

$ write sys$output "The two words are different."

$ goto finished

$same:

$ write sys$output "The two words are the same."

$finished:
```

The first line asks the user to input a word, a second word TEST is then set by the computer and assigned to the symbol WORD_2. The third line compares the two words and if they are the same, i.e. equal. (.EQS. is DCL's "equals" test), then the statement is "true" and the statement GOTO SAME is executed. This causes the program's execution to "jump" to the sixth line, i.e. the label SAME:, and continues execution from this point. The program's next line prints out a message, notifying the user that both words are the same and then finishes with the EXIT command. If, however, when the test on line 3 is made and the words are not the same, then the statement becomes false, the GOTO command is not executed, and the program continues with line 4 notifying the user that the words are different. The subsequent lines cause the program to "jump" to the EXIT label, which is the last line in the procedure.

VAX/VMS provides the facilities for other logical tests, as shown below:

Logical operators

X .or. Y	logical OR	test X or Test Y is true.
X .and. Y	logical AND	test X and Test Y is true.

Strings

A .eqs. B	equal	strings A and B have the same values.
A .ges. B	greater or equal	string A is greater or equal to string B.
A .gts. B	greater than	string A is greater than string B.
A .les. B	less or equal	string A is less or equal to the string B.
A .lts. B	less than	string A is less than string B.
A .nes. B	not equal	strings A and B have different values.

Values

A .eq. B	equal	values A and B have the same value.
A .ge. B	greater or equal	the value of A is greater or equal to the value of B.
A .gt. B	greater than	the value of A is greater than B.
A .le. B	less or equal	the value of A is less or equal to the value of B.
A .lt. B	less than	the value of A is less than B.
A .ne. B	not equal	the value of A does not equal the value of B.

Notice that some apply to symbols, others values (integers).

14.6.14 The IF-ELSE statement

In order to execute more than one statement if a test is "true", we place the THEN statement on the next line following the "test". Conditional on the "test" giving a "true" result, commands will be executed from this point onwards until an ENDIF statement is reached. Consider the following example:

```
$ inquire answer "Do you need instructions"

$ if answer .eqs. "YES"

$ then write sys$output "This program has been designed to"

$       write sys$output "help user run the various"

$       write sys$output "application programs on the computer"
.
.
.
$ endif

$ inquire name "Which package do you wish to run"
.
.
.
```

The first line asks the user if they need any help with the running of the procedure. By using the INQUIRE command, we read in the user's response to the question and store it in a symbol ANSWER. On the second line, we use the IF command to test if the answer is YES in uppercase. The IF statement does not perform character case conversion, so YES is not the same as (i.e. not equal to) Yes, but we have eliminated this problem by using INQUIRE, which converts all the user's input to uppercase. If we had used the READ command, which takes all input literally, we would have needed to write the first two lines as follows:

```
$ read/prompt="Do you need instructions" sys$command answer

$ if answer .eqs. "YES" .or. answer .eqs. "yes"
```

Even so, this does not allow for mixtures of upper- and lowercase characters, such as "Yes" or "yeS". This example also illustrates the relative merits of using INQUIRE in comparison with READ.

Returning to our original program, the IF statement on line 2 only checks to see if the answer is "yes", if the user has typed in any other word, the answer is taken to be "no". If the user types "yes", then the evaluation is "true" and the commands following the THEN statement down until the ENDIF statement, are executed. If the answer is anything but "yes", then the flow of execution in the procedure immediately jumps to the line following the ENDIF statement.

There is also an ELSE statement that can be used in conjunction with the IF statement to execute a set of commands if the test is "true" and another set if the answer is false. By modifying the example above we can print out a message notifying the user that instructions will not be given:

```
$ inquire answer "Do you need instructions"
```

```
$ if answer .eqs. "YES"
$ then write sys$output "This program has been designed to"
$      write sys$output "help user run the various"
$      write sys$output "application programs on the computer"
.
.
.
$ else write sys$output "No instructions will be given"
$      write sys$output "Type exit when finished"
$ endif
$ inquire name "Which package do you wish to run"
.
.
.
```

Notice in the example above that the ENDIF statement is placed after the ELSE section. The above procedure works as before when the user types "yes", but instead of skipping all the instructions when the user's answer is "no" (or anything other than "yes"), the procedure displays a brief message telling the user how to exit from the procedure. This message is not displayed if the user answers "yes".

To summarize, the general format is:

```
if ...
else...
endif
```

14.6.15 The CASE statement

The CASE statement can be considered to be an "extended IF-ELSE" statement. With the IF-ELSE statement, either one or the other section of the code is executed. This gives us a two-way choice that depends on the "truth value" being either "true" or "false". The CASE statement provides more choices: one of several blocks of code are executed depending on the value of a symbol. This is based on causing the flow of execution of the procedure to jump to one of a list of labels.

First, if we wish to check to see if the user's input is valid, we must list all the possible valid inputs. This list is essentially a collection of all the labels in the body of the CASE statement. We can compare the user's input with members of this list and produce an error message if a match is not found. Then we use a GOTO command to jump to that label and execute that section of code. At the end of the code there is a second GOTO to pass control out of the block, and back to the main section of the procedure. Consider the following simple example which uses the SHOW command to display various system details. The user types in the parameter for the SHOW command, such as USERS or SYSTEM, the procedure then goes to a label of that name and executes the instructions necessary to execute the DCL command, i.e. SHOW USERS or SHOW SYSTEM. The procedure will keep repeating until the user types EXIT.

The procedure starts with a comment explaining what it does. The second line is a list of the possible parameters, separated by full stops. They could in fact be separated by any symbol, as long as we specify which it is in the F$LOCATE command. The next four lines display to the users what the program does, by typing the text enclosed between the quotation marks onto the screen. The seventh line contains the label to which the program returns after each command has been executed. This causes the procedure to loop continuously until the user inputs EXIT. The next line prompts the user for input. The line after it compares the command entered by the user with each of the ones in the list PARAMETER_CHOICE. Notice the use of the parameter separators in quotation marks, in order to split the string into individual parameters. If a match is not found, then the procedure will GOTO the ERROR: label where it displays a message to the user listing the possible options. The procedure then returns (by going to the NEXT_PARAMETER label) and prompts the user for another parameter. If the parameter is valid, then the test will give a false result, the procedure will not jump to ERROR: but perform the GOTO statement following the test. By placing the symbol name in single quotes, the symbol "parameter" is first translated and the value (i.e. the string) contained in the symbol is then the "target" label for the procedure to "jump" to. Without the single quotes, the procedure would try and GOTO a label called "parameter", which is obviously not what we want in this instance. After the procedure has "jumped" to the label, and executed the code following that label, a second GOTO instruction causes the program flow to be returned to the label NEXT_PARAMETER, and the program cycle begins once again.

Below is the code for the command procedure, described above:

```
$! Procedure to perform a show command

$ parameter_choice = ".users.system.process.quota.exit."

$ write sys$output "This procedure runs the show command"

$ write sys$output "with the parameter specified by the user"

$ write sys$output "i.e Typing users will perform show users"
```

```
$ write sys$output "Type EXIT when finished"
$next_parameter:
$ inquire parameter "What would you like to show"
$ if f$locate ("."+parameter+".",parameter_choice) .eq. -
  f$length (parameter_choice) then goto error
$ goto 'parameter'
$users:
$ write sys$output "Performing - Show Users.."
$ show users
$ goto next_parameter
$system:
$ write sys$output "Performing - Show System..."
$ show system
$ goto next_parameter
$process:
$ write sys$output "Performing - Show Process..."
$ show process/full
$ goto next_parameter
$quota:
$ write sys$output "Performing - Show Quota..."
$ show quota
$ goto next_parameter
$error:
$ write sys$output "Sorry that command does not work !!"
$ write sys$output "Try USERS, SYSTEM, PROCESS or QUOTA"
$ goto next_command
$exit:
```

14.6.16 The EXIT and STOP commands

A procedure will stop running after it reaches its end, or when it reaches an EXIT or a STOP command. Both the EXIT command and the completion of the command procedure return the operation to the next higher level of DCL. If you are running a procedure interactively, this would be the DCL command level with the VAX/VMS dollar prompt. If you are running a command procedure from inside a second command procedure, then the operation will be returned to the originating procedure, at a position immediately after the call to the current procedure that just terminated. Unlike the command procedure, which finishes at its last instruction, the EXIT command allows us to return a STATUS value. This is a hexadecimal number which can be expanded to represent a VAX/VMS message code. You can obtain the status code by displaying the contents of the global symbol $STATUS.

For example, if during execution of a command procedure at DCL command level we press ⟨Ctrl⟩Y to terminate prematurely the procedure, the content of the symbol will then display to show the reason for the procedure's failure to complete.

```
$ @listing
⟨Ctrl⟩Y
INTERRUPT

$

$ show symbol $status
   $STATUS == "%X00030001"
```

However, allowing the procedure to complete normally, will give:

```
$ @listing
Job DIRECTORY (queue SYS$PRINT, entry 217) started on SYS$PRINT

$ show symbol $status
   $STATUS == "%X10000001"
```

We can see that in the first instance, the symbol $STATUS, contains an exit code of hexadecimal 30001, whereas a normal exit code of 10000001, was obtained by letting the procedure complete normally. By employing the IF statement to test the values of $STATUS a procedure can be written to perform various tasks depending on the error value, and hence the severity of the error, given by the contents of $STATUS.

The STOP command returns us to DCL command level, (i.e. to the dollar sign) regardless of the DCL level we are currently running at, and does not return a status.

14.7 Examples of Command Procedures

In course of using a computer system there are certain tasks that occur regularly. In this section we show with selected examples how to adapt DCL command procedures for these tasks. It is assumed that you will be able to expand and modify these examples for your own applications.

14.7.1 A command procedure to add two numbers

In this section we shall show two versions of a short command procedure called ADD1.COM. In the first version, the procedure prompts the user to input two numbers, adds them up, and finally displays the result.

```
$ inquire value_1 "Input first number : "
$ inquire value_2 "Input second number : "
$ total = 'value_1' + 'value_2'
$ write sys$output " The total is :''total'"
```

Running this procedure gives:

```
$ @add1
  Input first number : 15
  Input second number : 4
  The total is : 19
```

We can also create a second version of this procedure, which allows us this time to enter the values at the same time as we type the command to run the program. This is called using "command line arguments". The procedure is shown below:

```
$! This procedure adds two numbers
$ if p1 .eqs. "" inquire p1 "Input first number : "
$ if p2 .eqs. "" inquire p2 "Input second number : "
$ total = 'p1' + 'p2'
$ write sys$output p1, " + ",p2, " = ",total."
```

Notice that we check to see if both values have been given as command line arguments to the procedure. If not, then the procedure will prompt the user to enter the arguments as before. Also, the format of the output line, the last line of the procedure, has changed. Running this procedure (named ADD2.COM) gives:

```
$ add2 12 5
  12 + 5 = 17
```

14.7.2 A command procedure to simplify screen manipulation

With terminals such as Digital's VT100, VT200, and VT300 series it is possible to perform various screen functions. These include the use of large characters, characters in reverse video (i.e. dark characters on a light background), and blinking characters—or any combination of the above. There are also commands available for cursor and screen control.

The next command procedure is developed to be capable of assigning these special codes. Each code starts with ESC; this produces the same effect inside the file as obtained by a user pressing the ⟨Esc⟩ key on the keyboard, followed by a short character sequence, which is equated to a symbol. Typing the name of the symbol will cause that function to be performed, thus greatly simplifying the use of these "control codes". The process of changing the VDU display in this way is known as changing the "screen attributes".

The following procedure lists most of the special control sequences:

```
$     SAY          = "WRITE SYS$OUTPUT"
$     BELL[0,32]   = %x07
$     ESC[0,7]     = 27
$     BLINK        = "''ESC'[5m"          ! blinking display
$     REVERSE      = "''ESC'[7m"          ! reverse video
$     CHOME        = "''ESC'[H"           ! cursor home
$     CEOS         = "''ESC'[J"           ! cursor clear/screen
$     OFF          = "''ESC'[0m''ESC'(B" ! resets attributes
$     SAY CHOME,CEOS
$     SAY REVERSE,      "This should be in reverse video", OFF
$     SAY BLINK,         "This should blink ", OFF
$     SAY REVERSE,BLINK,"This should be in reverse video and
      blinking", OFF
```

Notice that the first line assigns WRITE SYS$OUTPUT to the symbol SAY; this avoids the need to type in the remainder of the procedure. Use of this technique later on in the file—for CHOME, CEOS (used in SAY CHOME, CEOS), and OFF—helps to simplify the file and to make it easier to understand.

Running the file (called VIDEO.COM) gives:

```
$ @video

This should be in reverse video
This should blink
This should be in reverse video and blinking
```

Each sentence should be displayed in the mode in which it is described by the text.

14.7.3 A command procedure to automate a number of related actions

We can combine a series of related commands that are routinely executed together into a single command procedure. These may correspond to the running of individual programs or processes. To execute these, it is then sufficient simply to execute the particular command procedure. For example, we show below a command procedure contained in a file called RUNNERS.-COM. This procedure will run two programs called A1 and A2, delete two temporary files called temp1.tmp and temp2.tmp, and finally display the quota status.

```
$ run A2
$ run A2
$ delete temp1.tmp;*
$ delete temp2.tmp;*
$ show quota
```

We can then execute the file and write the output into a file called RESULT.-LOG:

```
$ @runners/output=results.log
```

Alternatively, we could have redefined the output before executing RUNNERS.COM and collected everything in the file RESULTS.LOG. After the run is completed the output is redefined back to the screen:

```
$ define sys$output result.log

$ @runners

$ deassign sys$output
```

and to confirm that there is something in the file created, type:

```
$ directory/size/date result.log
```

From the system's response one can see whether the date and the length of the file correspond to one's expectations.

14.7.4 Command procedures dealing with data: file input/output

Two general cases occur when providing data for a program. In the first case, the data is written into a separate data file, using an editor such as EVE, or (for short files) the CREATE command, as shown below. We provide a few lines of telephone numbers:

```
$ create phone.dat
  Jim Brown      372
  Joe Smith      197
  Bill Taylor     725
  (Ctrl)Z

$ define sys$output telephone_update

$ run telephone_numbers

$ deassign sys$output
```

Here the program TELEPHONE_NUMBERS reads the data file PHONE.-DAT and writes its output to a file called TELEPHONE_UPDATE. After the program has completed its execution, the system output is once again returned to its default value, i.e. the screen.

In the second case, we provide data within the command procedure QSORT.COM. Thus the file, for the first run only, contains the commands shown below. For subsequent runs, of course, the first two commands corresponding to compiling and linking of the file are not required.

```
$ pascal qsort.pas   ! Compile QSORT.PAS

$ link qsort         ! Link QSORT

$ run qsort          ! Run QSORT

dat1.num             !inputfile for QSORT

temp1                !temporary file for QSORT

temp2                !temporary file for QSORT

sorted.dat           ! outputfile for QSORT
```

We then execute the procedure by giving the command @QSORT; this will compile, link, and execute a Pascal source code called QSORT.PAS. During runtime it will specify the data file to be sorted, assign names of two temporary files used within the sorting process, and write the sorted data into a file called SORTED.DAT.

Alternatively, redefining the input to the screen after the input file is named, using the command:

```
$ define sys$input sys$command      !input now from screen
```

will cause the interpreter to ask for the file names to be entered. In this case the output is also displayed on the screen.

```
$ run qsort            ! Run QSORT

dat1.num               !inputfile for QSORT

$ define sys$input sys$command

temp1                  !temporary file for QSORT

temp2                  !temporary file for QSORT

sorted.dat             ! outputfile for QSORT
```

Chapter

15

An Introduction to DECwindows

15.1 Introduction

Execution and use of the DECwindows interface requires a more advanced type of terminal, a suitable PC, or a Digital workstation. On account of the cost of suitable hardware, these interfaces are only normally available in small numbers in most establishments and particulary in educational institutes. We therefore present here only a brief overview of the use of DECwindows.

15.2 Overview of DECwindows

DECwindows is Digital's implementation of X Windowing version 11 software.

One of the major features of DECwindows is that it provides the user with a constant user interface over a wide range of hardware and software. In much the same way as VMS provides a constant user interface over a large range of VAX computers, DECwindows (which is essentially a revised version of X Windows for VAXs) provides a constant user interface over a range of different computer types. Thus, users will find that two computers from different manufacturers, which have a completely different hardware architecture, and different low-level languages, will be identical in operation. As X Windows (and so DECwindows) is implemented on computers by more manufacturers, the need to learn different operating systems will become less relevant.

The principle of DECwindows is to present a user interface to multitasking by using multiple windows on the display screen. Interaction of the user with the computer is via a pointing device (a mouse) which moves an arrow on the screen. The user moves the mouse to select the required window and then enters commands into that window via a keyboard (in the same way as entering commands at a terminal). The commands and their resulting execution are displayed in the window selected. Menus are provided to speed up certain processes, such as the starting, deleting, resizing, and the closing of windows. Icons, which are small drawings depicting an action or state (i.e. an icon representing a terminal may represent a window), are used to clarify the display.

Therefore, using icons and menus we can create a number of additional windows to carry out completely unrelated tasks. For instance, while in one window a program displays the current status of a process, in a second window using the mouse one can access a separate piece of software, or run through menus to select the desired action.

Thus DECwindows is a very powerful piece of software, which provides a user unfamiliar with VMS with a choice of options (via menus) at each stage. For the more competent VMS user, it provides a powerful development environment.

One major advantage between using a terminal connected to a VAX computer and using a VAXstation, which uses a large screened "bitmapped" display, is the ability to run windowing software.

The term "bitmapped" refers to the method whereby the screen is divided into a two-dimensional (x,y) coordinate system (graphics) in which each individual constituent of the screen is allocated a set of individual (x,y) values. The number of "bits" or (x,y) values determines the resolution of the image, i.e. its ability to display fine detail. Each bit can be individually accessed and activated.

The windowing software on a VAXstation can be one of two types—either a more basic system VWS (VAXstation Windowing Software), or more recently, DECwindows. Although both systems are supplied with the computer (from VMS version 5.1 onwards) only one type can be installed by the System Manager. The general user has no choice over which windowing system the computer is using.

Although VWS is still used, DECwindows is rapidly increasing in popularity. It not only provides more features and applications, but through its use of menus, it is also easier to use for a user unfamiliar with VMS.

Before looking briefly at DECwindows, let us first examine the general facilities a windowing system will give us.

15.3 The Need for X Windows

The computer environment is changing rapidly from large mainframe computers, to networks of smaller computers, e.g. PCs, and graphic workstations.

Each one of these network stations has access to software and hardware on other network stations. Networks often consist of computers and equipment manufactured by more than one manufacturer, each running a different operating system, with different applications software. This means that individual users have to familiarize themselves with a varying array of operating systems, interfaces and application packages. It was to overcome this problem by providing a consistent user interface, which is independent of software or hardware, that X Windows was developed.

The current implementation, X Windows version 11, was developed by the Massachusetts Institute of Technology (MIT) to provide two main functions: firstly as a windowing system, which uses the workstations graphic facilities, to provide an easy-to-use user interface that is independent of computer type and application. Secondly, as a development aid for various distributed applications. Since its introduction X Windows has become an industry standard.

Digital has enhanced X Windows to provide the same basic functions, along with some additional features. DECwindows using the workstation screen and a mouse provides a VAXStation user with the following facilities:

- *Graphic interface to VAX/VMS* The user interfaces to VAX/VMS via DECwindows. There are facilities for:

  (a) Starting and ending a session (i.e. log in and log out).
  (b) Running application software.
  (c) Creating, moving resizing and reducing windows to icons.

- *Constant user interface* Application windows which look and function the same regardless of the application. This consistency makes it easy to use for new applications.
- *Automated office* A variety of desktop tools (i.e. applications generally used in everyday office applications) such as: Bookreader, Calculator, Calender, Cardfiler, Clock, DIFF Document Viewer, EVE, FileView, Mail, Notepad Text Editor, Paint Graphics Editor, PostScript Previewer and DECterm.
- *Third-party applications* As DECwindows is an implementation of X Windows, all X Window applications, independent of manufacturer, will run on DECwindows.
- *Graphic library routines* Applications using these routines, which provide such things as drawing and window management, will run, without modification, on any of the models in the VAXstation range.
- *Libraries for use with text, graphics, and scanned images.*
- *Transparent access to other network computers.* DECwindows enables users to create a window onto another computer in the network, and then run any application on that computer, in the same way as if the window were a terminal wired directly into that machine.

- *VMS and Ultrix compatibility* Ultrix is Digital's implementation of the Unix operating system. Since both VMS and Ultrix use the same set of programming libraries and application programs, these can be moved between systems without the need for any modifications.
- *Extensible architecture* As new hardware emerges, DECwindows has the ability to accommodate these developments without the need for any modification, e.g. 3D graphics.

15.4 Using DECwindows

In this section below we give a simple example as a demonstration of how the DECwindows works.

Windows allow us to perform several tasks concurrently on the same screen. Each window represents individually the screen of a terminal. For example, we may edit a file, perform a directory command, and run a program, all at the same time, on the same screen but in different windows. We could therefore have the display shown in Figure 15-1 in three different windows at the same time. Note that it is not necessary for all the windows to be connected to the same VAX. By using the DECnet SET HOST command, we can connect the windows to any VAX(s) on the network. Therefore we are able to access any VAX in the network, from any window on our screen. We may thus have the processes shown in Figure 15-2 occurring and being displayed on the screen (in different windows) at the same time (i.e. concurrent operations).

Each window can essentially be seen as a terminal screen. DCL commands entered into any window will result in the same action in that window as would

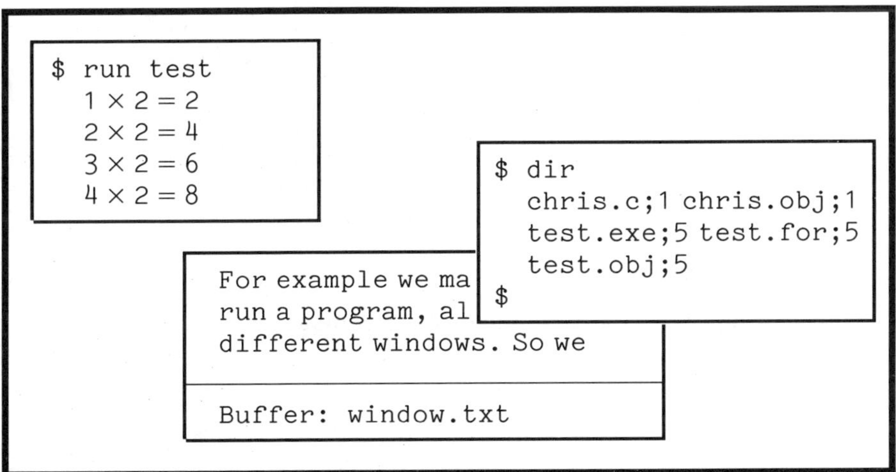

Fig. 15-1 An example of using DECwindows.

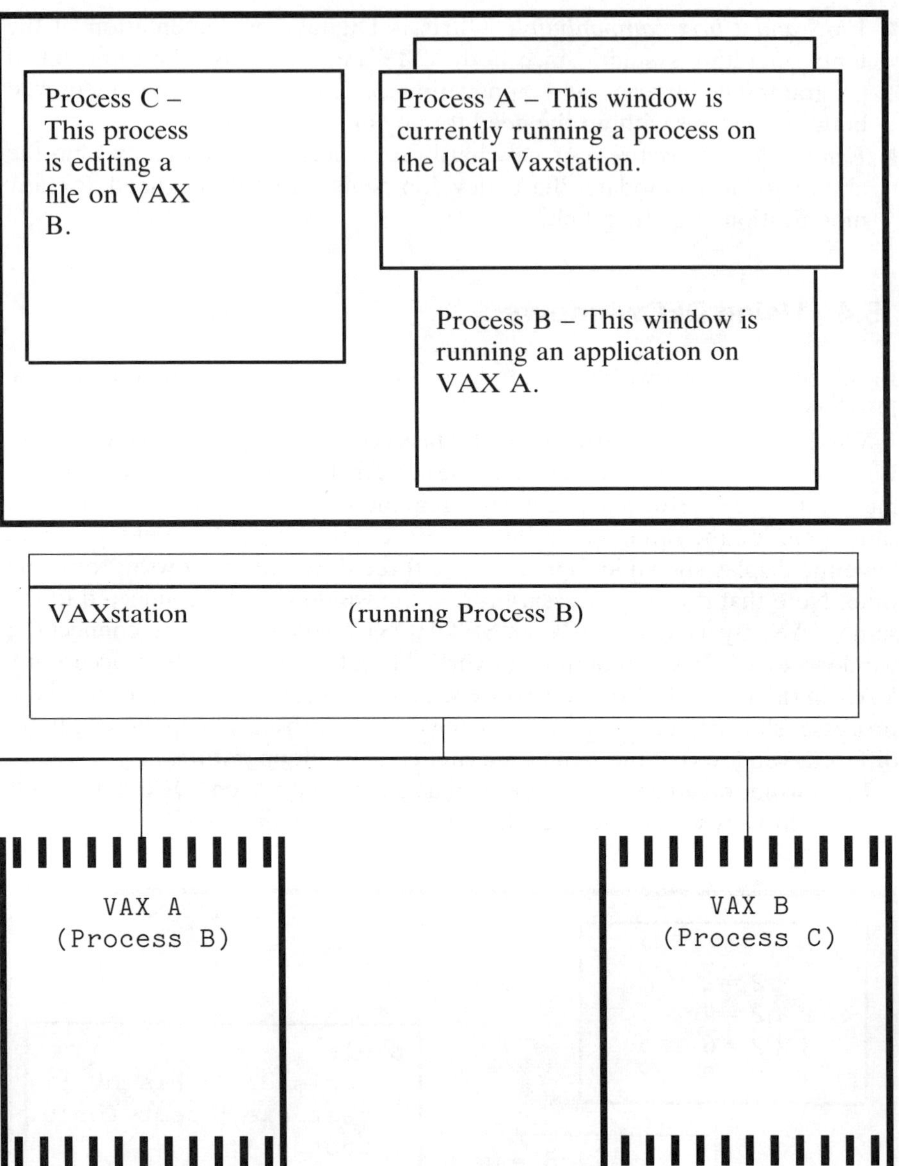

Fig. 15-2 Using DECwindows to access three computers concurrently.

```
FileView—DUA0:[STAFF.CHRISTOPHER]

Control  Customize  Views  Files  Applications  Help
                                  Bookreader
                                  Calculator
                                  Calender
                                  Clock
                                  Mail
                                  Notepad
```

Fig. 15-3 An example of DECwindows menu.

occur if the command was entered at a terminal. Although windows do possess the ability to perform graphical output, the workstation's mouse must be used to enter commands in a window. This mouse is used to place the pointer on the screen in the desired window. The left hand button on the mouse is then pressed to highlight that window and make it active. To make another window the current one, move the pointer to the menu for creating new windows and press the left hand button.

On color workstations all the colors can be adjusted (i.e. screen background, screen foreground, the window frame itself, and even the color of the pointer).

As well as being able to type commands directly into a window, in the same way as we would do on a terminal, it is also possible to use "pull-down" menus. Depending on the location of the pointer on the screen, a particular menu can be activated; the pointer is then moved down through the menu to select a particular option. A mouse button is then pressed, and the choice activated.

Figure 15-3 shows a typical example of a DECwindows menu. From the first menu (Control...Help) we selected "Applications", this then caused a second menu (Bookreader...Notepad) to "pop down". By moving the pointer down through this list we select "Mail" and then press the mouse button to run the mail application. The end result is the same as typing MAIL directly on a terminal.

This brief description on DECwindows has given a flavour of what is involved in window operations. If you have a suitable terminal available, we would strongly urge you to spend the few hours needed to familiarize yourself with the window operation and discover for yourself the advantages of using windows.

Appendix

Major File Types on VAX/VMS

File extension	File type
BAS	Program written in the BASIC programming language
B32	Program written in the BLISS-32 programming language
C	Program written in the C programming language
COB	Program written in the COBOL programming language
COM	Command procedure written in DCL
COR	Program written in the CORAL-66 programming language
DAT	A file containing data
EXE	Executable image (compiled program)
FOR	Program written in the FORTRAN programming language
LIS	File containing a listing, usually printed then deleted
LOG	Log file produced by batch queues
MAI	VAX/VMS mail file
MAR	Program written in the MACRO 32 assembler language
PAS	Program written in the Pascal programming language
SYS	VAX/VMS operating system file
TEX	Source file for Tex publishing system
TMP	Temporary work file
TXT	Text file

Appendix

B

Terminal Session

This appendix shows a typical terminal session to establish a simple working environment.

```
PCL Computer Services - VAX/VMS version 5.0 on Mole

Username: VAXVMS_18
Password:
Welcome to Mole, a VAX 6220 running VAX/VMS, version 5.3.
    Last interactive login on Wednesday, 19-APR-1990 15:12


PLEASE NOTE:
All users please note that all systems will be down this weekend
for monthly save/refresh. They will be back on Tuesday 30th May
1990.

$

$ set password
Old password:
New password:
Verification:

$ set terminal/inquire

$ show process

26-MAY-1990 10:59:59.72  RTA3: User: VAXVMS_18
Process ID:   00000271
                        Node: MOLE        Process name: "VAXVMS_18"
```

```
Terminal:           RTA1:  (MOLE::RAY)
User Identifier:    [EC330088,VAXVMS_18]
Base priority:      4
Default file spec:  DUA1:[EVEVMS.VAXVMS_18]

Devices allocated:  MOLE$RTA1:

$ set process/name="Ray Pretty"
$ show users
      VAX/VMS User Processes at 26-MAY-1990 11:01:21.27
    Total number of users = 3,  number of processes = 4

 Username       Interactive  Subprocess   Batch
 $OPER              2
 SYSTEM             1
 VAXVMS_18          1

$ show users/full
      VAX/VMS User Processes at 26-MAY-1990 11:02:29.03
    Total number of users = 3,  number of processes = 4

 Username   Process Name  PID       Terminal
 $OPER      $OPER         000003A4  OPA0:
 $OPER      MARKW         000003A8  LTA128:  (SYSTEM/PORT_4)
 SYSTEM     SYSTEM        000003C9  LTA141:  (MONKEY/PORT_12)
 VAXVMS_18  Ray Pretty    000003CA  RTA1:    (MOLE::RAY)

$ mail

MAIL> set mail_directory [.mail]
%MAIL-I-CREATED, USER1:[EVEVMS.VAXVMS_18.MAIL] created

MAIL> show all
Your mail file directory is USER1:[EVEVMS.VAXVMS_18.MAIL].
% MAIL-E-OPENIN,    error opening
    USER1:[EVEVMS.VAXVMS_18.MAIL]MAIL.MAI; as input
-RMS-E-FNF, file not found
%MAIL-E-NOMSGS, no messages

You have not set a forwarding address.
You have not set a personal name.
Your editor is EDT.
CC prompting is disabled.
Automatic copies to yourself are disabled.
Automatic deleted message purge is enabled.
Your default print queue is SYS$PRINT.
You have not specified a default print form.

MAIL> send
To:  vaxvms_18
Subj: test
```

```
Enter your message below. Press CTRL/Z when complete, or CTRL/C
to quit:
Hello Me,

This is a test to check that my mail is working. This message,
being the first one I receive, will also create a MAIL.MAI file.

                                         Bye

                                              Yourself
⟨CTRL⟩Z

New mail on node MOLE from MOLE::VAXVMS_18

MAIL⟩ set person "Ray Pretty"

MAIL⟩ set cc

MAIL⟩ set editor tpu

MAIL⟩ show all

Your mail file directory is USER1:[EVEVMS.VAXVMS_18.MAIL].
Your current mail file is USER1:[EVEVMS.VAXVMS_18.MAIL]MAIL.MAI;1.
No folder is currently selected.
The wastebasket folder name is WASTEBASKET.
Mail file USER1:[EVEVMS.VAXVMS_18.MAIL]MAIL.MAI;1
     contains 0 deleted message bytes.

You have 1 new message.

You have not set a forwarding address.
Your personal name is "Ray Pretty".
Your editor is TPU.
CC prompting is enabled.
Automatic copies to yourself are disabled.
Automatic deleted message purge is enabled.
Your default print queue is SYS$PRINT.
You have not specified a default print form.


MAIL⟩ exit

$ edit/tpu login.com
```

```
$! LOGIN.COM
$ dsd :== directory/size/date
$ dop :== directory/owner/protection
$ eve :== edit/tpu
$ set terminal/inquire
$ set process/name="Ray Pretty"
[End of file]

Buffer: LOGIN.COM                 Insert    Forward

Command: exit
```

```
$ @login

$ show symbol eve

EVE :== EDIT/TPU

$ create/directory [.progs]

$ set default [.progs]

$ eve hello.c
```

```
main()
{
printf("Hello,World\n");
}
[End of file]

Buffer: HELLO.C                   Insert    Forward

Command: exit
```

```
$ cc hello.c

$ link hello
%LINK-W-NUDFSYMS, 2 undefined symbols:
%LINK-I-UDFSYM,     C$MAIN
%LINK-I-UDFSYM,     PRINTF
%LINK-W-USEUNDEF, undefined symbol C$MAIN referenced
     in psect $CODE offset %X00000006
     in module HELLO file USER1:[EVEVMS.VAXVMS_18.PROGS]HELLO.OBJ;2
 %LINK-W-USEUNDEF, undefined symbol PRINTF referenced
     in psect $CODE offset %X00000013
     in module HELLO file USER1:[EVEVMS.VAXVMS_18.PROGS]HELLO.OBJ;2

$ define lnk$library sys$library:vaxcrtl

$ link hello

$ run hello

Hello,World

$ create/directory [.sources]

$ copy hello.c [.sources]

$ set default [.sources]

$ type hello.c

main()
{
printf("Hello, World\n");
}

$ print hello.c
Job HELLO (queue SYS$PRINT, entry 804) started on SYS$PRINT

$ show queue sys$print/all
Terminal queue SYS$PRINT, on MOLE::LTA11, mounted from DEFAULT
⟨Main System Printer⟩

  Jobname          Username      Entry  Blocks  Status
  -------          --------      -----  ------  ------
  HELLO            VAXVMS_18       804       1  Printing

$ set default [-]

$ show default
  DUA1:[EVEVMS.VAXVMS_18.PROGS]

$ directory [...]*.*

Directory DUA1:[EVEVMS.VAXVMS_18.PROGS]
```

```
HELLO.C;2              HELLO.C;1              HELLO.EXE;2
HELLO.EXE;1 HELLO.OBJ;2        HELLO.OBJ;1          SOURCES.DIR;1

Total of 7 files.

Directory DUA1:[EVEVMS.VAXVMS_18.PROGS.SOURCES]

HELLO.C;2

Total of 1 file.

Grand total of 2 directories, 8 files.
```

$ purge [...]*.*/log

```
%PURGE-I-FILPURG, DUA1:[EVEVMS.VAXVMS_18.PROGS]HELLO.C;1 deleted
(3 blocks)
%PURGE-I-FILPURG,    DUA1:[EVEVMS.VAXVMS_18.PROGS]HELLO.EXE;1
deleted (6 blocks)
%PURGE-I-FILPURG,    DUA1:[EVEVMS.VAXVMS_18.PROGS]HELLO.OBJ;1
deleted (3 blocks)
%PURGE-I-TOTAL, 3 files deleted (12 blocks)
```

$ directory [...]*.*

```
Directory DUA1:[EVEVMS.VAXVMS_18.PROGS]

HELLO.C;2              HELLO.EXE;2            HELLO.OBJ;2
SOURCES.DIR;1

Total of 4 files.

Directory USER1:[EVEVMS.VAXVMS_18.PROGS.SOURCES]

HELLO.C;2

Total of 1 file.

Grand total of 2 directories, 5 files.
```

$ logout/full

```
 VAXVMS_18    logged out at 26-MAY-1989 11:25:37.52
Accounting information:
Buffered I/O count:      684    Peak working set size:    512
Direct I/O count:        417    Peak page file size:     4917
Page faults:           11188    Mounted volumes:            0
Charged CPU time: 0 00:00:10.88 Elapsed time:    0 00:21:34.13
```

Appendix

C

Reference Data

In this appendix, we have collected together brief reference data under different headings in four main sections. Some of the data may be duplicated, but this is to give you a chance to find it quickly. Commands that are easy to use are only shown briefly here.

C.1 General Notes

- Summary of wildcard representation

Card	Represents
* (asterisk)	an entire "string"
% (percent sign)	a single character
... (ellipses)	current subdirectory and its subdirectories
- (hyphen)	one level up in directory structure; multiple hyphens refer to the corresponding level
. (period)	only one level below current directory
Combinations	
[* ...]	initiates action from top directory down (at least) 8 levels

- Qualifiers that regularly occur, such as /BEFORE [=time] and /AFTER [=time], are omitted.
- Use + (plus) or , (comma) to join together different files
- Time format is dd-mon-yyyy hh:mm, e.g. 03-JAN-1934 10:34

- The default directory can be represented by empty square brackets, [].
- To concatenate two files f1.TXT and f2.TXT using the COPY command:

```
COPY f1.TXT,f2.TXT f1.TXT
```

  Appends f2.TXT at the end of f1.TXT.
- To delete/stop a print job:

  1. SHOW ENTRY (note the entry/job number);
  2. DELETE/ENTRY = job number, or
  3. If already printing: STOP/ABORT.

- To duplicate an entire input directory structure, or to move an entire directory structure into another directory at the same, or at a different level:

```
BACKUP [current.*]*.*;* [Results.Save.*]*.*;*
```

  Note that the single asterisk in the output directory specification refers to the first subdirectory level in the input subdirectory. However, by using

```
BACKUP [Results.Save...]*.*;* [Current...]*.*;*
```

  the output directory structure follows the input directory structure from the first level that contained a wildcard.

C.2 Alphabetical List of Useful Commands

For a detailed description, see the appropriate section.

APPEND
Input file-spec [,...] output file-spec
Can use wildcards (for input)
Qualifiers: /CONFIRM, /LOG

CANCEL [process name] (see also STOP)
Cancel/Identification = PID (find PID from SHOW PROCESS)

CLOSE (see OPEN)

CONTINUE
Restarts processes interrupted by ⟨Ctrl⟩Y (see also SPAWN) (later)

COPY
Input file-spec [,...] output file-spec
Qualifiers: /NOCONCATENATE (produces individual output files), /CONCATENATE (default—produces single output file)

CREATE/DIRECTORY [directory name]
Qualifiers : /LOG, /PROTECTION

DEBUG
Must not use /NODEBUG
Stop execution using ⟨Ctrl⟩Y, then type DEBUG

DELETE
1. file-spec
   Qualifiers: /EXCLUDE=file-spec, /LOG
2. DELETE/key [key name] or /ALL

DIFFERENCES
Format: input1-file-spec [input2-file-spec]
Creates file-spec DIFF
Qualifiers: /IGNORE = (key word [,...]), /OUTPUT = [file-spec]
See also HELP for valid key words

DIRECTORY (see also CREATE)
Qualifiers: /COLUMN = n (with BRIEF only), /WIDTH CONTROLLED, /FULL, /OUTPUT [= file-spec] (if no output specified it produces DIRECTORY.LIS), /SIZE [= option] or /NOSIZE (default), /PRINTER, /SECURITY, /TOTAL, /VERSION = n

DUMP file-spec
Displays the file content besides a numerical form in ASCll conversion
Qualifier: /OUTPUT [=file-spec]

EDIT/TPU [file-spec]
Qualifiers: See text
EDIT/TPU/OUTPUT = Newfile.txt Oldfile.txt (Oldfile is edited; on EXIT Newfile is the updated version)
Special: EDIT/TPU ⟨CR⟩ creates buffer MAIN; then use command GET FILE ⟨CR⟩ edit. When finished specify output to WRITE FILE ⟨CR⟩

LEXICAL FUNCTIONS
General format F$ function-name ([args,...])
Note: Lexical functions are usually used with a "Routine" as shown in the following example to find all .COM and .DAT files:

```
$ START
$ COM = F$SEARCH (".COM;*",1)
$ DAT = F$SEARCH (".DAT;*",2)
$ SHOW SYMBOL COM
$ SHOW SYMBOL DAT
$ IF (COM.EQS. "") .AND. (DAT .EQS. "") THEN EXIT
$ GOTO START
```

Examples

F$ DIRECTORY	Returns current default directory name.
F$ PID (argument)	Returns the next process identification number in sequence.
F$ TIME	Returns time as dd-mm-yyyy-hh:mm:ss.cc.
F$ SEARCH (file-spec)	(see also under SEARCH) Searches a directory (file) and returns a full specification for the file.
F$ USER()	Returns the current user's identification code (UIC).

LINK file-spec[,...]
Invokes the VMS Linker.
Qualifiers: /MAP and one of /BRIEF, /FULL, or /CROSS_REFERENCE /DEBUG [file-spec] also produces /TRACEBACK
Example: $ LINK/MAP/CROSS_REFERENCE/DEBUG f1,f2,f3—the three object files are linked, producing an executable image f1.EXE as well as an f1.MAP global symbol file, together with the cross- reference in the file specified.

MERGE (see SORT)

OPEN and its associate CLOSE
Main qualifiers: /READ, /WRITE, /APPEND
Protocol: A new file has a single qualifier /WRITE. An existing file has qualifiers /READ and either /WRITE or /APPEND
Example: $OPEN/WRITE Output-file Results.OUT

.

.

.

$CLOSE Output-file (or Results.OUT)

PRINT
Qualifiers: /COPIES = n, /NOTIFY, /LOWERCASE (must be enabled) is able to print in both upper- and lowercase

PURGE [file-spec[,...]]
Deletes all but the highest numbered version
Qualifiers: /CONFIRM, /LOG

RECALL [command specifier]
Qualifiers: /ALL displays list of the commands used

RENAME input-file-spec[,...] output-file-spec
Qualifiers : /CONFIRM, /LOG, /NONEW_VERSION reports errors if these exist
Example: RENAME/NONEW_VERSION f1.DAT;3 F1.DAT creates same version number

RUN (image)
RUN (filename)
Example: RUN Myown or RUN Myown.EXE

RUN (process)
RUN file-spec
Qualifiers: /DETACHED (creates a sub or detached process; the process is deleted after the execution of the image), /BUFFER_LIMIT = quota, /DUMP

SEARCH file-spec [,...] search-string [,...] (see also F$SEARCH)
Enclose all—except capitals—in quotation marks
Qualifiers: /FORMAT=dump,/LOG,/NUMBERS,/STATISTICS, /WINDOWS [=(n1,n2)]
Example: $SEARCH/OUTPUT = found.DAT/WINDOW = 9 Stud.DIR Jim

Note: SET and SHOW are related commands

SET ACL (access control list)
Qualifier: /OBJECT_TYPE = file

SET BROADCAST = (Class-names[,...])
Selects recepients on whose terminal the messages will appear
Use HELP for class-list

SET DEFAULT (see text)

SET DIRECTORY directory-spec[,...]
Qualifiers: /LOG, /VERSION LIMIT[= n]

SET FILE file-spec [,...]
Qualifiers: /ACL (access control list), /CONFIRM, /LOG, /PROTECTION [= (code)]

SET HOST node-name
Qualifiers: /LOG [= file-spec] (without file-spec it is written into file SETHOST.LOG), /RESTORE saves and restores the current terminal characteristics

SET PROTECTION [= (code)] file-spec[,...]
Qualifiers: /CONFIRM, /LOG, /PROTECTION = (code)
Example: Input.DAT/PROTECTION = OWNER :R,W,E,D only the owner's protection is changed

SET TERMINAL
Qualifiers: /INQUIRE, /PAGE, /WIDTH
Example: SET TERMINAL/WIDTH = 132/PAGE = 60, i.e. 132 characters; 60 lines per page

SHOW PROCESS (process-name)
Qualifiers: /ALL, /PRIVILEGES, /QUOTAS

SORT/MERGE utility (see text)

SPAWN
Example

```
$ Run Myprogram
.
.
.
$ ⟨Ctrl⟩Y
$ SPAWN MAIL
MAIL⟩        and when finished
$ CONTINUE   (with Myprogram)
```

TYPE file-spec[,...]
Qualifier: /PAGE (one screen at a time)

WRITE (associated with OPEN; see text)

C.3 Frequently Used VAX/VMS Commands

C.3.1 General commands

$ SET PROMPT="PROMPT"	Set prompt to PROMPT.
$ SET PROC/NAME="PROC_NAME"	Set process name to correct type.
$ SET TERMINAL/INQUIRE	Set terminal to correct type.

$ SET TERMINAL/WIDTH=xxx	Set terminal screen width to xxx characters wide.
$ EDIT/TPU(/RECOVER) FILE.EXT	Edit "FILE.EXT".
$ FOR FILENAME (/DEBUG)	Compile the FORTRAN file filename. If using another language, substitute the compiler's name inplace of FOR, i.e. COB for COBOL, CC for C, and PAS for PASCAL.
$ LIN FILENAME (/DEBUG)	Link object file— filename.
$ RUN FILENAME (/NODEBUG)	Run image file—filename.
$ MAIL	Run the MAIL utility
$ PHONE	Run the PHONE utility

C.3.2 Looking at the system

The following commands display the entities referred to after SHOW:

```
$ show time
$ show device
$ show process
$ show system
$ show users
$ show queue sys$batch (/all /full)
$ show queue sys$print (/all /full)
$ show quota
$ show terminal
```

C.3.3 File and directory commands

$ DIRECTORY (/SIZE) (/FULL) (/DATE) (/OWNER) (/PROTECTION)	Lists files in the directory
$ TYPE FILENAME.EXT (/PAGE)	Lists content of a file.
$ CREATE/DIRECTORY [.DIRNAME]	Creates a subdirectory.
$ DELETE FILENAME.EXT;VERSION	Deletes a file or subdirectory.
$ COPY FILE1.EXT FILE2.EXT	Copies FILE1.EXT to FILE2.EXT.
$ RENAME FILE1.EXT FILE2.EXT	Renames FILE1.EXT to FILE2.EXT
$ PURGE (/LOG) (/KEEP=n)	Purges all, except latest n files.
$ SET DEFAULT [.DIRNAME]	Changes current directory.
$ SHOW DEFAULT	Shows current directory.

C.3.4 MAIL and PHONE commands

MAIL

$ MAIL	Runs the MAIL utility.
MAIL⟩ SEND (FILENAME)	Sends a message (or a file).
MAIL⟩ FORWARD	Forwards the current message.
MAIL⟩ REPLY	Replies to the current message.
MAIL⟩ MOVE FOLDERNAME	Moves to folder—foldername.
MAIL⟩ DELETE (RANGE)	Deletes current (or a range of) message(s).
MAIL⟩ EXTRACT FILENAME.EXT	Places current message in a file.
MAIL⟩ PRINT	Prints current messages.
MAIL⟩ SELECT FOLDERNAME	Selects a folder called foldername.
MAIL⟩ DIRECTORY	Lists all messages in the current folder.
MAIL⟩ DIRECTORY/FOLDER	Lists all folders.
MAIL⟩ EXIT	Leaves MAIL.

PHONE

$ PHONE	Runs the PHONE utility.
$ DIAL USERNAME	Phones username.
$ ANSWER	Answers an incoming call.
$ FACSIMILE FILENAME	Displays a file called filename.
$ DIR	Shows users on the system.
$ EXIT	Leaves phone.

C.3.5 EVE commands

Command: FIND STRING	Searches for string—STRING.
Command: REPLACE STRING1 STRING2	Searches for STRING1 and replaces it with STRING2.
Command: SPAWN	Temporarily leaves the editor.

Command: INCLUDE FILENAME	Includes file—filename—in current document.
Command: GET FILE FILENAME	Loads file—filename—into current document.
Command: LEARN	Teaches the editor a series of actions.
Command: EXIT	Leaves the editor, saving any changes.
Command: QUIT	Leaves the editor, deleting any changes.

C.4 Alphabetical List of Terminal Key Functions

C.4.1 VT100 key functions

⟨Ctrl⟩A	Switches between insert and overstrike mode.
⟨Ctrl⟩B	Recalls previous line.
⟨Ctrl⟩C	Interrupts and terminates current action.
⟨Ctrl⟩D	Moves cursor left one character.
⟨Ctrl⟩E	Moves cursor to the end of line.
⟨Ctrl⟩F	Moves cursor right one character.
⟨Ctrl⟩H	Moves cursor to the beginning of line.
⟨Ctrl⟩I	Tab (horizontal).
⟨Ctrl⟩J	Deletes previous word
⟨Ctrl⟩M	Line terminator (carriage return).
⟨Ctrl⟩O	Suspends/resumes echoing of output (on the screen).
⟨Ctrl⟩Q	Resumes output (after ⟨Ctrl⟩S).
⟨Ctrl⟩R	Refreshes current line.
⟨Ctrl⟩S	Stops output display on screen (⟨Ctrl⟩Q to resume).
⟨Ctrl⟩T	Displays process status
⟨Ctrl⟩U	Deletes characters from beginning of line to cursor
⟨Ctrl⟩V	Passes next character (or escape sequence) to the image without acting on it. Used mostly when control characters are placed in a text, to be acted on by an external device, such as a printer.
⟨Ctrl⟩X	Deletes characters from cursor to end of line, also purges the type-ahead buffer.
⟨Ctrl⟩Y	Interrupts current image.
⟨Ctrl⟩Z	End of file indicator.
⟨Ctrl⟩	Modifies another key; to pass on a special instruction.
ARROW DOWN	Recalls next stored line from line buffer to screen.
ARROW UP	Recalls previous line from line buffer to screen.
ARROW LEFT	Moves cursor left one character.

ARROW RIGHT	Moves cursor right one character.
BACKSPACE	Moves cursor to the beginning of the line.
⟨Ctrl⟩H	Moves cursor to the beginning of the line.
DELETE	Deletes previous character.
ESC	Begins escape sequence (from current action).
LINE FEED	Deletes previous word.
NO SCROLL	Suspends/resumes (display of) output.
RETURN	Line terminator (enter).
TAB	Horizontal tab.

C.4.2 VT200 and VT300 key functions

⟨Ctrl⟩A	Switches between insert and overstrike mode.
⟨Ctrl⟩B	Recalls previous line.
⟨Ctrl⟩C	Interrupts and terminates current action.
⟨Ctrl⟩D	Moves cursor left one character.
⟨Ctrl⟩E	Moves cursor to the end of line.
⟨Ctrl⟩F	Moves cursor right one character.
⟨Ctrl⟩H	Moves cursor to the begining of line.
⟨Ctrl⟩I	Tab (horizontal).
⟨Ctrl⟩J	Deletes previous word.
⟨Ctrl⟩M	Line terminator (carriage return).
⟨Ctrl⟩O	Suspends/Resumes echoing of output (on screen).
⟨Ctrl⟩Q	Resumes output (after ⟨Ctrl⟩S).
⟨Ctrl⟩R	Refreshes current line.
⟨Ctrl⟩S	Stops output display on screen (⟨Ctrl⟩Q to resume).
⟨Ctrl⟩T	Displays process status (enable with SET CONTROL=T).
⟨Ctrl⟩U	Deletes character from cursor to beginning of line.
⟨Ctrl⟩V	Passes next character (or escape sequence) to the image without acting on it. Used mostly when control characters are placed in a text, to be acted on by an external device.
⟨Ctrl⟩X	Deletes characters from beginning of line to cursor, also purges the type-ahead buffer.
⟨Ctrl⟩Y	Interrupts current image.
⟨Ctrl⟩Z	End of file indicator.
⟨Ctrl⟩	Modifies another key; to pass on a special instruction.
ARROW DOWN	Recalls next stored line from line buffer to screen.
ARROW UP	Recalls previous line from line buffer to screen.
ARROW LEFT	Moves cursor left one character.
ARROW RIGHT	Moves cursor right one character.
BACKSPACE	Moves cursor to the beginning of the line.

⟨Ctrl⟩H	Moves cursor to the beginning of the line.
DELETE	Deletes previous character.
ESC	Begins escape sequence (from current action).
LINE FEED	Deletes previous word.
F1 NO SCROLL	Suspends/resumes (display of) output.
F5 (Break)	Shuts down transmission line.
F6 (Interrupt)	Interrupts current image.
F10 (Exit)	Terminates the current command procedure or image.
F11 (Escape)	Begins escape sequence (from current action).
F12 (Backspace)	Moves cursor to the beginning of the line.
F13 (Line Feed)	Deletes previous word.
F14 (^ A)	Switches between insert and overstrike mode.
RETURN	Line terminator (enter).
TAB	Horizontal tab.

Index

Notes:
1. HELP topics: by invoking the HELP command with the topic name you can obtain information on the topic shown in the Index.
2. Key functions: for DCL and EVE editor keys, *see also* in Appendix C, pages 300–303 and in the Control Key table (Table 2.1).
3. The word following '*and*' points to an associated topic that might be of particular relevance.

@ at symbol, 38, 206, 227, 250
abbreviate, 20, 33, 52
abort a job or process, *see also* stop, 157
absolute:
  referencing of subdirectories, 99
  time *and* AFTER qualifier, 140, 180
Access Control Entries (ACE), 118
Access Control List (ACL), 35, 37, 118–119
Account user's, 5
Accounting information, 16
Ada programming language, 96, 208, 221
address
  and value assignment, 234
  see also MAIL, 152, 189
ADVICE *and*
  HELP facility, 33, 36, 38, 205
  HELP Library, 205
AFTER qualifier *see also* time specifications, 43, 45, 140
algorithm *and* program design, 158
ALL commmand procedure qualifier, 19, 20, 35, 37, 187, 202
alphanumeric, 76
alternative editor, 171
AND logical operator, 269
ANSI mode control sequence, 10
apostrophes *and* symbols, 225, 226
Append
  command, 213
  file operations, 266, 267
argument of a command, 4, 82, 199, 231, 238, 275
arrow key functions *and* cursor control, 55, 63, 66, 67, 83, 85
ASC translate codes, 210
ASCII (American Standard Code for

ASCII—*cont.*
Infomation Interchange), 93, 111, 172, 210
assembler language (low-level MACRO), 160–162
Assembler *and* source code translation, 160–162, 208
assign
command, 217, 218, 222–226, 232–234
and deassign, 29, 44, 45, 79, 254
editor key definition, 79
log file, 44, 45
input to a symbol, 262
qualifier, 19, 20, 35, 37, 187, 202
symbol to a command procedure, 257
asterisk (*) *and* symbols, wildcards, 38, 68, 220, 248
at symbol (@), 38, 206, 227, 250
attach name in MAIL, 192
ATTACH, 33, 36, 176
attributes
MAIL, 183
PASCAL compiler, 41
screen display, 276
Autobaud *and* terminal setting, 10
automate tasks *and* DCL command procedures, 22, 255, 277
Automatic copies and purge in MAIL, 189, 190
AUTO_PURGE in MAIL, 190
AWAIT, 211

background
processes and SPAWN, 125, 128, 130, 131
screen manipulation, 276
Backspace *and* control keys, 28, 31, 55
BACKUP *and* HELP display, 34, 39, 109
backwards *and* EVE editor commands, 30, 51, 54
banner *and* print mode, 147, 152, 153
BAS BASIC high-level language, 96, 159
BASE
priority, 20, 144, 156
sys$print printer specification, 20, 24, 25, 144, 156
BASIC high-level language, 34, 159, 160, 208, 213
BATCH, 35, 37, 135, 203
Batch
job, queues *and* processes, 19–20, 23–24, 136, 147, 228, 253–256, 260, 262
queues *and* operations, 137, 143, 144, 256
baud data transfer rate terminal specification, 11
before *and* time specification, 141, 169, 182, 191
BEFORE, 182
BELL, 212, 276
binary code, 163
bit
relation to
WORD (= 2 bytes = 16 bits), 112
longword (= 4 bytes = 32 bits), 112
unit of computer data, 11
bitmapped display on VAXstations, 281
BKSPACE EVE editor command, 52
BLINK *and* video setting, 276
BLISS computer language, 159, 160
block
mode terminal setting, 10, 63, 66, 67
of text in EVE operations, 48, 63, 66
unit of disk data storage, 14, 15, 19, 25
boolean logical operator, 268
boot start-up operations, 238
BOTTOM EVE editor command, 62, 66, 79
BRIEF HELP topic, 35, 37, 202
Broadcast communication and terminal command, 10, 35, 37
buffer, 53, 54, 62, 63, 66, 67, 71, 109
and screen management routines, 212
EVE
editor command, 82, 83
editor storage space, 50, 57, 62, 81–90
buffered I/O count, 16
build DCL command line, 17, 21
BULLETIN HELP topic, 34, 39
BURST *and* printer output, 149
byte elementary unit of computer data, 14, 189

cable Ethernet DECnet network, virtual and wire connections, 11, 26
CAL HELP topic, 34

calculate
  and program example, 164–169
  using lexical functions, 215, 230, 232
  using symbols and numbers, 167–170, 222–227
CALL using Run–Time Library, 34, 213–214, 259
CANCEL HELP topic, 34
CAPITALIZE WORD EVE editor command, 77
carbon copy MAIL, 177, 178, 182, 189–190
CASE statement *see also* IF statement
  selection in program construct, 271–272
CC carbon copy MAIL facility, 177, 189
cc call to VAX C language compiler, 160, 166–168
CENTRE LINE EVE editor command, 77
central processing unit (CPU), 1, 2, 12, 16
CEOS cursor clear screen sequence, 277
CHANGE, 54
CHANGE DIRECTION EVE editor command (forward, reverse), 54
CHAR
  Screen Management Library routines
  SMG$DRAW_CHAR output specified character, 212
  SMG$DRAW_CHARS delete specified character, 212
  STR$DUPL_CHARS copy a character n times, 213
char character type in source code, 166, 167, 172
character letter or symbol *and* key commands, 28, 52, 53
CHECK PASCAL parameter HELP, 41
CHECKDISK command, 227
child and parent processes SPAWN and DCL level, 125–128, 131–133, 217
chips, 2
choice *and* the CASE statement, 271–274
CHOME screen attribute cursor home, 276
CLOCK set by the system function F$TIME, 229
clock *and* time specification, 8, 140, 141, 229
CLOSE
  file after use, 55, 146, 267
  HELP display, 34
COBOL high-level language, 34, 159, 160, 164
code source program language expression, 92–96, 158–172, 271–278
colon *and* MAIL, 184, 219, 220, 246, 247, 263
COM command file type specifier, 163, 169
combination of upper and lower case characters for DCL commands, 17
command SET and SHOW are main commands of VMS in conjunction with arguments, 4
command VAX/VMS Digital Command Language DCL, 17
commands most frequently used
  assign (*and* deassign), 44, 45
    (recall *and* edit), 27
  control keys, 5
  define function keys, 31
    and /terminate qualifier, 31
  directory or dir, 49
  edit/tpu filename, 50
  EVE *and* DO key 51
  line
    build-up, 21
    editing, 28
  login logout, 7, 8
  logout/full, 4, 16
  print filename, 40
  print/delete filename, 40
  recall/all, 29
  recall n (n < 20), 29
  recall argument, 30
    (recall *and* edit), 27
  set
    host/log, 46
    password, 13
      /generate, 13
      /secondary, 13
    prompt, 9
    terminal, 5
      /device=Vt100, 10
      /hardcopy, 45
      /inquire, 9
      /line_editing, 29
      /speed=1200, 11
      /unknown, 9

commands—*cont.*
/width=132, 10
show
(main), 22
and HELP, 35
default, 44
device, 25
device dua (of name dua), 25
key/all, 33
network, 25
process, 24
que sys$print (shortened to), 20
queue sys$print, 19
/all, 20
/full, 20
quota, 15
system, 19
terminal, 10
time, 8
users, 8, 16, 23
users/full, 22
structure
$ prompt, 18
command naming, 18
qualifier, 18
value, 18
comment, 180, 256, 261, 272
common comparison of file contents, 176
COMMON, 113, 236, 240, 246
communicate, 46
phone utility 174, 193
COMP HELP topic, 38, 39
compare *and* differences, 119–121, 244, 271
COMPARE, 213
compile source code, 41, 76, 160–171, 208, 215, 278
compiler, 160–162, 167, 171
COMPRESS, 176
concatenation (joining together), 112, 113, 225
conceal information, 239
concurrent, 2, 130, 193
concurrent operations on same screen using DECwindows, 283
conditional operations, 268
conditions *and* SEARCH operations, 117
confirm *and* delete, 114
CONFIRM qualifier, 149
connect to other computers SET HOST, 46
CONNECT, 34
console, 39
CONTINUE, 34, 111, 126, 243
continuation, *see* hyphen
CONTROL, 12, 19, 144, 264
convention file naming, 94
conversation *and* the PHONE utility, 194, 196–199
CONVERT, 34
COPIES, 110, 149
copy DCL command, 21, 22, 112–113, 117–121
copy EVE editor command, 62–67, 84, 85, 88–90
copies, qualifier for
print command, 149
MAIL command, 189, 190
COR, 159
CORAL language, 159, 160, 208
counting *and* numbers, 222, 223
CPROLOG language, 34
CPU (*see* Central Processing Unit)
CPUMAXIMUM, 144
crash, 49, 60, 143
create
command files .COM, 249
procedure for BATCH file, 137, 138, 143, 253
directory, 100, 101
file, 107, 108
HELP Library, 205, 208
logical name, 233–236, 239
MAIL folder, 185–187
subprocess (i.e. a job) SPAWN, 125, 128
CREATION of a process SPAWN, 125
CRON, 39
CROSS_REFERENCE file in PASCAL compilation, 41
CRT terminal attribute, 10
CTRL LIB$DISABLE_CTRL disable interception of CTR characters, 210
CTRL LIB$ENABLE_CTRL enable interception of CTR characters, 210
CTRL B redisplay last command with cursor at end, 28
CTRL C cancel listing of MAIL folder, 183, 210
CTRL C cancel current process, 5
CTRL L TAB creation, 12

CTRL O proceed with display of next file (of a group, TYPE command), 111
CTRL R terminate LEARN process in EVE editor, 73, 74
CTRL T display status message, 12
CTRL Y handling CONTROL=Y and NOCONTROL=Y, 264, 265
CTRL Y interrupt display of file CONTINUE or STOP (TYPE command), 111
CTRL Y interrupt process, 243, 274
CTRL Y interrupt process for SPAWN then LOGOUT and CONTINUE, 126, 127
CTRL Z end of file, 176
Ctrl keys
  DCL line editing commands, 28–31
  EVE editor commands, 52, 55, 57, 73, 74, 78, 81
  PHONE text formatting, 196
  see also Appendix C, 301–303
cursor
  and screen manipulation commands, 276
  control in
    EVE editor, 50–56, 58–63, 66–70, 73–78, 82, 83, 85, 87–90
    PHONE utility, 196
  movements, 55
    with DCL line editing commands, 28
customize environment
  DCL level, 249, 251
  MAIL, 175
cut-and-paste EVE editor operations, 59, 62

dark screen display, 276
DATATRIEVE *and* HELP, 34, 208
Date *and* AFTER time format specification, 140, 184, 186, 188, 214
DBG debugger, 172, 173, 236
DBMS, 19, 34
DCL commands and qualifiers
  assign, 44, 45
  deassign, 45
  define/key, 31
  line editing, 28
  print, 43
  recall/all, 29
DCL—*cont.*
  type, 43
  (*see also* Commands; Qualifiers; Show; Set)
DCL command line build-up, 20–22
DCL (Digital Command Language)
  structure
    $ prompt, 18
    command naming, 18
    qualifier, 18
DCL command procedures, 253–254
  assign, 254
  comments ($!), 255
  deassign, 254
  default logical names, input/output, 259
  executing, 256
  levels, 259
  running, 256
    from within a second, 257
    over DECnet, 258
DCL syntax rules, 260
  case statement, 271
  commands, 260
  comments, 261
  continuation, 260
  close, 267
  CTRL Y handling, 264
  data, 260
  error handling, 263
    set on *and* noon, 263
    $severity, 263
      0 warning, 263
      1 success, 263
      2 error, 263
      3 information, 263
      4 fatal, 263
  exit, 274
    status value, 274
  goto, 267
  if statement, 268
    logical operators, 268, 269
  if-else, 269
    endif, 269
  inquire, 270
    nopunctuation, 262
    global, 262
  labels, 261
    call, 262
    goto, 262
    gosub, 262
  read, 265

DCL—*cont.*
prompt= , 265
open, 266
read, 266
append, 267
error= , 267
read, 265
prompt= , 265
labels, 271
stop, 274
DECIMAL, 111, 222
DECnet, 23, 26, 27, 46, 155, 177, 197, 256, 258
DECtalk, 209
DECwindows multitasking, concurrency, multiple windows, 280–285
def default, 102, 103
DEFAULT, 20, 32, 33
define
key in
DCL, 31, 32
EVE editor, 80, 81
library referencing, 163, 168
symbols
global, 219–227, 230, 233, 239–244, 247–251, 257, 277–279
hexadecimal *and* octal symbols, 224, 225
local, 217, 218
DEFKEY, 31, 32
DEFQUEPRI, 154
DEL delete key, 12
DELETE
/entry qualifier to stop a job running, 144, 145, 157
authority for files, 92
command, 15, 34
file, 40
files using wildcards and qualifiers, 98, 100, 113, 114
in EVE editor, 55, 62, 63, 66, 67, 82
library information, 204, 205
line editing command, 28–31
MAIL, 184
qualifier for print queues, 150
subdirectory, 105–107
symbol, 220
using a command procedure, 277
DELKEY, 33
delta time definition, 140, 142
DEPOSIT in debugger, 34, 172
dial PHONE, 194, 197, 199
difference between files, 119–122
DIFFERENCES command for files, 34, 120–122
DIFFS, 121
digits, 93, 95, 111
dir *see also* Directory, 29, 101–108
direction *and* EVE editor commands, 54, 55, 61, 62, 69, 70
directory *and* files, 15, 27, 91, 96–119
directory *and* file protection, 117–119
disable automatic copies in MAIL, 189
disaster *and* recovery, 59
Disconnect terminal attribute, 10
diskquota, 5, 14, 19
dollar ($) default systems prompt, 7–9
downtime, 7
DUMP, 34, 93, 111, 112
DUPL, 213

echo *and* no echo terminal attributes, 10
edit
/tpu filename entering EVE editor, 50
/tpu/recover filename retrieve alterations after a crash, 60
DCL command line editor commands *and* use, 27–31
EDT editor, 34
ENCRYPT HELP topic, 34
endif terminator of a boolean test of if .. then .., 269–271
ENLARGE WINDOW, 87
ENTRY qualifier and delete print queue, 157
enquire qualifier for terminal type, 61
ERRORLOG SYSERRORLOG faults data store, 236
ESC escape key, 116, 276
EVE Extensible Vax Editor, *see also* TPU, 34, 40–43, 48–61, 67–90
commands protocol
buffer, 82–83
delete, 82
get file, 82
go to, 83
messages, 83
show, 83
buffers, 83
system buffers, 83
write file, 83
change direction, 54

EVE—*cont.*
entering commands, 51
erase line, 56
exit, 56
find, 54
forward direction, 54
help, 52
include file, 71
insert/overstrike mode, 53, 55
learn a series of keystrokes, 73
mark (*and* GOTO), 76–77
move
by line, 54
by word, 54
cursor, 55
with arrow keys, 55
(CTR)E to end of line, 55
(backspace) to start of line, 55
overstrike/insert mode, 53, 55
quit, 56, 57
recover, 60
repeat (*and* LEARN combination), 75
replace dialogue, 69, 70
restore (cancel the last action of one of the following), 56–58
erase
word, 56
line, 56
previous word, 56
start of line, 56
reverse direction, 54
spawn (*and* logout), 75, 76
status line, 50
wildcard
find, 68
match of characters (*) and (%), 69
control key commands for vt100, *and* vt200 terminals, 52, 53
(CTR)B recall, 52, 53
(CTR)E end of line, 52, 53
(CTR)R remember, 52, 53
(CTR)U erase to start of line, 52, 53
(CTR)V quote, 52, 53
(CTR)W refresh, 52, 53
copy text between two files, 84
insert here, 84
remove, 84
select, 84
DCL, 79

EVE—*cont.*
define key, 79
initialization file *and* saving key definition, 80–81
section file *and* saving key definition, 80
tpusection default file extension, 80
edit
single file using two windows, 87–88
two files using two windows, 89–90
enter commands protocol, 51
press do, 51
enter command, 51
press return, 51
windows, 87
delete, 87
enlarge, 87
next, 87
one, 87
previous, 87
shrink, 87
split, 87
two, 87
keys, 60
(bkspace) start of line (vt100), 52
(CTR)H start of line (vt200), 53
delete, 55
direction, 61
forward, 61
reverse, 61
do, 51, 66
find, 60
F10 exit (vt200), 53
insert, 62
insert here, 63
remove, 62, 63
select, 62, 63
keypad, advanced actions
(bottom) end of file, 55
(find) next occurrence of a string, 55
(move by word) next word, 55
(next screen) next screen, 55
(previous screen) previous screen, 55
(top) top of file, 55
text
block of
copy, 63, 66
delete, 63

EVE—*cont.*
move, 63, 66
copy, 62, 63
delete, 62, 63
formatting commands
capitalize word, 77
centre line, 77
fill, 77
paragraph, 78
range, 78
insert page break, 78
set, 78
left margin n, 78
nowrap, 78
right margin n, 78
tabs at n, 28
tab, every n, invisible, movement spaces, visible, width n, 78
lowercase word, 78
uppercase word, wrap, 78
shift, left n, right n, 78
insert, 54
move, 62, 63
replace, 54
reverse direction, 54
move cursor, 55
with arrow keys, 55
(CTR)E to end of line, 55
(backspace) to start of line, 55
exclude qualifier, 249
executable image, process, 95, 162–164, 213
EXIT EVE editor command, 52, 56, 57
expire *and* password, 13, 141

FACSIMILE, 199
FATALSYNTAX error, 166, 167
fault page, 16
faults restart, 139
file
copy, 112
concatenate, 112
delete, 113, 114
qualifiers
confirm, 114
since=date, 114
diff difference, 119
qualifiers
ignore, 120
merged, 120
match=n, 121

file—*cont.*
HELP, 114
noconcatenate, 112
protection (*and* directories), 117
attributes, 117–118
read
write
execute
delete
system
owner
group
world
and ACL, ACE, 118–119
purge, 114
qualifiers
keep=n, 114
log, 114
qualifiers
protection, 113
replace, 113
since=date, 114
rename, 115
search, 115
qualifiers, 116–117
Find *and* EVE editor, 52, 54, 55, 68
flag *and* page, 150
FLUSH buffer, 212
folder *and* MAIL, 174, 178–192
FORMS qualifier for paper size in print, 152
Fortran high-level language, 17, 22, 96, 153
Forward *and* EVE editor, 50–57, 61–68
FORWARD set FORWARD command in MAIL, 189
full qualifier, 16, 20–25, 36–37

ge logical operator tests if the first integer expression is greater or equal to the second, 269
ges logical operator tests, as above but for strings, 269
GENERIC HELP topic, 20, 35, 37, 156, 202
GETJPI *see* F$GETJPI symbols and lexical function assignments, 210, 229, 230, 250
GETSYI see F$GETSYI symbols *and* lexical function assignments; get system information, 210, 228, 229

global symbols, 217–226, 257, 258, 262, 274
GLOBAL symbol qualifier, 262
GOTO *and* MARK command; LABELS, 76, 267–269, 272
GO TO *and* MARK EVE editor command, 83
GOSUB MARK *and* LABELS, 34, 262
GRAPHICS HELP topic, 34
graphic
  library routines for DECwindows, 283
  workstation DECwindows, 281
group
  membership *see also* ACL, 92, 117, 118
  table
    GRPNAM privilege, 235, 236
    GRPPRV privilege, 235, 236
    see also logical names, 233–247, 250, 253
gt logical operator tests if the first integer expression is greater than the second, 269
gts as above but for strings, 269

halt process execution (CTR Y), 243
HANGUP the phone, 199, 209
hardcopy terminal qualifier, 28, 42, 45
header
  MAIL qualifier, 179
  printer qualifier (*and* noheader), 137, 152
help commands
  DCL
    help, 33–34
      DBG> help (in the debugger), 173
      delete, 114
      show, 35
      show queue, 35
      show queue/full, 35–37
      sort, 112
        /output=sort.log log*, 122
  EVE, 52, 53
  MAIL, 175, 199
HELP Library, 201–207, 237, 245, 246
HELPLIB *see* HELP Library, 33, 40, 204, 205, 246
Hex, 223–225, 227, 229, 231, 232
hexadecimal
  and DUMP, 111
  and STATUS value display, 274
  numerical values, 222–224
HIB process status, 19
hibernating process, 126, 128, 132
Hints HELP topic, 34
hlb library type, 204, 205, 207
hlp library type, 203–207, 246
Home directory, 92, 100
HOST, SET ... command, 46
Hour-time specifier, after QUALIFIER, use, 140, 141, 145, 146
hundredths time specifier, 142
hyphen
  (-) wildcard for directory referencing, 101
  DCL command line continuation and prompting, 21, 22, 119, 260

icon, mouse *and* menus on DECwindows, 281
ID (Process IDentification), 23, 25, 133
IDENT (IDENTIFICATION qualifier) with PID, 133, 134
identical *and* difference between files, 119, 120
IDENTIFIER *and* Access Control List ACL, 119
IF boolean operator if ... then, 34, 253, 268–271, 274
IGNORE qualifier *and* differences, 120–122
image *and* .EXE (program image files), 162–164, 168–171, 208
IMAGELIB *and* LINK and Run-Time routines, 213
INCLUDE EVE command ... file, 71, 73, 84
inherit protection, 113
INIT EVE$INIT, see initialization file, 34, 79–81
initialization file, 34, 79–81
Input default I/O logical names, 259, 277
INPUT, system table definition, 236, 241, 259, 265
inputfile *and* outputfile after processing, 278, 279
INQUIRE
  DCL command (procedures), 262, 265, 270

INQUIRE—*cont.*
qualifier terminal set-up, 5, 34, 45, 165, 193
insert
EVE editor *and* overstrike mode, 50, 52–56, 67, 71, 88, 89
HERE EVE editor KEY, 52, 53, 62
INTERACTIVE mode *and* batch jobs, 136, 138, 139
interface user-machine, 2, 160, 164
Interpreter language, 148, 160
INTERRUPT *and* CTR Y command, stop/exit, 274
INTRUSION HELP topic, 35, 37
invoke language compiler/assembler, 160
IO (input/output), 12

JOB
HELP topic, 34, 35, 37
logical name ; job table LNM$JOB_xxx, 130, 234–235
JOBDELETE entry from a queue, 157
Jobname trace of progress, 143, 144
join copy *and* concatenate files, 112
joining lines in EVE editor, 55, 56
JourNaL JNL files created by EVE editor, 148
journal back-up data of EVE editor session, 60
Journaling status in file attributes, 109

keep qualifier
and logfile, 142, 143
and purge, 114
Kermit HELP topic, 34
key
and sort utility, 122–124
define in EVE *and* section files, 79, 80, 81
line editing commands table *and* use, 28–31
programming functions, 31–33
Keyboard *and* key functions, 11, 12
control, 12, 111, 127, 176
delete, tab, 12
shift, return or entry, 11
Keypad
and debugger, 171, 173
and keyboard commands EVE editor, 51–53, 60, 73–75, 173
keystrokes *and* LEARN in EVE editor, 73, 74
killed processes SPAWN, parent *and* child, 130, 133

L EVE command replace string, 70, 196, 211
L PHONE text formatting (CTR L) clear text from your window, 196
label name assigned to a
device, 25, 96, 99
location in a file, 76, 261, 262, 266, 272
statement, 260, 265, 267–269
LABELS print paper FORM qualifier for size of paper, 152
language
DCL (Digital Command Language) *and* commands, 17, 22, 253
high-level, 41, 96, 159–165, 208, 213, 214, 253
LSE (Language Sensitive Editor), 159
laser printer type, 147, 148, 155, 192
LAST HELP topic, 176, 231
LATCP HELP topic, 34
le logical operator value less than or equal, 269
les logical operator string less than or equal, 269
LEARN EVE Editor Command a sequence, 59, 73–75
left arrow key, 28, 81
left EVE editor command shift window, 78, 79
LENGTH lexical function F$LENGTH, 230, 232
level
command procedure level, 259, 263, 274
and logical name translation, 241
error severity, 263
lexical functions
F$EXTRACT, 231, 232
F$GETJPI, 229, 230
F$GETSI, 228, 229
F$LENGTH, 230, 231, 232
F$PROCESS, 230
F$TIME, 229
LFfill HELP topic, 10
lib Run–Time library routines, 208, 213–215, 237
Library
and logical name definition, 241, 243

Library—*cont.*
accessing other HELP libraries @ (at) command libname, 38
HELP library
changing the content, 201–203
creating other library, 205–206
HELPLIB.HLB in SYSHELP directory, 33, 201
LNK$LIBRARY and SYS$LIBRARY assignment, 163
other libraries qualifiers : create, library, 207–208
redirecting HELP
output, 40
using assign command, 44
using output qualifier, 44
using SET HOST/LOG command, 46, 47
qualifier to access another HELP library, 40
VAX/VMS common Run-Time library, 208–215, 237
licence identification of VAX/VMS software, 229
life of symbol and logical name definitions, 216
lifetime of program, 158
line *and* screen-size specification, 10
command line
build-up and DCL prompting, 21, 22, 28
editing commands, 28–32
the EVE status line (*see* EVE commands for line specifics), 50
LINEFEED, 28
link
network, 26
programs *and* files, 162–164, 208, 278
and the VAX/VMS Debugger, 170–173
LIS, 167, 169, 170, 245, 255
lis file type, 167
list
programs, 167
qualifier, 161, 162
search list logical name, 247, 248
LNM process table, *see also* logical, 44, 45 205, 234–236, 240–245, 247, 248
Local
and global symbols, 217, 218
terminal state, 10, 26
LOCC LIB$LOCC library routine find a character, 210
LOCK, 211, 212
LOG
delete/purge *and* log the process, 105, 106, 115
file *and* batch job report, 138
name qualifier, 143
set HOST/LOG logfile creation, 46
logical command *and* attributes, 240, 243, 247, 248
logical names
definition, 238, 240
translation, 244–247
and tables, 233
group table LNM$GROUP_xxx, 235, 236
job table LNM$JOB_xxx, 235
process table LNM$PROCESS, 234, 235
system table LNM$SYSTEM, 236, 238
operators, 268–271
login, 7
.com and file
automatic definitions, 163, 255
environment customized with symbols, 249–252
example program, 139
link$library SYS$LIBRARY definition for inclusion, 168
MAIL :== MAIL/EDIT to include, 178
see also SETUP.COM file, 80, 81
store symbols, 217
logout
.com file, 50, 254
and full qualifier, 4, 8
LONGWORD, 112
LSE (Language Sensitive Editor), 159
LSEDIT HELP topic, 34
LTA 1186 reference format to terminals, 18
lt logical operator value less than, 269
lts logical operator string less than, 269

MAI MAIL message file, 96
MAIL
across DECnet, 177
command
DIRECTORY, 189

MAIL—*cont.*
SELECT, 187, 188
SEND, 176, 177
delete and recover, 184, 185
distribution list, 179, 180
environment
AUTO_PURGE, 190
Carbon Copy (CC), 177
CC_PROMPT, 190
EDIT qualifier, 178
EXTRACT files, 178, 179
FILE, 191
FOLDER, 191
MAIL_DIRECTORY, 191
PERSONAL_NAME, 192
QUEUE, 192
SET editor, 190
SHOW all, 89, 192
subdirectory creation, 191
folder, 180, 181
creation MOVE, 185–187
MAIL holds read and retained messages, 175
NEWMAIL holds unread messages, 175
WASTEBASKET holds messages to be deleted, 175
HELP topic, 34
invoke, 175
messages
directory, list of qualifiers, 182, 183
reading, BACK, NEXT, SEARCH string, printing, 181, 182
MOVE to destination, 185, 186
Set folder wastebasket, 184
symbol to run mail editor, 150
mailbox, 200
margin, 78, 81
MARK and GOTO, 76, 83
match
and differences, 120, 121
qualifier, 116, 121, 122, 213
and search string, wild cards, 61, 116, 117
Member of the same group (group ID number), 92
MERGE HELP topic *and* SORT, 34
MERGED files, 120–122
MESSAGE
HELP topic, 34
MESSAGE—*cont.*
SYSMESSAGE directory of system error messages, 237
window in EVE, 83, 237
minus sign in comparison with the hyphen ;time specification, 142
Minute time specification, 140–142
MODULA high-level language, 34
MOVE by
line EVE editor command, 54
word EVE editor command, 54
multitasking *and* windows on VAXstations, 281
multiple windows on VAXstations, 281

NAME
file *and* directory, 94–100
LOG NAME qualifier, 143
PERSONAL_NAME in MAIL, 189, 192
prompted for by MAIL (and VMS), 176
qualifier for print banner, 152, 153
SPAWN and NOLOGICAL_NAME, 131
NAND logical operator, 117
nes logical operator, 269
NET SYSNET, 235
network, 23–27, 29, 46, 146, 155, 193, 194, 200, 238, 256, 258
network *and* Ethernet DECnet, 26, 46
network stations *and* DECwindows, 282
NETWORK HELP topic, 35, 37
NEW qualifier
ACL *and* ACE, 118
for MAIL, 183
NEWFOLDER MAIL, 187
NEWMAIL, 175, 179–181, 185, 188
next
screen EVE editor keypad command, 52, 53
window EVE editor command, 87
No list of negation HELP topics, 10
NOANALYSIS, 41
NOBJECT, 166, 167
NOBROADCAST, 195
NOCC, 190
NOCONCATENATE, 112
NOCONTROL, 264
NOCROSS, 41

node name, 19, 26, 46, 47
nodebug, 171
NODIR, 249
NOEDIT, 250
NOENABLE, 20, 156
NOEXACT, 116
NOFLAG, 150, 151
NOHEADER, 179
nolog, 139
NOLOGICAL, 131
NOMARKED, 183
NOMSGS, 185
nonalphanumeric, 116
NOON, 263, 264
nooptermize, 162, 170, 171, 221
NOPRIV, 106
nopunctuation, 261, 262
NOR, 117
nor, 70
NOREPLACE, 113
NOREPLIED, 183
NOSYMBOL, 131
NOTES, 150, 220, 221
NOTES printer qualifier, 150, 153
NOTIFY printer qualifier, 153
NOTRAN, 240
noverify, 256
NOWAIT, 126, 128, 130, 136
Nowrap, 78
NUMBER, 224
Numbers
  and character strings, 226–227
  and symbols assignment, 222
NUMBERS, 278

OBJ object file, 95
OBJECT library qualifier, 207, 208
OCCAM computer language, 34
OCTAL qualifier and DUMP command, 111
Octal numbers and symbols, 222–227, 229, 231, 232
offset in combination time, 142
OLB object library extension, 207, 208, 213
ON command
  (CTR)Y handling, 264
  error handling SET ON SET NOON, 263, 264
ONE Window in EVE, 87, 89
ONLY qualifier /READ_ONLY, 139
OPEN
  file *and* close file, 265–267
  HELP topic, 34
Operators logical, 269
OPTIMIZE *and* NOOPTIMIZE qualifiers, 162, 170
OR
  logical operator, 269
  MATCH qualifier *and* SEARCH, 117
OUTPUT
  obtaining, 42–47
  qualifier
    files *and* directories, 110
    redirect, 27
overdraft *and* directory quota, 15, 19, 32
overstrike mode in EVE editor, 50, 53–55
owner's privilege for directories and files, 106
ownership, 91

p1 p2 command line arguments, 275
page
  and printing of files, 147, 149–155, 251
  and terminal status, 10
  BREAK EVE editor, 78
  fault, 16
  FLAG page, 152
  paged display with symbol assignment, 251
  qualifier for display of files, 111
  system report, 19
  UP, DOWN EVE editor commands, 81
paged in or out for Virtual Memory operations, 2
pagefile disk area allocated for Virtual Memory operations, 2
PAGES qualifier for printer, 153, 154
paragraph EVE editor command, 77, 78
parameter
  DCL Command field referencing, 18, 19, 30, 35, 36
  example in command procedure, 272, 273
  filename, 96
  symbol, 265
  system for printer DEFQUEPRI, 154
parent
  directory, 101, 102, 105, 106, 109, 119

parent—*cont.*
  process SPAWN, 125–128, 130–134
Parity in terminal status, 10
PAS PASCAL language type, 50
Pascal high-level language, 95–99, 159–161, 171, 278, 279
PASSALL print qualifier, 154
password, 5–7, 12–15, 92, 259
Pasthru HELP topic, 10
PATCH HELP topic, 34
path directory, 38, 256
Peak *and* accounting information, 16, 139
pending, 130, 148, 153
percent sign (%) *and* wildcards use, 98
PF1–4 function keys on VT100 terminal, 31–33
PF17–20 function keys on VT200 terminal, 31–33
phone, 193–200, 209, 278
  %HUNGUP *and* EXIT finish the call, 197
  %(CTR)Z finish the call, 197
  answer accept call, 195
  command window entry key, percentage key (%), 197
  commands, 198
    FACSIMILE, 198
    HELP, 198
    HOLD, 198
    REJECT $PHONE then %REJECT, 198
  dial
    and PHONE equivalence, 194
    computername::username, 194
    username, 194
  directory show users, 194
  disable terminal SET TERMINAL/NOBROADCAST, 195
  percentage key (%) entry to command window, 197
  SET TERMINAL /NOBROADCAST disable terminal, 195
  text formatting key table, 196
  username make the call, 193
  utility, 193–200, 209, 278
PID Process Identification Number, 23, 133, 230
port, 10, 146, 147
precedence of local over global symbols, 217
previous EVE editor command
  screen, 55, 87
  word, 56
print, 181, 182, 189 192, 228
  display, show queue SYS$PRINT and qualifier, 156
    All, 156
    FULL, 156
  manipulate with qualifiers:
    ENTRY and DELETE, 157
    STOP and QUEUE/ENTRY, 157
  priorities, 137
  queue table, 135
  submit a job, 145
  SYS$PRINT default print queue name, 147
    file using wildcards, 148
    filename, 148
    (path) filename in other directory, 148
    qualifiers, 149
      burst, 149
      confirm, 149
      copies, 149
      delete (after printing), 150
      flag (first page), 150
      forms (paper size), 152
      header, 152
      name, 152
      note, 153
      notify, 153
      pages (selected section only), 153
      passall (supress special characters), 154
      priority (in queue), *and* system parameter DEFQUEPRI, 154
      queue (place in another queue), 155
      remote (computer on other node in DECnet), 155
      restart *and* STOP/QUEUE/RESTART, 155
      trailer, 155
process
  background processes, 125
  child *and* parent process relations, 125
  creation, 125
  HELP topic, 35

process—*cont.*
process table LNM$PROCESS TABLE, 234–235
define logical name, 239, 240
conceal *and* translation *and* USER MODE, 239, 240
show F$PROCESS lexical function, 230
show PROCESS/full, 230
SPAWN, 125
command attach, 131
(CTR)Y return to DCL level, 126
logout, 126
continue, 126
qualifiers
nological_names, 131
nosymbol, 131
nowait, 128
output, 130
process (another), 131
subprocesses (jobs), 125
creation, 125
format specifications, 125
techniques *and* examples, 126–128
SUBMIT, 125
background processes, 125
child *and* parent process relations, 125
program
compile/assemble, 160, 161
qualifiers
list, 161
optimize *and* nooptimize, 162
debug, 162
enter (PF3), 171
step, 172
examine, 172
deposit, 172
help, 173
key display (PF2), 173
development, 158–173
editors: EVE and LSE, 159
link *and* C runtime library SYS$LIBRARY:VAXCTRL, 162
object module .OBJ, 163
run, 163
programming languages *and* type extensions, 158
prompt
($!) comment format in command procedures, 255

prompt—*cont.*
($@) format to execute command procedures, 255
DCL
default $ and changing it, 8, 9
to build up a command line, 21, 22
DEBUG format, 172
EVE editor, 61, 69, 75, 76, 83
HELP topic, 34
MAIL format, 175
qualifier for the READ command, 265
set for subprocesses, 132
protection file and directory
delete, read, write, execute, 92
SET FILE/PROTECTION, 105, 113, 117–119, 219, 249
system, owner, group, world, 92
PURGE, HELP topic, 34
purge, 15, 76, 114–115, 170, 188, 190, 288, 289, 292, 299, 302
PUT HELP topic, 210

Q (CTR)Q restart after (CTR)S command, 12, 70, 196
qualifiers *see also* Appendix C2, 294–298
after
=date specification (see time), 140
=TODAY, 141
all, 19
append, 266
before=YESTERDAY, 98
blocks, 112
brief, 15
burst, 149
cc_substring=text, 182
confirm, 114, 149
copies=integer, 149
create, 205
debug, 162
delete, 118, 150, 204
device=VT100, 10
edit MAIL, 178
end_of_file=label, 266
entry
=integer, 157
=name, 136
error=label, 267
exact, 116
exclude
=names, 98
=specification, 249

qualifiers—*cont.*
extract, 179
flag
and noflag, 150
=all, 151
folder, 183
forms =labels (etc), 152
from_substring=text, 183
full, 15
global, 262
hardcopy terminal, 45
header, 152
identification=name (or ident), 133
inquire terminal, 171
keep, 142
keep=integer, 114
key
name, 31
=(position:AA, size:BB) sort, 122
library, 208
line_editing, 29
list, 167
log, 46
log_name, 143
match *and* logic operators, 116
name="name1", 152
new, 118, 183
noheader, 179
[no]marked, 183
nopunctuation, 262
[no]replied, 183
note="message", 153
notify, 153
nowait, 128
object, 207
optimize *and* nooptimize, 162
output, 110
output=filename, 27
page, 111
pages=(start, finish), 153, 154
passall, 154
priority=integer, 154
process, 238
prompt=specification, 265
protection, 219
protection=( ), 113
queue=name, 138, 155
read, 266
read_only, 139
records, 112
recover, 60

qualifiers—*cont.*
remote, 155
replace NOREPLACE, 113
restart, 143, 155
since
=date, 183
=TODAY, 114
size, 110, 219
specification=filename, 122
speed=9600, 11
start=start_point, 183
subject_substring=text, 183
terminate, 32
total, 109
to_substring=text, 183
trailer, 155
type=unknown (terminal), 40
user_mode, 240
width=132, 10
write, 266
queue:
batch, 136, 144–146
batch, default SYS$BATCH, 137
DEFQUEPRI, 154
HELP
SHOW QUEUE list of parameters *and* qualifiers, 201–202
SHOW QUEUE/FULL, 35–37
topic, 34
LIB$GETQUI, 210
manager, 137
print, default SYS$PRINT, 147
set, 192
show, 143, 192
SYS$BATCH, 144
SYS$BATCH/all, 144
SYS$CONTROL, 144
SYS$CONTROL/all, 144
SYS$PRINT, 19
SYS$PRINT/all, 19, 20
SYS$PRINT/full, 20
table, 135
USERS$BATCH, 138
QUIT
EVE editor, 52, 56–58, 76, 81, 82
HELP topic, 176
QUOTA
disk, 14, 15
show, 19
quotation marks needed, 31, 60, 116, 218, 219, 232, 263, 272
QWERTY keyboard, 11

radix, 222, 223
READ HELP topic, 34
read
  authority for files, 92, 117–119
  command, 265–267, 270, 278
  MAIL, 181, 265, 266, 267, 270
  open file for read, 146, 266, 267
Readsync terminal setting, 10
recall
  all (last 20 commands), 251
  commands, 27–31
Record
  and sort facility, 122
  format in file specification, 109
RECORDS qualifier for file size, 112
RECOVER
  deleted messages in MAIL, 184
  qualifier in EVE editor, 60
recover a deleted message in MAIL, 184
redirect output, 27, 40, 130, 260
REJECT PHONE call, 199, 200
REMOTE printer qualifier, 155
REMOVE
  EVE editor key command, 52, 62, 88–90
  HELP topic, 176
RENAME
  command to change directory or file specifications, 115
  symbol to rename commands, 251
repeat EVE editor command, 75
REPLACE
  EVE editor command, 69, 70
  text in library, 204
REPLY MAIL HELP topic, 176
REQUEST HELP topic, 34
Restore EVE editor command, 56
Resume after exit from EVE to SPAWN, 127
RETURN
  HELP topic, 34
  key, 11
reverse direction EVE editor command, 54
right arrow key, 54–56
RING phone, 212
RUN
  HELP topic, 34
  programs *and* command procedures, 227, 276–279
RUNOFF text formatter, 34
Run–Time library, 213–215
RWED file protection specifiers, 109, 219, 220

save
  extended eve
    default extension TPU$SECTION, 80
    eve savekey, 80
  key definition in section file EVE editor, 80
scrolling screen stop (CTR)S resume (CTR)Q, 12
SEARCH
  and FIND key in EVE editor, 61–63, 247
  command for a string in files, 115–117
    and qualifier
      EXACT, 116
      MATCH, 116
  HELP topic, 34
  list logical names, 247–249
  string in MAIL, 181
seconds *and* time specification, 140–142
section file save key definition EVE editor, 80
select
  key in EVE editor, 52, 62, 85
  MAIL command, 187, 188
SEND
  EDIT MAIL command, 176–179
  files in MAIL, 178–179
  MAIL
    across DECnet, 177
    command, 176–179
set
  auto_purge, 190
  cc_prompt, 190
  control=Y, 264
  default, 100, 106
  directory, 119
  editor tpu, 190
  EVE editor text formatting list, 77–78
  file filename specifies current MAIL file, 191
  file/protection, 106
  folder foldername, 185
  global symbol, 226
  host/log, 46
  noon error trapping off, 264
  on error trapping on, 264
  password, 13

set—*cont.*
/generate, 13
/secondary, 13
personal_name, 192
prompt, 9
protection, 298
terminal, 5
/device=vt100, 10
/hardcopy, 45
/inquire, 9
/line_editing, 29
/nobroadcast, 195
/speed=1200, 11
/unknown, 9
/width=132, 10
text formatting list (EVE), 77–78
verify, 256
SETUP .COM initialization file (EVE) alternate to EVE$INIT, 81
SEVERITY error handling set on valid, 263
Shift left n *and* right EVE editor, 79
show
(main), 22
all in MAIL, 189
and HELP, 35
auto_purge, 190
cc_prompt, 190
default, 44
device, 25
dua (of name dua), 25
entry, 157
key/all, 33
logical SYS$OUTPUT default setting, 44
mail_directory, 191
network, 25
process, 24
/full, 273
que sys$print (shortened to), 20
queue
sys$batch, 143
/all, 144
sys$control
/full, 144
sys$print, 19
/all, 20
/full, 20
quota, 15
symbol time, 146
system, 19
show—*cont.*
terminal, 10
time, 8
translation, 104
users, 8, 16, 23
/full, 22
SHRINK *and* WINDOW EVE editor command, 87
since = today time qualifier for files, 114
SORT, 277–279
HELP topic, 34, 50
utility, 122–124
source code high-level language, 159
spawn
attach command to a process, 131–134
HELP topic, 34
qualifier
identification, 133
nological, 131
nosymbol, 131
nowait, 76, 126, 127, 128, 129, 130, 131, 132
output, 130
process, 131
subprocesses, 125–132
temporarily exit from EVE editor, 75, 76
SPLIT WINDOW EVE editor command, 87–89
startup file, 80
stop command, 111, 157
store a sequence by LEARN command, 73
string, 228, 269
subdirectory, 92, 93, 99–106, 114, 191, 251, 257
changing, 103–104
create, 100–101
delete, 105–107
referencing, 99–103
submit batch files, 137–146, 253
qualifiers
after, 140
log name, 143
restart, 143
subprocess
in EVE editor, 76, 79
job table and P I D, 234, 235
see spawn, 125–128, 131, 132, 212
subroutine command procedure levels, 259

SUBSTRING accessing in MAIL, 182, 183
suspend job execution, 126, 140
symbol
  abbreviating names, 220–221
  and lexical functions (*see also* lexical functions), 228–232
  as values for other symbols, 232–233
  assignment for EVE, 50
  assigning values to, 222, 224
  global, 217, 218
  local, 217
  nosymbol qualifier in SPAWN, 131
  predefined, 221, 222
  to add character strings, 225
  to add values, 224, 225
  to run command procedures, 227
  to run programs, 227
  to store character strings, 225, 226
  useful, 249–252
  using, 218–220
SYS$BATCH default batch queue, 130
SYS$COMMAND source from where DCL commands are read, 234
SYS$DISK default disk, 235
SYS$ERROR destination for VAX/VMS to send error messages, 235
SYS$NET defined during task-to-task DECnet operations, 235
SYS$OUTPUT default logical name to which DCL writes output, 235
SYS$EXAMPLES directory of system examples, 236
SYS$HELP directory for VAX/VMS help library, 237
SYS$INPUT default logical name input device, 236
SYS$LIBRARY directory for programming libraries, 237
SYS$LOGIN the default directory name for login, 235
SYS$MANAGER directory of system files, 237
SYS$MESSAGE directory of system error message files, 237
SYS$NODE DECnet node name for the host node, 237
SYS$PRINT default print queue, 147
SYS$SYSROOT directory for the system directories, 238
SYS$SYSTEM directory for VAX/VMS operating system codes, 238
system logical name tables, 233–238

Tab
  DCL, 12, 28, 60, 78
  PHONE, 196
terminal
  set *and* show commands, 5
  qualifiers
    /device=vt100, 10
    /hardcopy, 45
    /inquire, 9
    /line_editing, 29
    /nobroadcast, 195
    /speed=1200, 11
    /unknown, 9
    /width=132, 10
text
  file, 93
  formatting list (EVE), 77–78
time specification, 140–142
  absolute, 140–141
  combination, 142
  delta, 141–142
timesharing, 1
top
  EVE editor
    command, 53, 62
    HELP topic, 53
  level home, main directory, 103–104
TPU (Text Processing Utility)
  EVE Extensible Vax Editor, 48, 50, 75, 80
  MAIL edit, 178, 190, 250
  VAXTPU, 48
TRAILER page, 155
TRANSLATION show command, 35, 37, 242, 243, 245
transparent access to other computers *and* DECwindows, 282
txt file type specification, 40
type command display content of a file (on the VDU), 93
TYPE command procedures over DECnet, 258

UIC
  and group table LNM$GROUP_xxx, 235, 236, 250

UIC—*cont.*
  and symbol call to F$GETJPI (get job process information), 250
  see also ACE (Access Control Entry) and ACL (.. List), 118, 119
  user identification code, 6, 14, 15, 118, 119
UNDSYM undefined symbol VMS message example, 218
undelete text EVE editor RESTORE, 56
UNHOLD phone command, 199
Unix operating system, 251
UNKNOWN terminal type qualifier, 9, 40, 45, 46
UNLOCK HELP topic, 34, 36
unplugged phone, 195
unread MAIL, 175, 181, 183, 189
up arrow key *and* (CTR)B RECALL commands *see* RECALL, 29, 30, 56
UPCASE STR$UPCASE convert to uppercase, 213
UPPERCASE WORD EVE editor *and* CAPITALIZE, 77, 78
user
  constant interface on DECwindows, 282
  identification code UIC, 6
  response time, 136
username name assigned or a text string selected as a parameter, 6
user's directory directory file or top directory, 91

Value acts as parameter to a qualifier, 18
values *and* variable use in program examples, 166–169
VAXCRTL SYS$LIBRARY:VAXCTRL C language run-time library, 139, 163, 168
VAXstation, 281
  Windowing Software VWS, 281
VAXTPU Vax Text Processing Utility *see* TPU and EVE editor, 48
VDU video display unit attributes, 276
verify set *and* noverify commands, 256, 258
video display unit setting attributes VDU, 276
violation of system protocol ie file protection, 105, 106
virtual connection on DECnet network, 26
Virtual Memory *and* page file of computer memory VMS, 2
Volume mounted disk or tape's name, 25, 96, 99
VT100 ;VT200 ;VT300 terminal types, 11

WAIT LIB$WAIT wait for a specified time to elapse, 210
Warning
  see Error handling and SEVERITY, 263
  system message on violation of protocol, 13
WASTEBASKET *and* MAIL, 174, 175
watch progress of a job with SHOW QUEUE command, 143
wildcard character referencing (*see also* Appendix C, 293), 37
  asterisk (*), 37
  combination [...]*.*;/log, 107
  ellipsis (...), 101
  hyphen (-), 101, 102
  percent sign (%), 98
  period (.), 100
  subdirectories
    absolute and relative, 99–111
    use of square brackets [ ], 99
Wildcard FIND in EVE editor, 68, 69
windows
  EVE editor operations, 59, 87–90
  DECwindows
    interface, 281–282
    using, 283–285
  X windows, 281–282
WKS file type, 112
WORD
  definition (= 2 bytes=16 bits), 112
  longword definition (= 4 bytes=32 bits), 112
  parameters in EVE editor commands, 52, 54, 55, 77, 78
World file ownership attribute no access rights, 92
Wrap
  set EVE editor command, 78

Wrap—*cont.*
terminal attributes, 10
write
and command procedure files, 22, 253, 254
permission in file attributes, 92, 118, 119
WRITE qualifier with OPEN command for files, 266, 267

X Windowing and DECwindows, 280–283